P9-ARQ-920

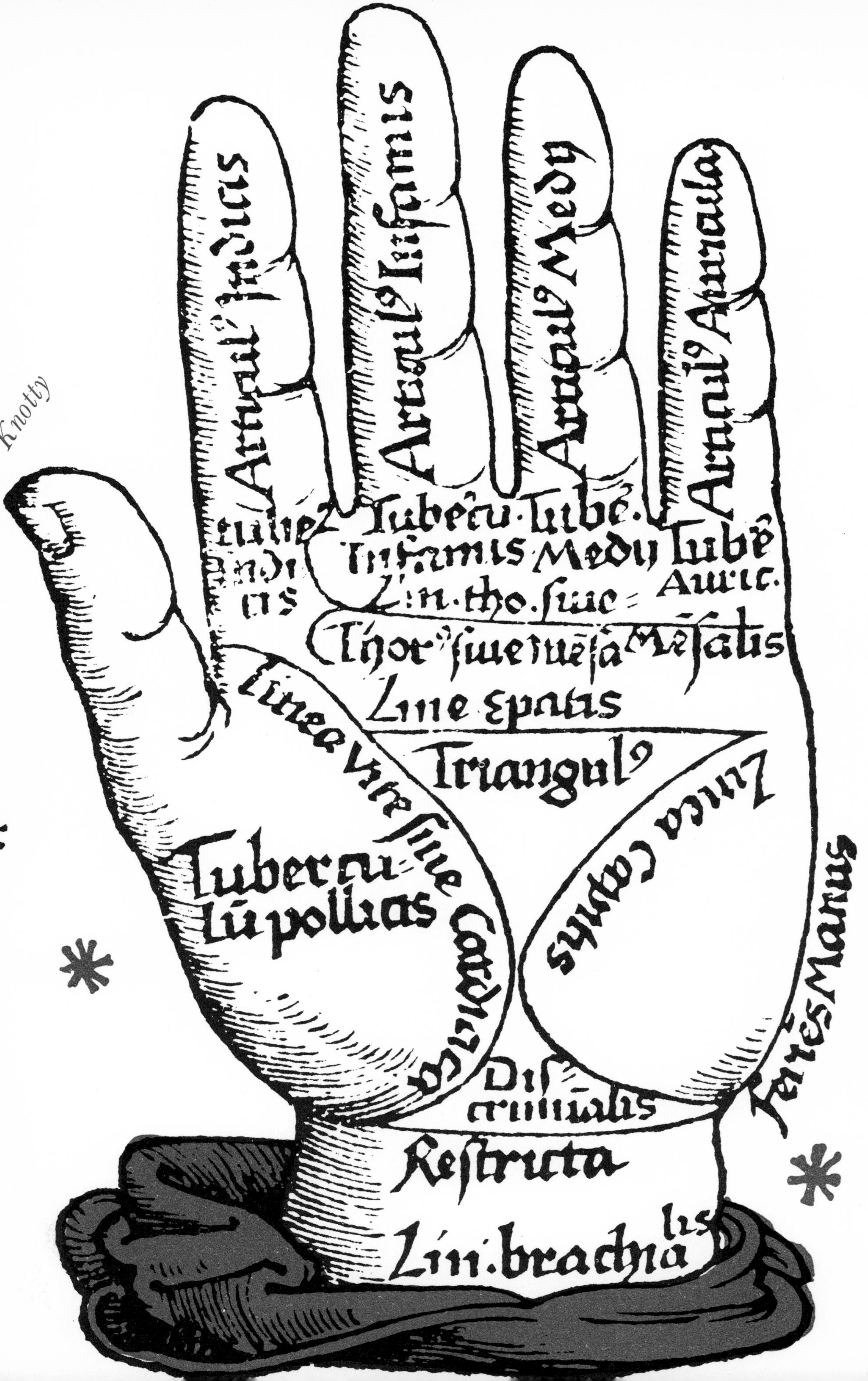

The Knotty

Articulꝰ Indicis

Articulꝰ Infamis

Articulꝰ Medy

Articulꝰ Auricula

Tubeꝰ Indicis

Tubercu. Tube.

Infamis Medy

Tubē Auric.

Lin. tho. siue

Thorꝰ siue mēsa

Mēsalis

Line epatis

Triangulꝰ

Linea vite siue Cardiaca

Tuberculū pollicis

Linea capitis

Fetēs Manus

Dis criminalis

Restricta

Lin. brachialis

The Book of Palmistry

Fred Gettings

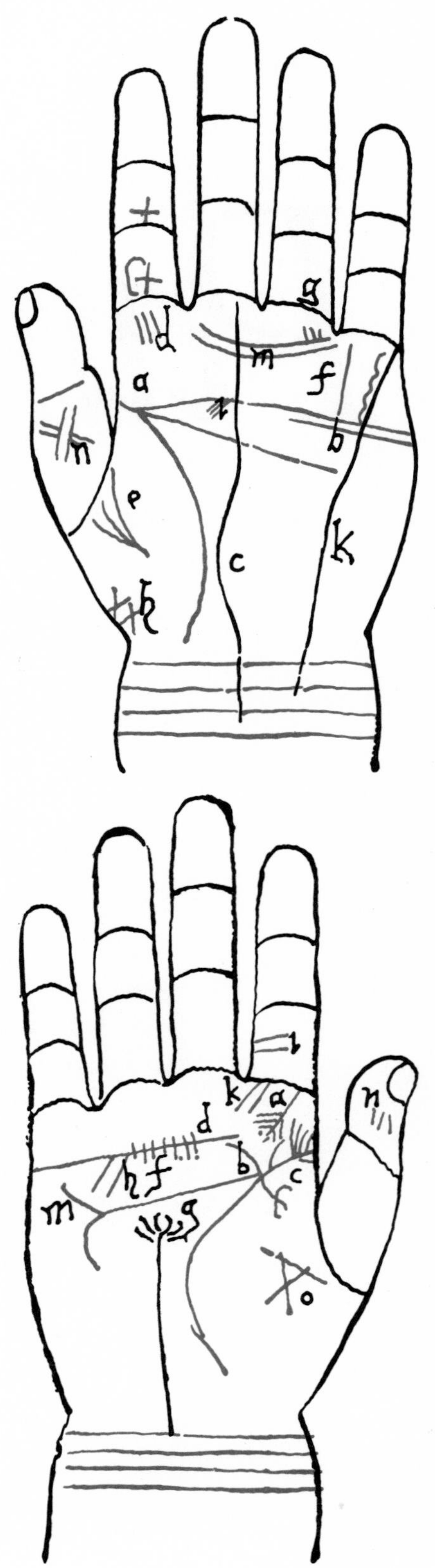

ISBN 0 85674 014 4
Published by
Triune Books, London, England

Printed in Spain by
Printer Industria Gráfica SA, Tuset 19,
Barcelona
San Vicente dels Horts
Depósito legal B18975–1973
Mohn Gordon Ltd, London

Contents

Introduction 7
The form of the hand 21
The lines of the hand 89
The Heart line 97
The line of the Head 107
The line of Life 117
Subsidiary lines 123
Conclusion 139
References 142

1

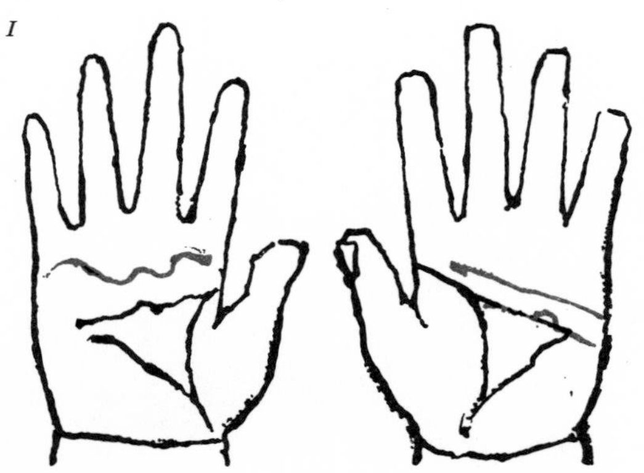

1. A sixteenth century drawing of a malformed heart line, relating to emotional disturbances. (after Taisnier)

2. A modern print, with a heart line ending under the middle finger. See text opposite.

3. A seventeenth century hand, showing major lines and their planetary rulers. The Heart line is in colour. (after Fludd)

2

Introduction

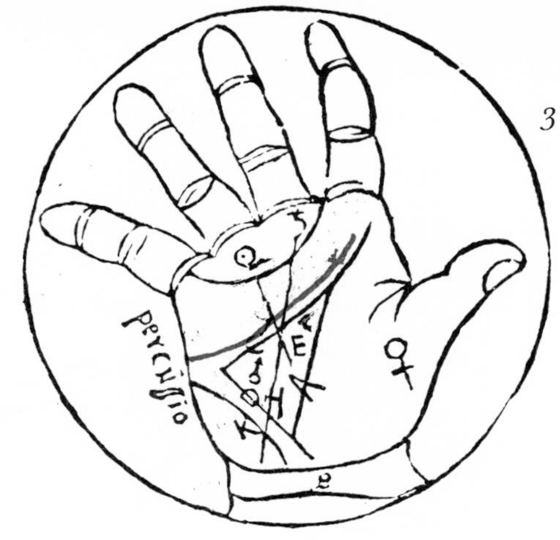

3

The aim of this book is to explore the world of traditional palmistry in the light of its application to modern teachings concerning the form of the hand. Palmistry of earlier days was quite unlike the palmistry of today, and yet some of the older forms of teachings connected with the hand still have a validity and interest in their own right, even though these may be merely entertaining or histrionic in their implications. For example, one seventeenth century treatise on palmistry tells us that:

> When the line of Heart runs across the palm of the hand, and finishes underneath the middle finger, without terminating in a fork, then this is a sign of man who will run into the danger of dying through his own negligence . . . (1)

Now this line is a relatively common one, in fact, and such a gory reading must have impressed or upset many people. Not surprisingly therefore, by the nineteenth century such a blood and thunder interpretation was no longer considered applicable, and the identical line merely

> shows the sensualism in the affections of one whose love is tinged with the idea of pleasures from sexual relations . . . (2)

With typical lack of respect for tradition a modern reading of this common line virtually reverses the interpretation, for we learn that the presence of this line in a hand may lead us to 'expect a more inhibited and less physical approach to sex'.

These three very different 'readings' of a single line may well lead us to ask whether there is any truth at all in the idea that the hand may be examined with a view to revealing personality or destiny. Certain it is that the vast literature relating to palmistry is very often contradictory, even about the most fundamental lines in the hand, with the result that the casual observer may be tempted to reject the hotchpotch of superstitions and halftruths as no longer applicable to the modern age. However, anyone who investigates such literature more than casually cannot help being impressed by the tenacity of certain ideas connected with the hands, as with lines on the hand. As Desbarrolles, the famous French palmist, says:

> It is good to seek for the meanings of popular traditions; there is always evidence of a *something* which has preserved the idea from oblivion. Good sense is often hidden beneath a cloak of folly, and the people gather them together; but adepts should apply themselves to the separation of the nuggets from the dross. (3)

Very often the nuggets of palmistry are not very deeply buried. For example, while we note above the wide divergence of opinions concerning an identical line of Heart, we cannot but observe that there is a connecting thread which links this divergence in an unexpected way. In each case there is reference to emotional states, and it has always been held that the line of Heart links with the emotions, even at a time when this line was not specifically called 'line of Heart'. We nowadays have no doubt that emotional attitudes are linked with sexuality, which is why the modern interpretation of the line is imbued with interpreting sexuality; and yet,

4

Tout exemplaire non revêtu de la signature de l'auteur sera réputé contrefait.

Ad. Desbarrolles

No 831.

4. Autograph of the famous French chiromancer Desbarrolles.

5. Title page of Desbarrolles' most influential book on palmistry.

6. Included in this seventeenth century diagram is the reading for a double line beneath the thumb, reputed to show 'loss of chastity'. (after Belot)

5

CHIROMANCIE NOUVELLE

EN HARMONIE AVEC LA PHRÉNOLOGIE ET LA PHYSIOGNOMONIE

LES MYSTÈRES

DE LA MAIN

RÉVÉLÉS ET EXPLIQUÉS

ART DE CONNAÎTRE LA VIE, LE CARACTÈRE, LES APTITUDES ET LA DESTINÉE DE CHACUN D'APRÈS LA SEULE INSPECTION DES MAINS

PAR AD. DESBARROLLES

CINQUIÈME ÉDITION

Revue, corrigée et augmentée d'explications physiologiques

PARIS

LIBRAIRIE DU *PETIT JOURNAL*

21, BOULEVARD MONTMARTRE, 21

Droits de traduction et de reproduction réservés.

even here we find a direct connexion with teachings which are over five hundred years old, for this line is linked by a mediaeval palmist with 'those partes that longe to the begetyng of chylder', or in other words to the sexual organs themselves!

Palmistry has of course become much more sophisticated since those times, and with the sophistication there has developed an abtruse complexity which often confuses the laymen, as well as those who wish to study palmistry for themselves. One cannot put the clock back and resurrect the ancient, unsophisticated palmistic techniques, for these are linked with a view of mankind which is no longer tenable. The version of mankind five hundred years ago was more clearly concerned with the balance between Heaven and Hell, or, put it another way, the perilous balance between Heaven and Hell was more readily appreciated in those days: black lines on white backgrounds marked moral issues, and villains were booed, heroes cheered, in a way which would nowadays be quite inconceivable. Line markings which indicated 'loss of chastity' or 'incest' or even 'sodomy' led to hell fire, and had different meanings to such people in fear of sins which will scarcely raise an eyebrow in the modern 'liberated' age. Not only have social mores changed, and not only is our type of sophistication of a different quality; our attitude to man has fundamentally changed. Because of this we have different questions to ask of the hand, though we must not delude ourselves into thinking that the questions are any more or less important. The average subject who consults a palmist now wants to know when she will get married, how many children she will have, and if her husband will ever be rich enough, just the very questions which were no doubt asked a thousand years ago.

In fact, the major changes which have occurred in palmistic doctrine over the past few hundred years have not been in terms of the questions put to the palmist, or in terms of the answers given or promised by palmists, but in terms of the view of the nature of knowledge. There has been a distinct and important move from the study of particular symbols within the hand, such as individual lines and curious formations, to the study of the hand as a whole, regarded as a unity of structure and lines. This corresponds to a general move from the interpretation of the world through platonic symbolism to the interpretation of the world through holism. A seventeenth century French palmist might well say that two lines below the thumb nail will indicate 'loss of chastity' (figure 6), and, life being what it is, he would as likely as not be right. A seventeenth century English palmist might see a similar arrangement of three lines below the thumb nail as indicating a great need for fidelity, the loss of which will invariably result in the unfortunate subject being hanged (figure 121). Few, if any, modern palmists would go quite so far as pinning their hopes and fears on one or two relatively unimportant lines in such a way: this is a kind of palmistry which has long been out of date, and which survives only in the very worst of the crude palmistry books which appear nowadays. In modern times the

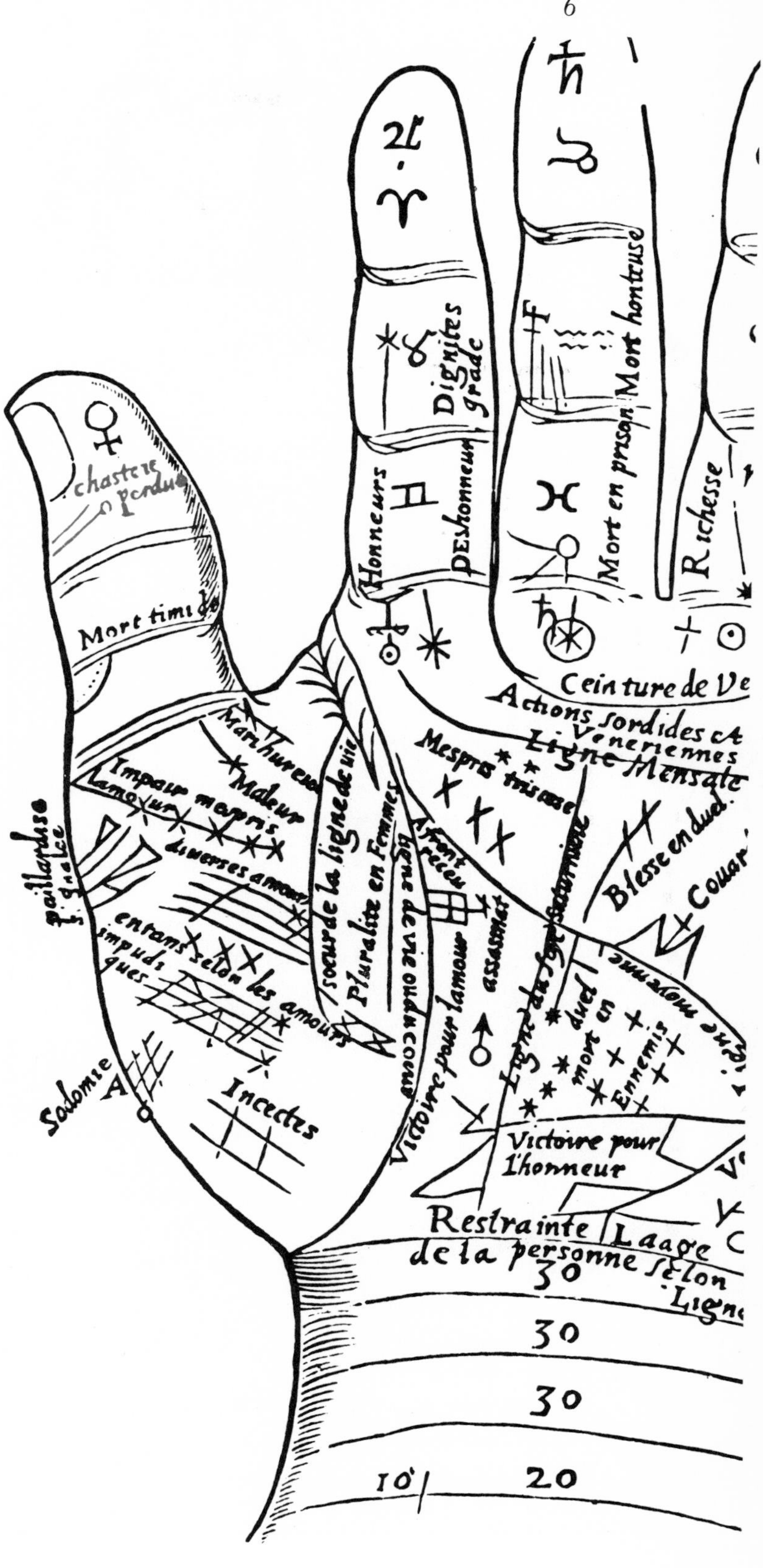

6

7

8

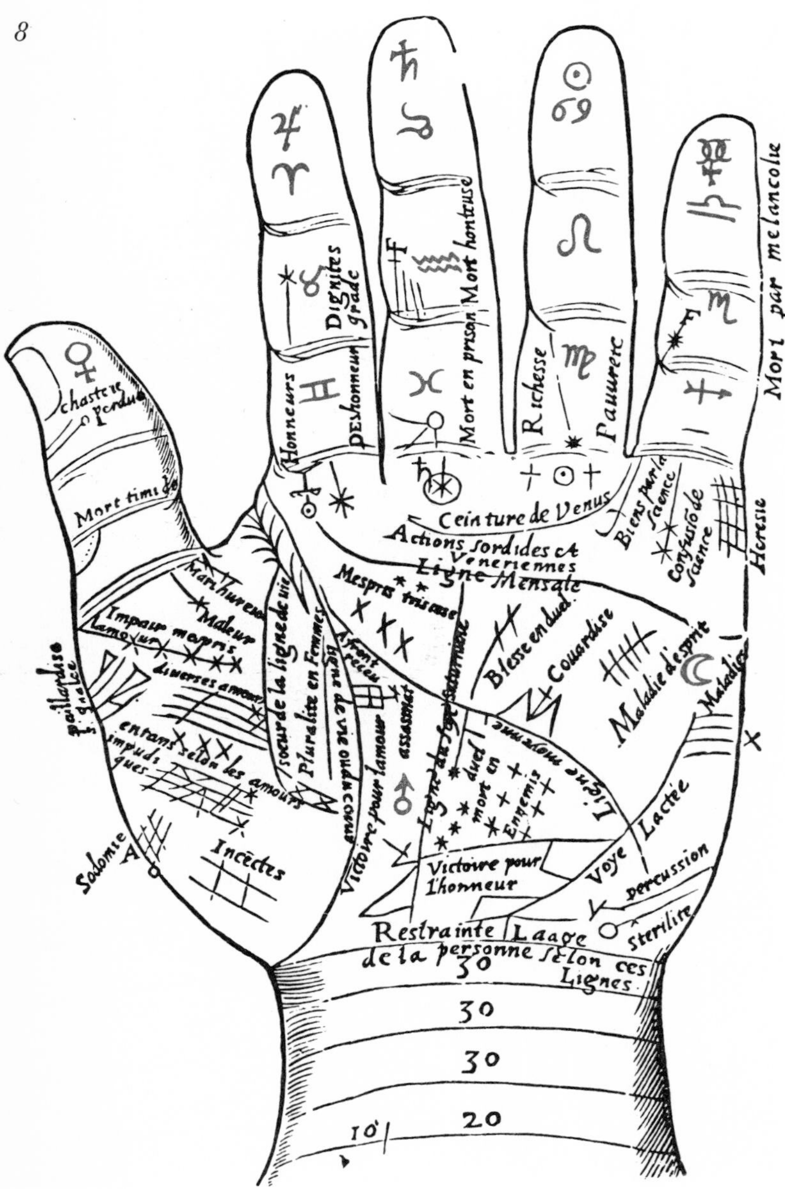

professional palmist will balance one factor against another, with the result that virtually identical linear markings will be interpreted quite differently when they appear in hands of a different quality or structure. The hand as a whole must be interpreted, and the individual lines, textures and papillary patterns linked together in such a way as to present a picture of the whole man, rather than to attempt to portray a fixed, and often all too dramatic, image of a particular disposition or tendency from one single line or element in the hand.

There are, then, very many different ways of looking at the hand, all linked by the underlying belief that the hand itself reflects the temperament and personality of the possessor. What has changed is the view of how this reflection may be interpreted. In the past, reliance was placed upon individual symbols, with the result that the tradition was founded on line markings: the early palmistry books concentrated mainly upon the meanings of the lines, and special signs in the hand, whilst the form of the hand was itself largely ignored. The term *chiromancy*, which means literally 'fortune telling by the hand', was reserved almost exclusively for predicting the future and reading character from the lines of the hand, to such an extent that by the time it was considered important for palmists to study the form of the hand as an aid to prediction and character reading an entirely new term, *chirognomy*, had to be coined. Modern palmistry makes use of both chiromancy and chirognomy in the evaluation of character and in prediction, yet the division of the study into two

7. *Jean Belot, an important seventeenth century French palmist.*

8. *A plate from Belot's textbook on palmistry, showing his system of planetary and zodiacal relationships to different areas of th hand. This system is no longer used.*

9. *Title page of an English translation of the most important and influential books on palmistry in the sixteenth century, by Indagine.*

10. *Photograph of the hand compared with a print of the same. The study of hand form is called* chirognomy, *whilst the study of the lines is called* chiromancy. *Both are combined in most modern palmistic systems.*

9

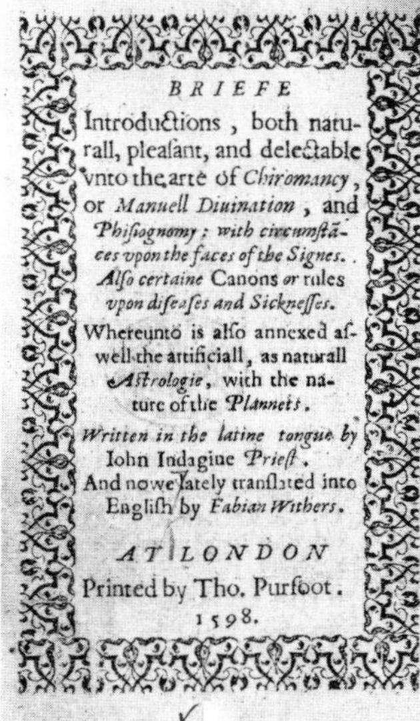

BRIEFE

Introductions, both naturall, pleasant, and delectable vnto the arte of *Chiromancy*, or *Manuell Diuination*, and *Phisiognomy: with circumstāces vpon the faces of the Signes.* *Also certaine* Canons *or* rules *vpon diseases and Sicknesses.*

Whereunto is also annexed aswell the artificiall, as naturall *Astrologie*, with the nature of the *Plannets*.

Written in the latine tongue by Iohn Indagine *Priest*. And nowe lately translated into English by *Fabian Withers*.

AT LONDON

Printed by Tho. Purfoot. 1598.

10

areas has of necessity, and for good historical reasons, been preserved. It is for this reason that the present book has been divided into two parts: in the first we examine the teachings attached to the study of the form of the hand, whilst in the second we examine the rich tradition attached to the study of the lines of the hand. The major problem which faces all serious students of palmistry is that whilst it is possible, and indeed inevitable, that these studies be approached separately, these must be yoked together in practice, when it comes to actually attempting to 'read' a hand. What may appear to the student poring over a book on palmistry as theoretically satisfying, if not exactly exciting, clear and watertight, only too easily dissolves into a nebulous haze of conflict when he is given a real living hand to pore over. This is because it is extremely difficult to move from theory into practice in this field where even the most simple theory is hedged in with qualifications and amendments. There is no easy remedy for this haze of conflict, for the inner panic which faces any student of palmistry who finally has a living hand pushed between him and his books, and is asked, 'tell me about myself, when will I get married, how many children will I have, do I have a long life line?' and so on, almost interminably. There is no easy remedy, but there is a remedy–*practice*. With practice, the rules ancient and modern will begin to take on a significance quite unexpected in the face of contemporary superstitions connected with the inner and outer life of man. But practice must begin with theory, and im-

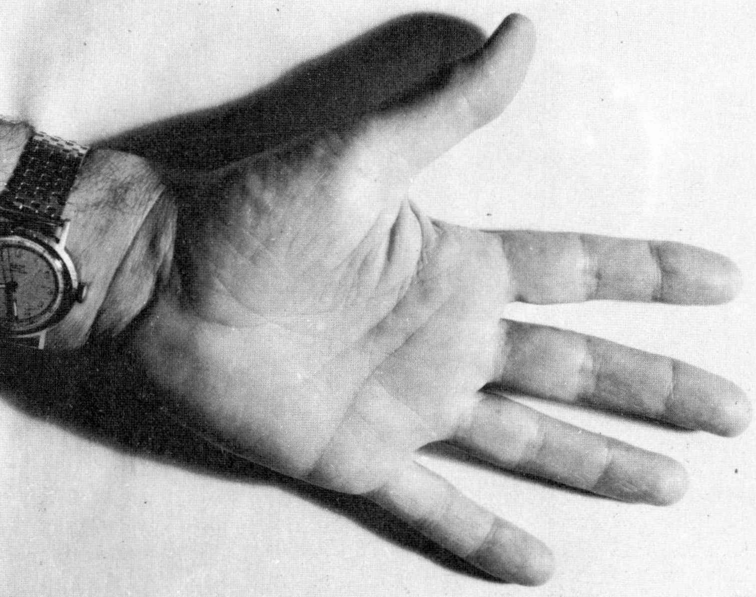

11

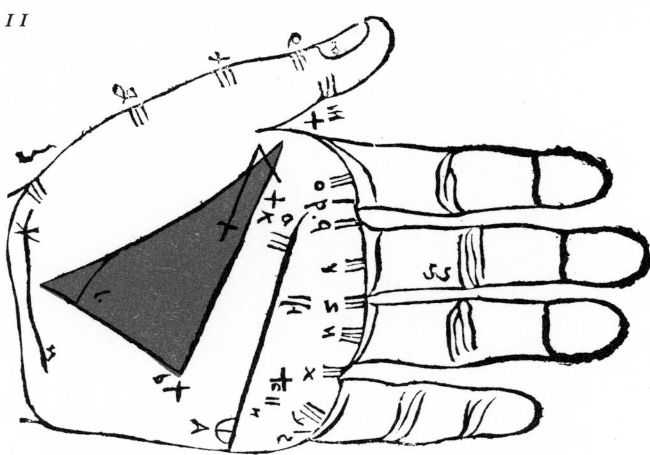

mediately the question is raised by any serious student: *which theory?* It is towards this end–answering the questions as to which theory may be most profitably studied–that the present book has been designed.

One might say that there is no such thing as palmistry: there are only palmists. Each palmist evolves his own system, mainly through trial and error, with the result that when he teaches his system to students, or puts his experience into book form, he tends to *add* to the palmistic tradition, to refine on it. For example, in the past hundred years alone we have seen at least a dozen different methods of classifying hand forms introduced, and five or six of these are still in common use. This must inevitably confuse any student who is prepared to study palmistry, for it is important that he should be certain which is the best form of palmistry to which he may apply his attention. There is a great need for a book which discusses the more important of the palmistic systems in order that those interested in palmistry may determine which particular system or systems they may usefully follow to satisfy their own requirements. A bird's eye view of the more valid palmistic systems will be both interesting and practical: interesting from an historical point of view, for those who wish to enlarge their boundaries in a field which they have already studied, and practical in that it will enable the student and the layman alike to decide for themselves which system he may most usefully put his faith in until such time as he may develop his own theories and systems, based upon practical observations.

An anthology of the kind presented here raises in the mind of the author many disquieting thoughts–the fact that there are a multitude of different palmistic systems, a multitude of excellent teachings, from which one might cull interesting beliefs in order to instruct and entertain. However, space precludes anything more than a brief survey of the more important systems, which are presented in such a way as to indicate the variety of concepts about the nature of the hand in relation to the ancient belief that the hand mirrors the personality and destiny of the subject. Again, a serious limitation is that one may consider only those theories which may find some applicability with regard to contemporary thought concerning the nature of man. Many of the early beliefs are now completely outmoded in terms of the contemporary image of man–which does not mean, of course, that they are no longer valid –and it would require much effort to understand many of these beliefs. For example, most comments on the dependence of man upon such spiritual hierarchies as the angels, archangels, and other even higher beings, tends to fall on sterile ground in an age in which the very existence of the spirit itself is doubted and openly denied. At the same time, the nature of the occult system is such that it has protected much which will be of value to mankind in his coming spiritual development, and for this reason it is difficult for us to avoid using certain occult terms, especially in regard to the astrological doctrines. The doubts raised by such terms, and by the richness of the associations, finds no

12

11. Diagram based on a sixteenth century German print, showing the triangulum, *an area regarded as being of the greatest importance in early palmistry, though completely ignored nowadays.*

12. The ancients appear to have virtually ignored the different papillary patterns on the finger ends, which are now held to be of the greatest importance in palmistic interpretation.

place in regard to the modern systems of 'palmistry' which have been propounded by many psychologists in the present system. Certainly there has been much honest endeavour here, in the attempt to arrive at the truth concerning the hand in relation to personality, but it is not so much in the end-product that one finds doubt–indeed, there has been a remarkable substantiation of the traditional palmist systems in the majority of modern research. The doubts arise because of the nature of the picture of man which such systems attempt to describe. It is easy for us to see that no one may establish a valid picture of the inner and outer nature of man, in its full spiritual, psychic and material implications, until the reason for the existence for man has been discovered. Yet, in spite of this, psychologists, and not only psychologists, are constantly attempting to say *what* man is, to paint him in the round, both spiritually and physically, without knowing *why* man is. The majority of classifications which have arisen from such sources have, of necessity, been based on attempting to describe relationships between hands and certain mental states, and even diseases. Worse has followed however, for portrayals of hand forms in relation to purely theoretical diseases have arisen–a hand type, for example, which is said to be that of the schizophrenic, now exists, in spite of the fact that there is no agreement, even in medical circles, as to what schizophrenia is. The difficulties are obvious, and so it is with no regret that I have found it necessary to exclude almost all the research which has been done by psychologists in the field of

13

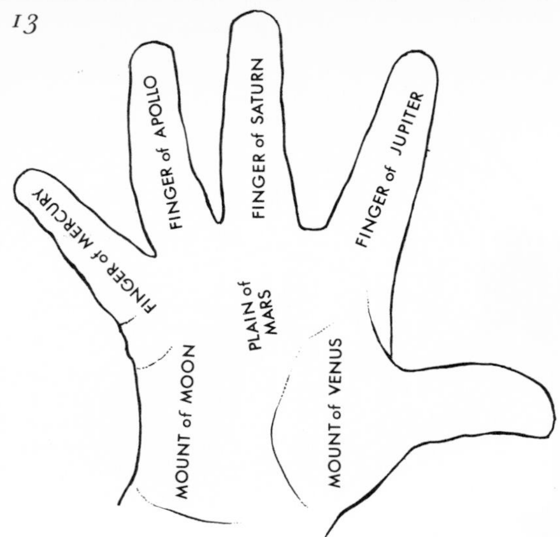
FINGER of MERCURY
FINGER of APOLLO
FINGER of SATURN
FINGER of JUPITER
PLAIN of MARS
MOUNT of MOON
MOUNT of VENUS

14

13. *The major areas of the hand.*

14. *Whilst the lines change only to a small extent, and this always significantly, the form of the hand changes fundamentally with natural growth. For this reason chirognomical study with children is difficult.*

15. *A sixteenth century hand system. (after Indagine)*

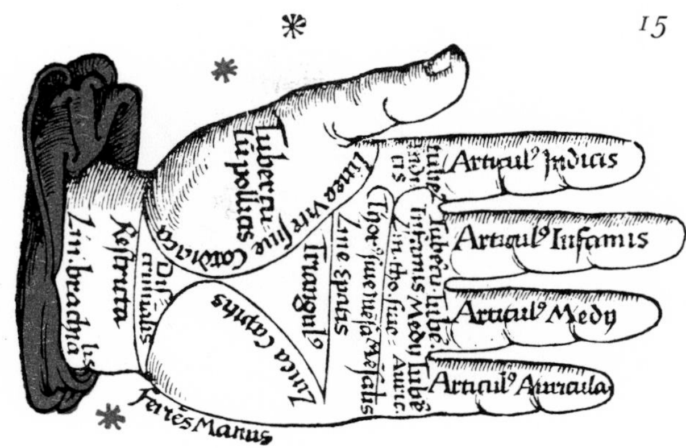

palmistry–which, incidentally, such researcher scrupulously avoid calling 'palmistry'–in our present century.

It will facilitate matters if the reader learns by heart the few traditional names associated with the fingers, mounts and lines on the hand, as set out in figures 13, 16, 18.

A brief survey of the nomenclature may be of value at this point. The fingers are related to self expression of the personality, in contrast to the palm of the hand, which is regarded in modern palmistry as the reservoir of energies used in the expression of self. In the older systems of palmistry, the three phalanges of the fingers were held to represent the three spirits or souls of man–the top phalange relating to spirit or 'ego' or thinking, the second phalange to 'soul' or feelings, and the third to the 'vegetative soul' or body, though in some systems (figure 22) the first was taken as relating to the mental world, the second to the practical world, and the third to the material. In some cases, particularly in the seventeenth century, the twelve phalanges of the four fingers were, almost inevitably, named after the twelve signs of the zodiac (figure 6, for example), though the significance of this designation was rarely expounded upon. The general consensus of opinion is that the four fingers now rule specific fields of self expression. The finger of Jupiter is the *indicator,* the finger which points into the world: this rules over the ambitions of the native, and expresses the manner in which he relates to distant objectives and to spiritual ideals. The finger of Saturn is the *mediator,* the finger to which the other fingers gather, and this expresses the inner balance established within the personality between spiritual and material demands: it stands between external and internal forces (figure 13). The finger of Apollo, the ring finger, is related to emotional self expression, and hence to emotional relationships and to creativity. The finger of Mercury, the small finger, is linked with sexuality and with money. Strengths and weaknesses in such fingers, represented by length or by the papillary patterns upon them, as well as by deviations from the norm, spark off energies and predispositions in terms of the planets with which they are associated: the nature of these planets is discussed on page 48 forward.

The thumb stands apart from the other fingers, and is more rooted in a deep materiality, through its heavy 'third phalange' of the mount of Venus. It is ruled by the materialistic, energetic and egocentric Mars, and is itself an indicator of willpower. In the traditional system it is not uncommon for palmists to refer to the top phalange as relating to will power, and the middle phalange to 'logic', suggesting that it is possible to determine thinking and emotional capabilities from the thumb alone.

In the traditional system as represented in the nineteenth century, the palm was divided into seven main areas. Under each of the fingers were the finger mounts, named after the relevant fingers (figure 30). The central area of the hand was called the Plain of Mars, and below this, on either side, were placed the large mounts of Venus and Moon. The finger mounts were interpreted in terms of

16

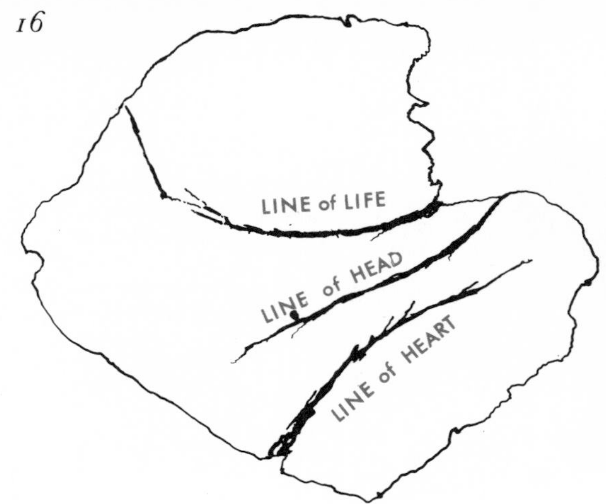

16. The three main lines of Life, Head and Heart.

17. The three main lines are found on almost all hands, though sometimes the last two combine to form one single line which runs across the entire hand. This line is called the Simian.

18. The Girdle of Venus, and lines of Apollo and Saturn. The latter two balance and complement each other—Apollo rules creativity and expansion, whilst Saturn rules control and restriction.

19. The three lines noted above may be traced in this print, which is representative of a fairly typical example of each.

17

their size in relation to the area of emotionality signified by the fingers, whilst the plain of Mars was examined for indications of temper and aggressive instincts. Venus was the repository of the passions and energies relating to health, happiness and even sexual attraction. The Moon was the fount of imaginative faculties, and was examined for mystical strains, sensitivity, and, by the blood and thunder palmists, for signs of insanity. In certain systems we find a mount of Mars, above the mount of Moon and below the mount of Mercury, and yet in other systems (figure 30) a 'lower Mars' above the Mount of Venus, and under Jupiter. These combined to give an area of Mars running right across the hand in a wide band, indicating aggression, temper and resistance, in that order, from the thumb to the percussion (figure 152). The hand at figure 30 represents the culmination of the nineteenth century tradition as preserved by the American palmist Benham, though it must be understood that certain earlier systems employed quite different hand divisions and different nomenclatures. In particular a great deal of attention was placed by mediaeval palmists on the 'triangulum' (figure 11) in the central part of the palm. The modern tendency has been to revise even the nineteenth century system, and to place less emphasis on the finger mounts, and upon the Mars band, even dispensing entirely with all three areas of Mars, and reading Martian influences entirely from the thumb itself. The system of astropalmistry has modified the nomenclature, in order to represent the entire hand as a miniature zodiac (figure 74).

The names of the lines on the hands have changed considerably during the past few centuries, though the general trend of interpretation—that is, the meaning accorded to the lines—has changed only very little. The three main lines of Life, Head and Heart are still interpreted as relating to physical health, mentality and the emotions respectively, whilst many of the very ancient traditions concerning their points of origin and insertion appear still to be valid. There is much more variation in connexion with the interpretation of the line of Saturn, sometimes called the line of Fate, and at one time called the line of Death, but the general idea is that this line is linked with the way in which the subject reaches his standing in life—certainly the line has nothing to do with 'fate' or with 'death'. The line of Apollo is interpreted in terms of creativity and versatility, whilst the Girdle of Venus is taken as a sign of either over-emotionalism or, in certain hands, of what they used to call in divorce courts 'excessive sexual demands'. In the system of astropalmistry these two lines are interpreted together. The line of Mercury is nowadays called the line of Intuition, and is related to just that faculty in the human psyche. If we use Benham's picture as a guide to the nomenclature, we might as well refer to his words, for these are more explicit than most:

> The line of Heart will show the strength or weakness of the affections, and the physical strength of the heart. The clearer, more even, and better-colored the line is, the

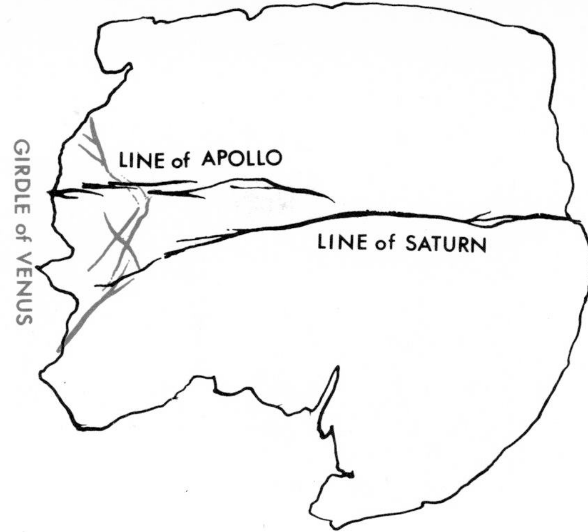

18

19

20

21

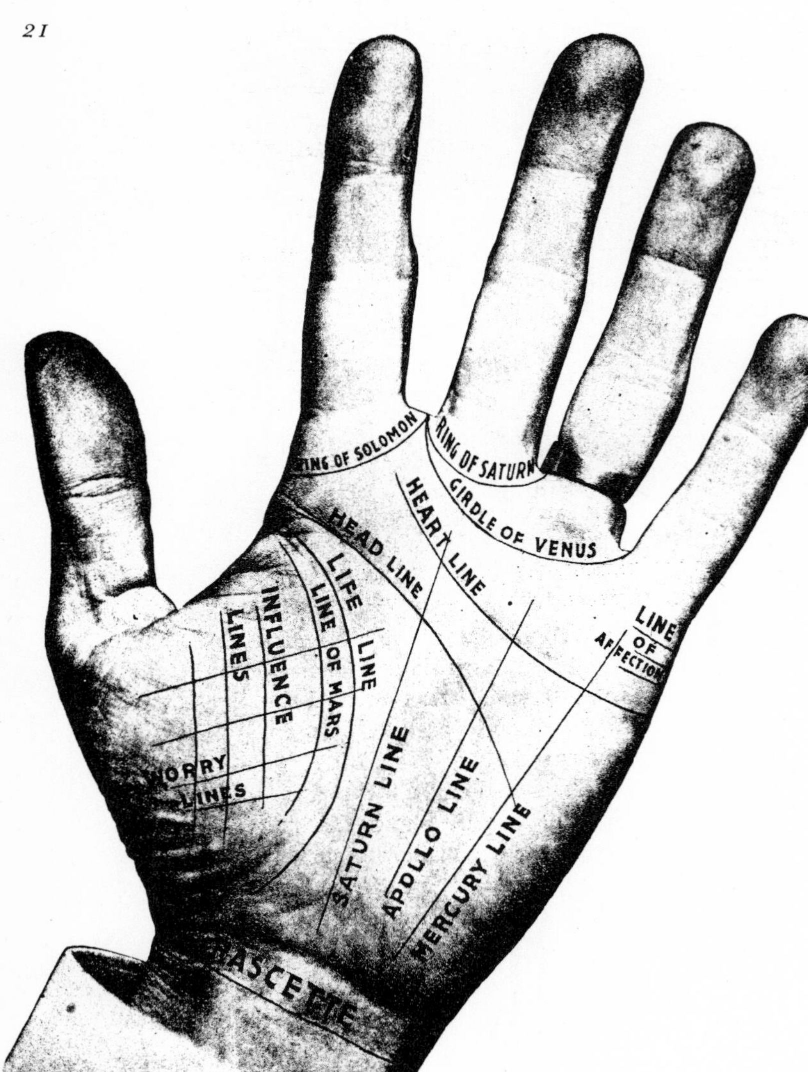

PLATE B

better the heart's action, and the more constant the affections.

The line of Head will show the strength of the mental powers, and the physical strength of the brain. The clearer, more even, and better-colored it is, the better the concentration of the mind, the self-control, and the less danger there is from brain disorders.

The Line of Life shows the strength of the constitution, the kind of strength, whether muscular robustness, or nervous energy, and, as physical strength is a great factor in human life, this line is most important.

The line of Saturn accentuates the Mount of Saturn, and shows that the balancing qualities of that type are present. One who has these restraining elements is less liable to do foolish things, and the course through life is likely to be more even and smooth. The more even, clear, and straight this line is, the more even the course through life will probably be.

The line of Apollo accentuates the Mount of Apollo, and brings out strongly the brilliant qualities of that type. The clearer, more even, and better-colored this line is, the more creative power in art, or productive money-making quality in business the subject has. The lines of Saturn and Apollo do not show defects of health. The line of Mercury, often called the line of Health, distinctly shows health difficulties.

(4)

The numerous subsidiary lines have been accorded too many various interpretations

20. The American palmist Benham laid great emphasis on the importance of assessing character from the manner in which a person carries and uses his hands. These nine diagrams from his textbook are almost self-explanatory.

21. Benham's system of line nomenclature.

22. The system used by the nineteenth century French palmist Desbarrolles, linked with the Kabbala.

22

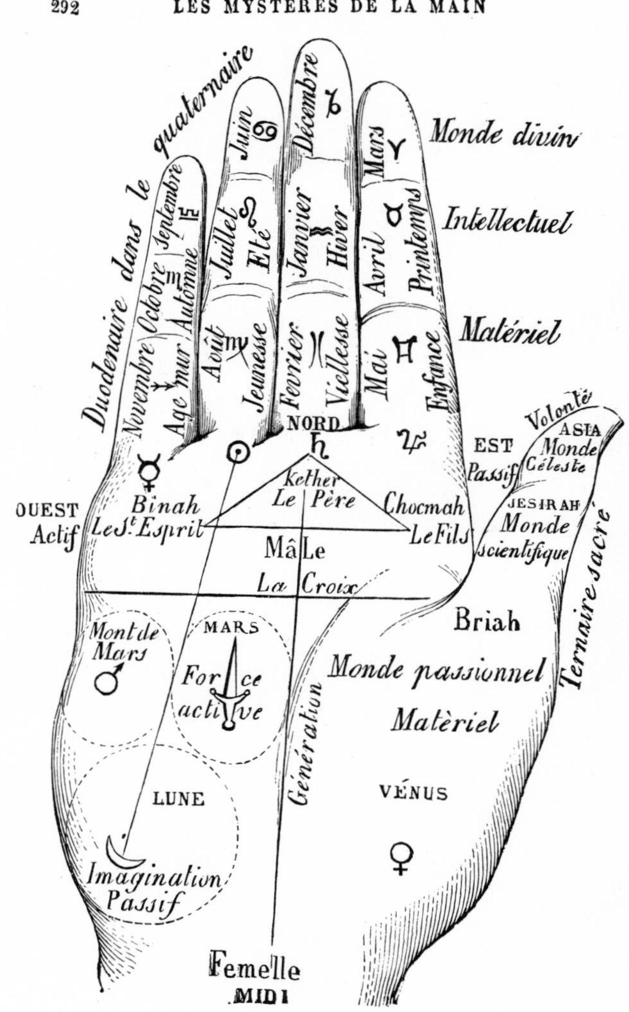

to be dealt with here, and we must take only those shown at figure 21, from Benham's book, as being worthy of note, though we must consider even these in a fairly negative manner. The line of Affection, which is more properly a series of small lines in the upper part of the percussion, do *not* indicate the number and quality of marriages as is so often believed: it is not clear in fact what these lines relate to at all, but we may as well dispense with this pernicious and worrying superstition here and now. The influence lines can be interpreted in terms of external influences affecting the life of the subject no more than can the so-called 'worry lines' relating to worries: it is hard to understand how these traditions emerged and survived for so long. The Ring of Solomon, like the Ring of Saturn, has the effect of isolating the planetary forces from the rest of the hand, but there is little agreement in the tradition as to how these lines are to be interpreted. In any case, the tendency nowadays is to regard the subsidiary lines as having importance only as conductors of energies from one part of the hand to another, and their significance may be understood only in terms of the particular areas involved.

We must not forget also that both gesture and posture are important in arriving at a clear understanding of a subject's personality. Benham's drawings (figure 20) have more than an antiquarian interest, for they point to the truth that no more than we may separate the hand from personality than from the rest of the human frame. Hand gesture is important in character reading.

23

23. *A rascette line, from an early book by B. Cocles. This line, or series of lines, was held to be very important in interpretation by early palmists, though it is largely ignored today.*

24. *The modern tendency is to give predominance in readings to the structure of the hand as a whole, and to relate to this structure the interpretation of individual lines.*

25. *The palmistic systems up to the nineteenth century tended to disregard entirely the form of the hand, and interpreted lines along a system of fixed symbols quite unrelated to the hand upon which they were found.*

24

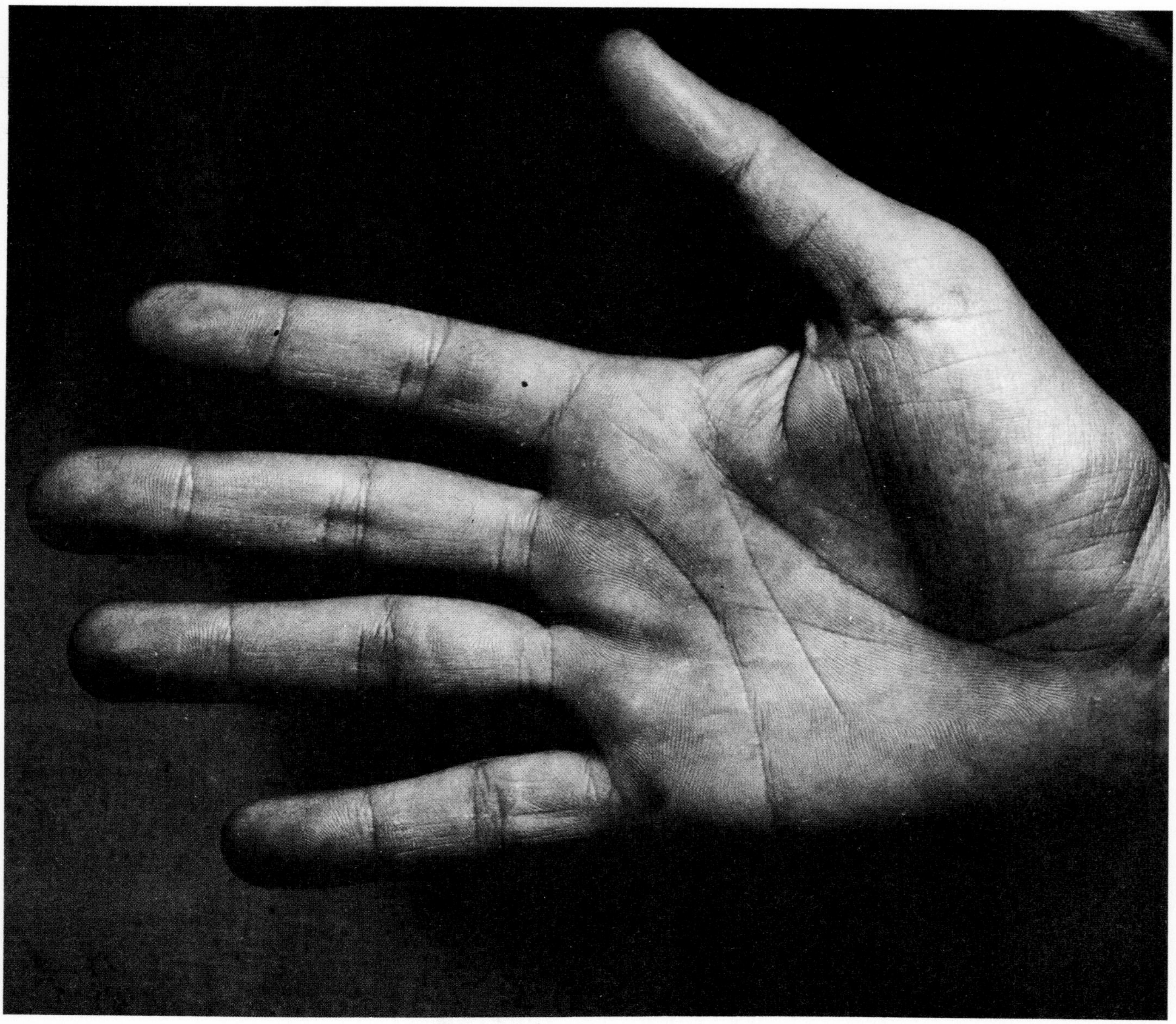

The form of the hand

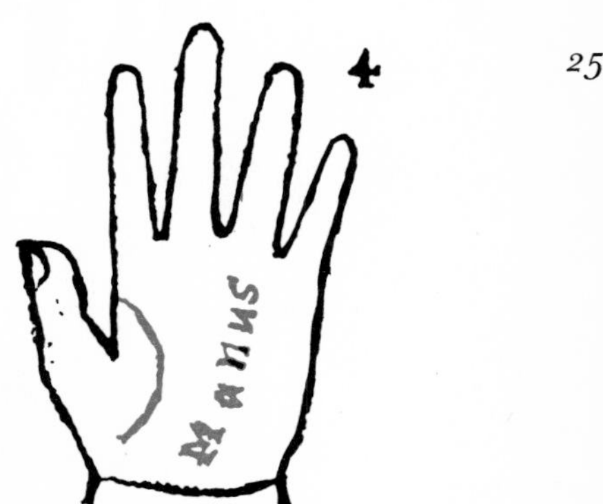

4 *Manus oblongæ, & digiti crassiunculi*

If a hand is stiff and hard, opening with difficulty to its full extent, it betrays stubbornness of character. (4)

One could scarcely find a more clear indication of the underlying theory of palmistry–that the hand is a material reflection of spiritual qualities, that the outer form reflects the inner power. It is almost on the same level as ordinary character analysis in which we all indulge when we assume that because someone is smiling, they are happy . . . Unfortunately, not all palmistry is quite so simple as this, and any student of the subject will find a whole battery of traditions concerning the relationship between hands, details of hands, and line structures, which are extremely complex, and which may even appear to be illogical in their application to personality. This is particularly so when one attempts to make predictions concerning the future of a person from line markings on the palmar surface of the hand. As Heron-Allen, the nineteenth century palmist, says:

> It is in dealing with future events and their traditional signs that the Cheirosophist finds the greatest difficulty and room for the greatest doubt. Thus, in the case of sudden deaths and unforseen calamities, we cannot satisfactorily account for the signs which predict them; but it is a fact that certain traditional signs are accepted by schools of Cheirosophy to indicate certain unforeseen occurrences, and until they shall fail to predict correctly, we must accept them and retain them, but use them and cite them warily and discreetly. Cardan remarked that of forty-five persons to whom Barthelmy Cocles had predicted a sudden death, only two failed to fulfil his prediction. (5)

Fortunately, the prediction of sudden death is far far away from ordinary run-of-the-mill palmistry, which is mainly concerned with reading character from the hand, and from the nature of the personality, based on the assumption that a particular life pattern which will lead almost inevitably to certain 'events'. The main body of palmistry, especially in earlier forms, consists of a collection of aphorisms which connects certain structures and formations in the hand to distinctive personality traits and certain psychological propensities.

When for example, John Gaule wrote in anger against astrologers and palmists, he frequently parodied their styles, as though to mock them: in choosing to rail against palmistry, he in fact gave us a pretty accurate summary of certain of such aphorisms connected with the art:

> A great thick hand signes one not only strong but stout; a little slender hand one not only weak but timorous; a long hand and long fingers betoken a man not only apt for mechanical artifice but liberally ingenious; but those short on the contrary note a foole and fit for nothing; a harde, brawny hand signes dull and rude; a soft hand witty but effeminate; an hairy hande luxurious; long joints signe generous, yet if they be thick withal, not so ingenious. Short and fat fingers mark a man out for intemperate and silly; but long and leane for witty; if his fingers crook upwards that

26

27

154 LES MYSTÈRES DE LA MAIN.

lois de la raison qu'à la seule condition qu'elles lui seront physiquement profitables; elle se soucie beaucoup moins

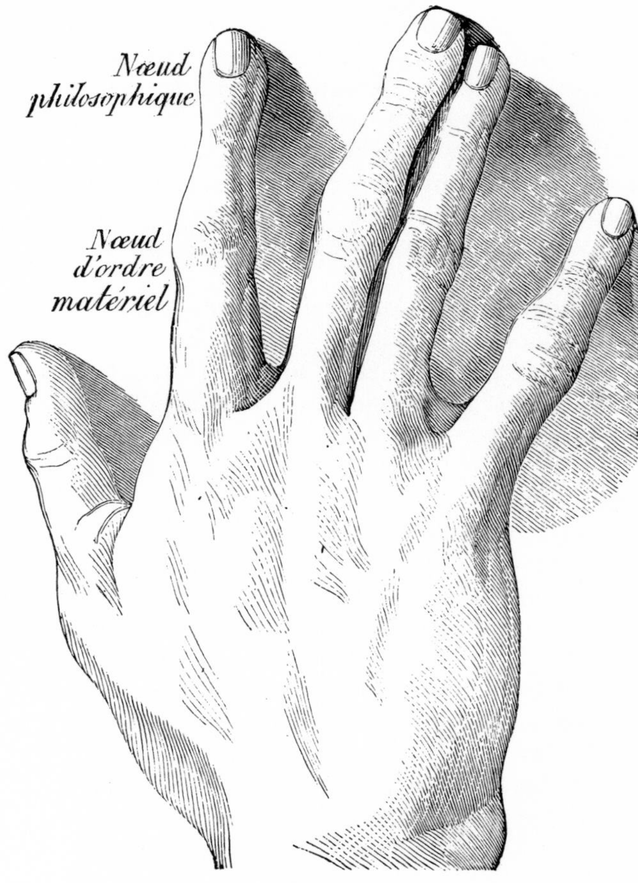

26. A nineteenth century system of interpreting the associations of the three phalanges.

27. A nineteenth century interpretation of the associations of the finger joints. 'Smooth' joints and 'Knotty' joints were differentiated: 'Knots' were held to be barriers to the life forces which passed through the hand and fingers.

28. What the palmists of previous centuries might regard as spatulate fingers, indicative of practicality, may nowadays be regarded as indicative of pulmonary troubles.

> shows him liberal, if downward niggardly . . . (6)

The traditions linked with the fingers are extremely interesting as examples of direct observation: the general quality of aphorism indicating that thick fingers indicate a love of ease and luxury, whilst supple or elastic fingers indicate mental dexterity, curiousity and extravagance. Short fingers are indicative of a more thoughtful and quiet nature, and so on. When one goes a little deeper into the theory of palmistry, however, one leaves behind such simple concepts, and this clarity and simplicity of aphorism is lost: the main teaching is (in regard to fingers, for example) that the three phalanges of the fingers relate to different 'faculties' in the human psyche:

> Thus, the first phalanges of the fingers represent the intuitive faculties, the second phalanges represent the reasoning powers, and the third or lowest phalanges represent the material instincts. Thus, therefore, if the third phalanges are relatively the largest, and are thick and full by comparison with the others, the prevailing instincts will be those of sensuality and of luxury; if the second phalanges are the most considerable, a love of reason and reasoning will be the mainspring of the life, whilst with a high development of the first (or exterior) phalanges the intuitive and divine attributes will be the prevailing characteristics of the subject. (7)

This is a nineteenth century attempt to rationalize the three parts of the fingers, and in some ways it differs only slightly from the earlier attempts to link each of the phalanges with one

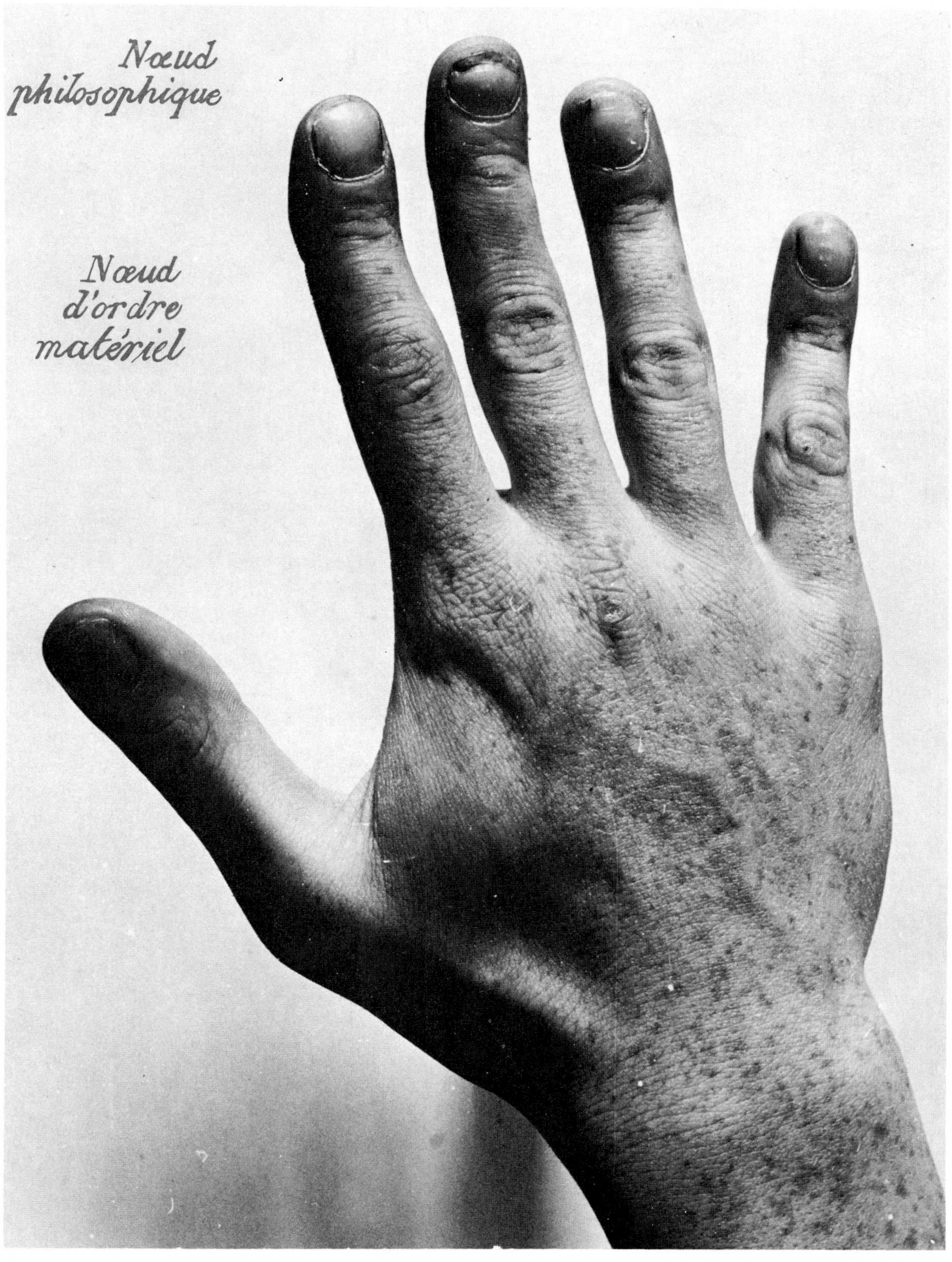
Nœud
philosophique
Nœud
d'ordre
matériel

29

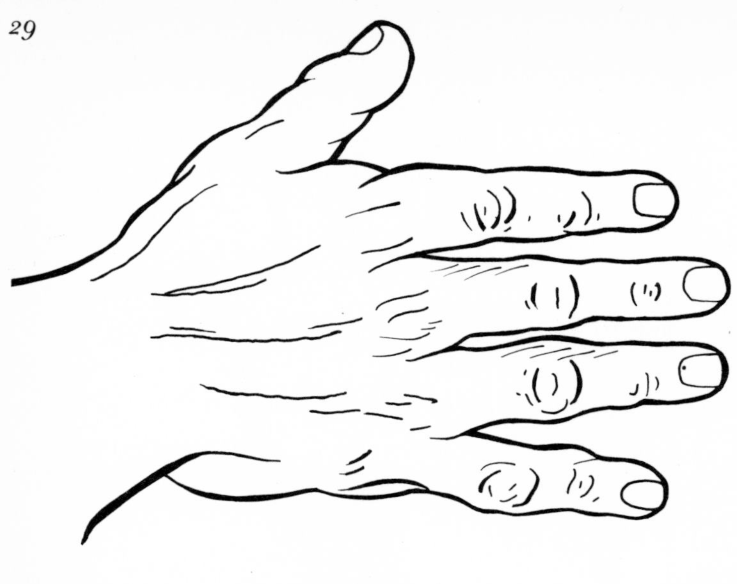

30

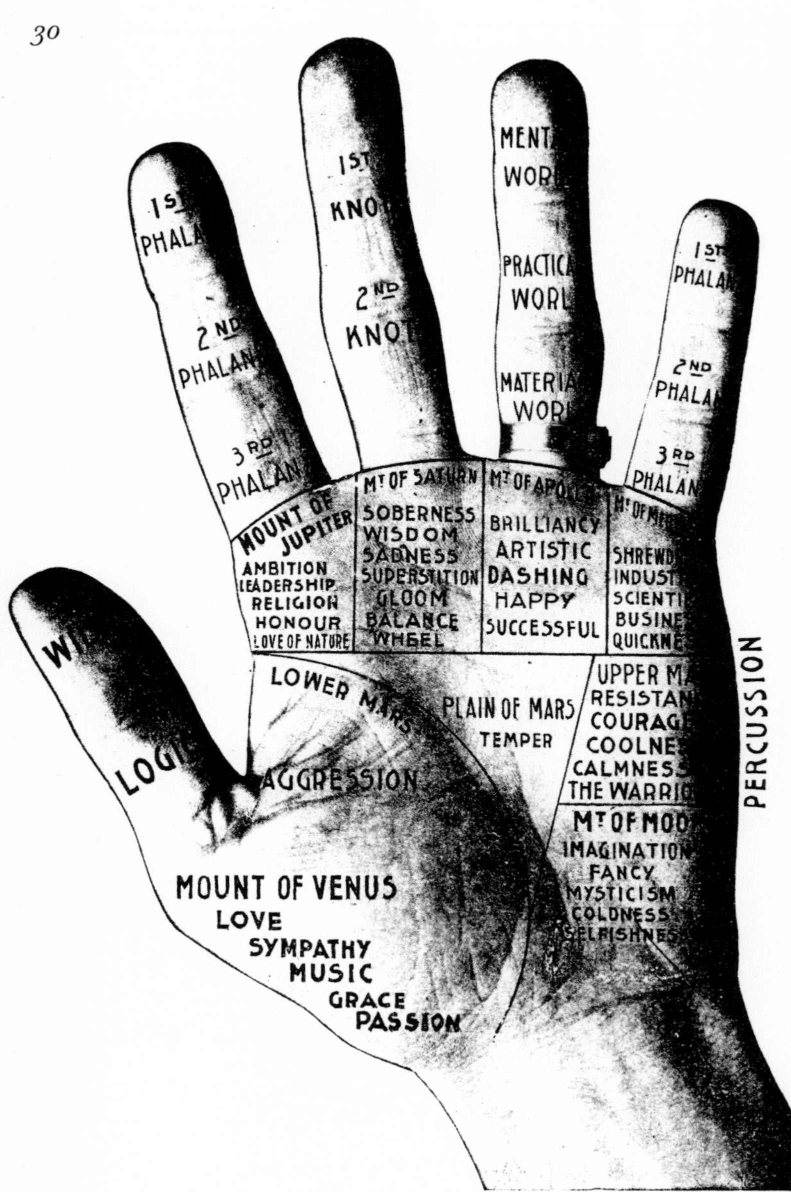

of the signs of the zodiac (figure 6). One feels that the system was rather hamstrung by the wish to relate the physical body to the triad of spirit, soul, and body which permeates occult teachings. The real significance of the fingers was understood only a little later, when it was grasped that such terms as 'long fingers' and 'short fingers' meant almost nothing except in relation to the hand as a whole. Once this fact had been realized, the way was open for the integration of the fingers into the hand– instead of cutting the fingers into three, the fingers were related to the structure from which they sprang, to the palm surface, and it was possible for the palmist to see the hand as a whole. After this, it was possible to establish classifications of the hand into different types, some of which had long fingers, some of which had short, some of which had knotty fingers, and so on. Even with the development of such 'hand types', which began its most healthy phase in the middle of the nineteenth century, the tendency was still to cling to descriptions of particular hand types, which were supposed to link up with certain psychological dispositions: the so-called spatulate hand, for example, was meant to indicate an active personality, and so on.

Of the several systems of such hand classifications which have survived, and which are still used by certain palmists today, the oldest is that instituted by the Frenchman D'Arpentigny, who claimed to have been introduced to the art of palmistry by a Spanish gypsy girl. He was perhaps following the old astrological tradition which centred around the 'seven' planets when he classified hands into seven

29. The back of an Elementary hand, in D'Arpentigny's system. See text below.

30. Benham's system of hand-zone nomenclature.

31. The Elementary hand in D'Arpentigny's system.

32. A plate from Benham's classic 'The Law of Scientific Handreading'.

31

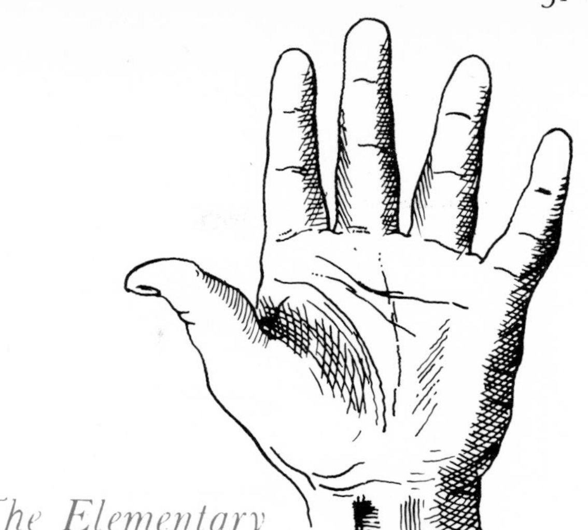

32

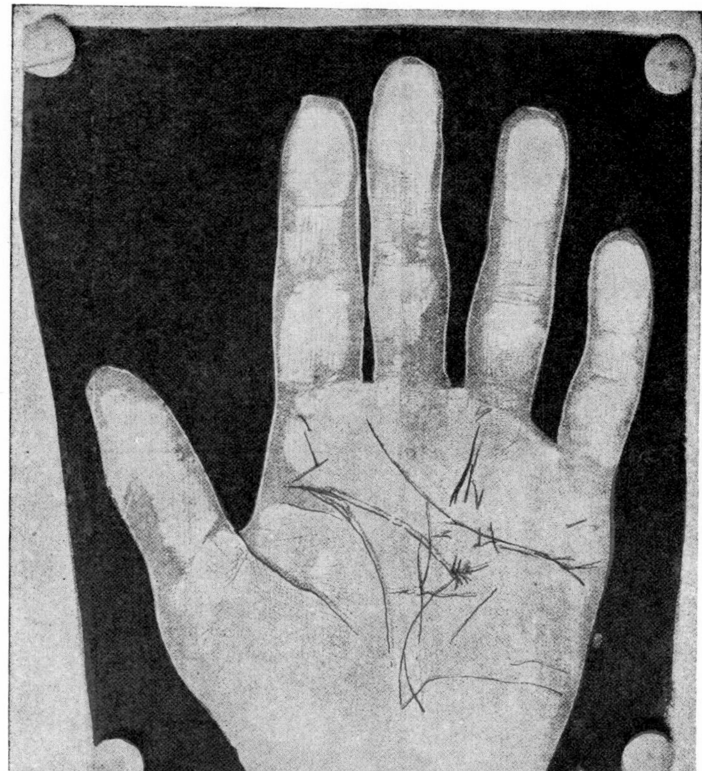

ALBERT J. FRANTZ

The murderer of Bessie Little of Dayton. This case was a celebrated murder mystery. Frantz was convicted on circumstantial evidence, and electrocuted November 19, 1898. His death is indicated on his Head Line.

types—the Elementary, the Spatulate, the Conical, the Square, the Knotty, the Pointed, and the Mixed. This seven-fold classification has taken such a hold of palmistry, mainly through the dubious offices of Count Louis Hamon, better known as 'Chiero', who adopted D'Arpentigny's system as his own, that it is worth while examining the teachings which draws a correlation between these seven hand types and the psychological states which they reflect. Whilst one may examine the original drawings of these hands, as reproduced in the relevant places, it is also interesting to see how these do in fact correspond to hand types which may be discovered today. The main failing with the D'Arpentigny classification is that it was not complete, and that the six main hand types do not between them cover all the different hand types which may be discovered in actual fact: the basis of division was not strictly logical. It is for this reason that the seventh, the so-called 'Mixed' hand was included in the list, for this very conveniently included all other hands which did not fall into the net of the described six. His system of classification is none the less worth close attention:

The Elementary or Necessary Hand (figure 31). This is so called because it belongs to the lowest grade of human intelligence, and seems only to be gifted with the amount of intellect requisite to provide the merest necessities of life . . . Such a hand as this betokens a crass and sluggard intelligence, incapable of understanding anything but the physical and visible aspect of things, a mind governed by custom and habit, and

33

A FEW EXTRACTS FROM CHEIRO'S AUTOGRAPH-BOOK.

The Duke of Newcastle.

Cheiro has told my past and immediate future with wonderful accuracy, especially with regard to certain coming events which he could not possibly have known.

Oscar Wilde.

Indeed, Cheiro, the mystery of the world is the visible, not the invisible.

Mark Twain.

Cheiro has exposed my character to me with humiliating accuracy. I ought not to confess this accuracy, still I am moved to do it.

34

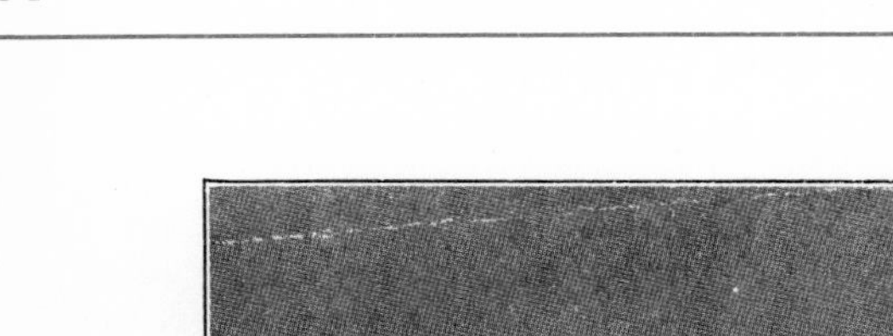

not by inclination or originality. Such a character, inaccessible to reason from sheer want of originality, of intellect to understand it, is sluggish, heavy, and lazy as regards any occupation beyond its accustomed toil. It has no imagination or reasoning power, and will exert itself mentally or physically so as to obtain that which is absolutely necessary to its existence. Thus in war such hands will only fight to defend themselves, and not for glory or honour; such people fight with a brutish ferocity, but without any attention to the arts of modern warfare . . . (8)

Not for the Elementary the delicacies of modern reciprocal annihilation – fists and bayonets will suffice! In fact, joking apart, this description of the temperament associated with the kind of hand portrayed is far from unbiased, and one suspects that D'Arpentigny was being bugged by his social position. He was relatively speaking a man of leisure, of the upper class, and this probably meant that his acquaintance with the peasant stock would be slight yet would compel such an interpretation as the one quoted above. Cheiro, who took over D'Arpentigny's system piecemeal, pictures the type in almost cruel terms:

They have little or no control over their passions; love of form, color, and beauty does not appeal to them . . . Such people are violent in temper, passionate but not courageous . . . They possess a certain low cunning, but the cunning of instinct, not of reason. These are people without aspirations; they but eat, drink, sleep and die. (9)

The possessor of such a hand form is not quite

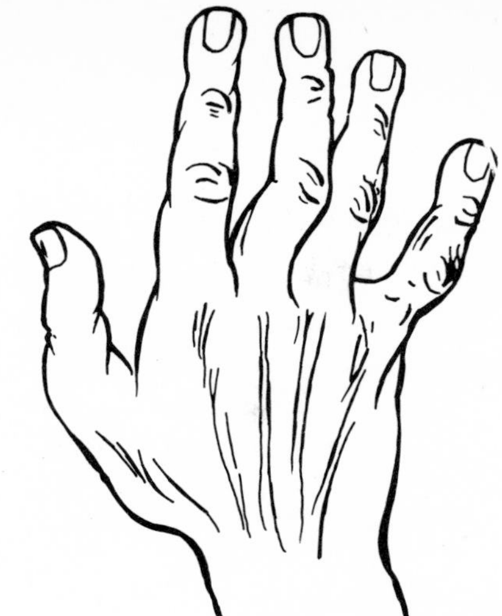

35

33. Some of the 'unsolicited testamonials' from a nineteenth century edition of 'Cheiro's' 'Language of the Hand'.

34. Portrait of 'Cheiro', whose system of palmistry was scarcely original, but who undoubtedly possessed some clairvoyant ability.

35. A back view of the Spatulate hand in D'Arpentigny's system, reproduced from 'Cheiro's' book. 'Cheiro' took over D'Arpentigny's system wholesale, and virtually without acknowledgement.

so crass as the description would have us believe: as we shall see, this type of hand is often found among artists and people otherwise creative, and also summarizes intelligence, though the most primitive types certainly do qualify for D'Arpentigny's description. In certain respects this hand closely corresponds in form to the Earth hand of a later classification.

The Spatulate, or Active Hand (figure 35). The great pronounced characteristics of this type are: action, movement, energy; and, of course, the harder or firmer the hand, the more pronounced will these characteristics be. A man of this type is resolute, self-confident, and desirous of abundance rather than of sufficiency; . . . he will be more active than delicate, more energetic than enthusiastic; in love he will be more constant and faithful (though less tender and affectionate) than the conic or pointed-handed subject, by reason of his want of inclination towards things romantic and poetic . . .

They are only very slightly sensual, and are greedy rather than epicurean; they like travelling about and seeing new places; being very self-confident, they have no objection to solitude, and are clever to all utilitarian sciences, which enable them to shift for themselves.

A man of the spatulate type admires architecture, but likes it to be stupendous rather than ornate. They are great arithmeticians, and to please them things must be astonishing and exact, representing a large amount of physical labour. With them the artizan is more considered than the artist; they appreciate wealth rather than luxury, quantity rather than quality. A town, to suit their views, must be clean, regularly built, substantial, and of business-like appearance.

These subjects will be fond of order and regularity because of its appearance, and they will arrange and tidy things more from the desire to be *doing* something than from the love of tidiness itself.

Their laws are strict and often tyrannical, but always just; and their language is forcible rather than ornate. They are brave, industrious, and perservering; not cast down by trifles, but rather courting difficulties so as to surmount them. They desire to command, and are intolerant of restraint, unless for their individual good. They are most tenacious of what is their own, and are always ready to fight for their rights. (10)

Perhaps a little unfair to Heron Allen to link this hand more with the Scots than with the English because of the 'industry, perseverance . . . economy, caution, and calculation' which is associated with the type! One suspects that it is actually the *consistency* of the hand which is more important than the spatulate shape, for should this hand be soft, then the entire character of the personality changes, and is left, as it were, hanging upside down:

When the spatulate hand is very soft the spirit of action will have a powerful enemy in an innate laziness. Such a subject will be a late riser, and a man of sedentary habits; but will love the spectacle and noise of action and movement. He will like to travel and hear about travels, but he will travel

36

37

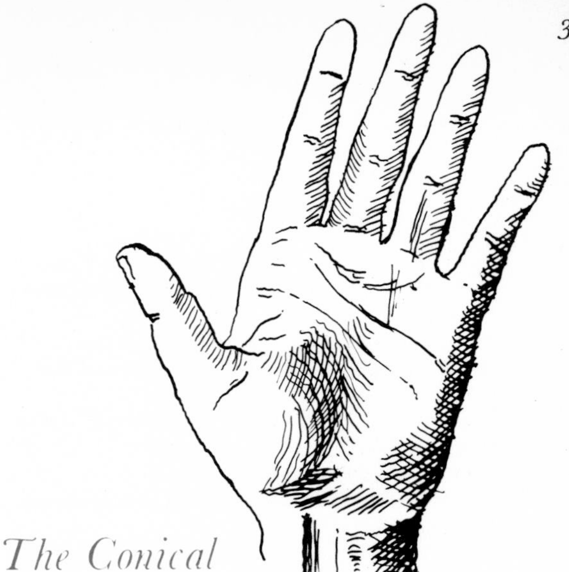

The Conical

comfortably, preferring to hear and read about the actions and movements of others than to be active and energetic himself. (11)

Scarcely the description of the active personality so far associated with the Spatulate hand. Cheiro has a different view of the two types of spatulate:

> . . . the spatulate hand, when hard and firm, indicates a nature restless and excitable, but full of purpose and enthusiasm. When soft and flabby . . . it denotes the restless but irritable spirit. Such a person works in fits and starts, but cannot stick to anything long. (12)

He summarizes the type with the key words 'intense love of action, energy, and independence.'

With the third of D'Arpentigny's hand formations we discover various qualifications which appear to subdivide the hand into three further categories.

> The Conical, or Artistic Hand (figure 37). It is subject also to three variations of formation and concomitant chararacteristics which modify the indications of the type as regards the ends to which it works. Firstly, a supple hand with a small thumb and a developed though still medium palm. This hand is drawn invariably to what is actually beautiful in art. Secondly, a large hand, rather thick and short, with a large thumb. This hand is endued with a desire of wealth, grandeur, and good fortune. And, thirdly, a large and very firm hand, the palm highly developed. This formation indicates a strong tendency to sensuality. All three are governed by inspiration, and are absolutely unfit for physical and mechanical pursuits; but the first goes into a scheme enthusiastically, the second cunningly, and the third with an aim towards self-gratification.
>
> Such a subject will be ruled by impulse and instinct rather than by reason or calculation, and will always be attracted at once by the beautiful aspects of life and matter. He will prefer that things should be beautiful rather than that they should be useful. Attracted by ease, novelty, liberty, and anything which strikes his mind as being pleasant, he is at the same time vain, and fearful of ridicule; enthusiastic, but outwardly humble, and his prime motive powers are enthusiasm and impulse, rather than force or determination. Subject to the most sudden changes of temperament, he is at one moment in the seventh heaven of excitable hopefulness, and the next in the nethermost abyss of intangible despair. Unable to command, he is incapable of obedience. He may be attracted in a given direction, but never driven. The times of a domestic life are unbearable to him. At heart he is a pure Bohemian. In lieu of ideas he has sentiments. Light-hearted, open-handed, and impulsive, his imagination is as warm as his heart is by nature cold . . .
>
> Subjects of the artistic type are not nearly so capable of constancy in love as their square or spatulate brethren and sisters, for they are so apt to fall in love on impulse, and without consideration, whereas with the spatulate, true love (as are all other

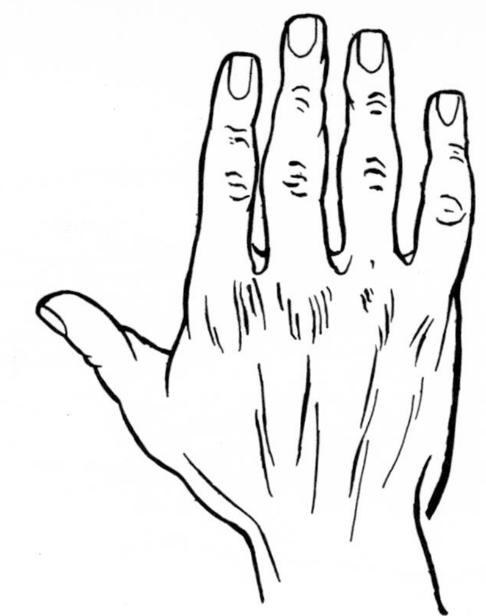

36. The back of the Conic hand in D'Arpentigny's system of classification.

37. The conic hand, from the textbook by Heron-Allen.

38. The back of the Square hand of D'Arpentigny's system, as depicted by 'Cheiro'.

39. The Square hand, from Heron-Allen's 'The Science of the Hand'.

> subjects) is a matter of reason and calculations. (13)

One supposes from such a commentary that the modern equivalent phrase for 'artistic' would be 'neurotic'. It is perhaps in this sense that D'Arpentigny's classification is weak, for it is quite unreasonable to assume that one particular hand formation indicates the artist; after all, there are artists and artists, and we will find the artistic temperament, as well as an artistic ability, linked with all hand formations. Certainly it is symptomatic of a strange vision of the universe to separate the practical from the artistic, and then to insist that the artistic type is 'absolutely unfit for physical and mechanical pursuits'. (14) Perhaps we may infer that D'Arpentigny didn't know many artists, or that the sensitive souls he did know were fairly neurotic.

> The Square or Useful Hand (figure 38).
> The leading instincts on which this hand founds all its characteristics are perseverance, foresight, order, and regularity. To these hands the useful is far preferable to the beautiful; their great passion is organisation, arrangement, classification, regularity of form and outline, and the acceptation of things prescribed and understood as customary . . . They are only romantics within the bounds of reason, and are constant in love, more from a sense of the fitness of things than from depth of feeling . . .
>
> They cherish their privileges, preferring them to complete liberty; and they have a passion for varied experience, which they are always ready to pay for . . .
>
> They are slaves to arrangement–that is,

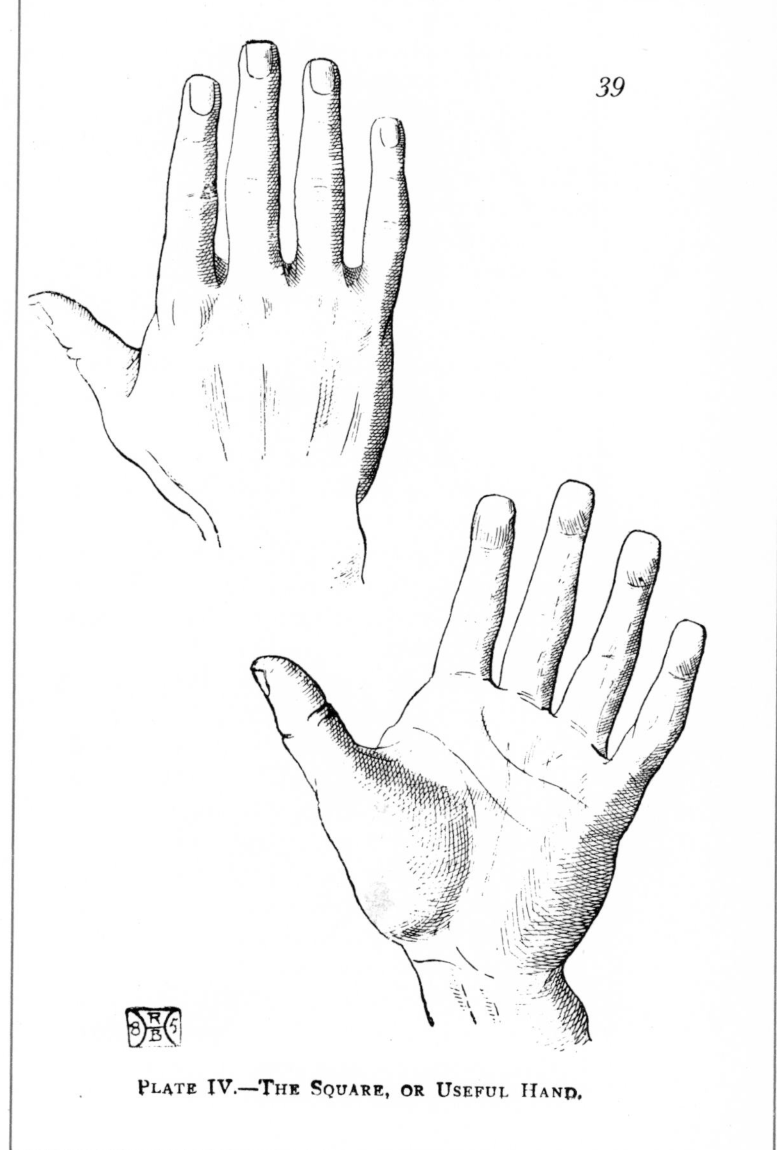

PLATE IV.—THE SQUARE, OR USEFUL HAND.

40

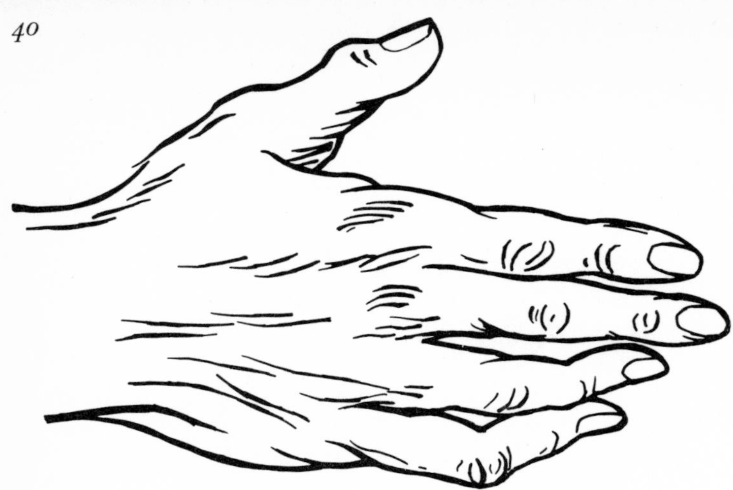

40. The back of the Knotty hand, according to 'Cheiro'.

41. The Philosophic hand, from Heron-Allen's 'The Science of the Hand'.

42. A page from Indagine's book on Chiromancy, dealing with the plain of Mars.

41

PLATE V.—THE KNOTTY, OR PHILOSOPHIC HAND.

11

> they have a place for everything, and everything is in its place; unless their fingers have also the joints developed, it is quite possible (if not probable) that their rooms and cupboards may be outwardly very untidy. but, nevertheless, they always know where everything is. As a rule, they will only comprehend things as far as they can positively see them, having themselves far too well under control to allow themselves to launch into enthusiasm; they are, therefore, strong disciplinarians, prone to details, fond of minutiae . . . Square-handed people can always govern the expressions of their faces, their language, and their looks; they are most averse to sudden changes or circumstances . . . They dress very quietly, but always very well, and they avoid studiously anything like ostentation or display in matters of eccentricity, ornament, or jewellery, excepting on fitting occasions, when their magnificence is striking from its good taste. (15)

The salt of the earth, this square-handed type, but could there be an element of boredom around them, for 'they make many acquaintances, but few friends'? Not merely boredom, but even an element of tyranny:

> Good sense, therefore, is the guiding principle of the square type, but, were the world wholly populated by them, fanatical 'red-tapeism' and narrow-minded despotism would be universal. (16)

Even so, in comparison with the Elementary hand, one would infinitely prefer to meet a Square-handed person when alone on a dark night. Cheiro emphasises their *conformity*:

42

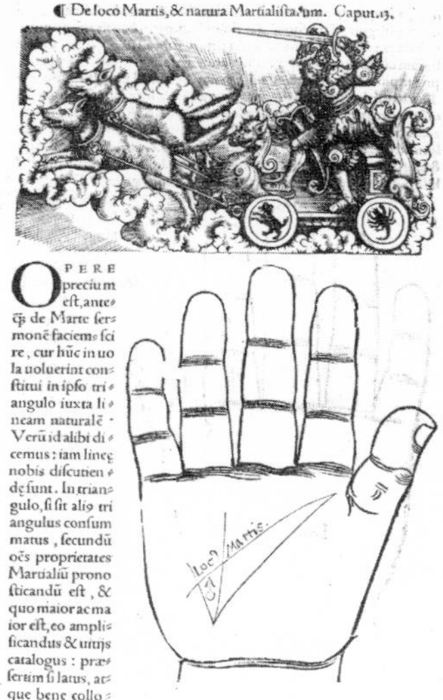
¶ De loco Martis, & natura Martialiſta.*um. Caput.13.

OPERE precium eſt, anteq̃ de Marte ſermonẽ faciem, ſcire, cur hũc in uola uoluerint conſtitui in ipſo triangulo iuxta lineam naturalẽ. Verũ id alibi dicemus: iam lineę nobis diſcutiendę ſunt. In triangulo, ſi ſit aliꝰ triangulus conſummatus, ſecundũ oẽs proprietates Martialiũ pronoſticandũ eſt, & quo maior ac maior eſt, eo amplificandus & uitijs catalogus: præſertim ſi latus, atque bene collo-

People with such a hand are orderly, punctual, and precise in manner, not, however, from any innate grace of nature, but more from conformity, to custom and habit. They respect authority, they love discipline, they have a place for everything and everything is kept in its place . . . They respect law and order, and are slaves to custom; thus are not quarrelsome, but are determined in opposition . . . (17)

One of the major characteristics of the type, hinted at by Cheiro, but not stated, is the love of rhythm, which is a kind of 'patterned order in time'.

The Knotty or Philosophic Hand (figure 41). The great characteristics indicated by this type of hand are–analysis, meditation, philosophy, deduction, poetry of *reason*, independence, often deism and democracy, and the search after, and love of, the abstract and absolute truth. The development of the joints gives this hand calculation, method, and deduction; the quasi-conic formation of the exterior phalanx gives it the instinct of poetry in the abstract, and beauty in things real; and the thumb gives it perseverance in its metaphysical studies . . .

Such subjects like to account for everything, to know the reason of everything, whether physical, metaphysical, psychological, or psychic; their ideas they form for themselves, without caring in the least for those of other people; their convictions–religious, social, and otherwise–are only acquired as the result of careful analysis and considerations of the questions involved; love, instinct, faith, are all made subordinate to reason, which is the principle more powerful with them than rule, conventionalism, inclination, or love, except in matters of religion, for their religion is one rather of love and adoration than of fear and conventionality. It is thus that among the subjects of this type we find a large proportion of persons who become known as sceptics of various kinds, for they look upon doubt and scepticism as one of the first necessary evils of life, which will give way to reverance and adoration, and therefore do not in any way worry themselves on this account.

They are just, (from an intuitive sense of justice and a discriminating instinct of ethics,) unsuperstitious, great advocates of social and religious freedom, and moderate in their pleasures. It is in these respects that they differ so totally from the subordination and conventionalism of square-fingered hands. (18)

Here we have the intellectual salt of the earth, so to speak, though we cannot help thinking that this Knotty hand was the one which D'Arpentigny himself possessed. We would all like to think of ourselves as 'seeking the truth in all things, and in all things directed by reason, and by common sense directed by will', as the nature of the type was epitomized. 'They like to be distinct from other people,' writes Cheiro, 'and they will go through all kinds of privations to attain this end . . .' Perhaps we are all like this, though not quite so ethereal as Cheiro further images the type:

Theirs is the peace of the aesthetic; theirs the domain beyond the borderland of

43

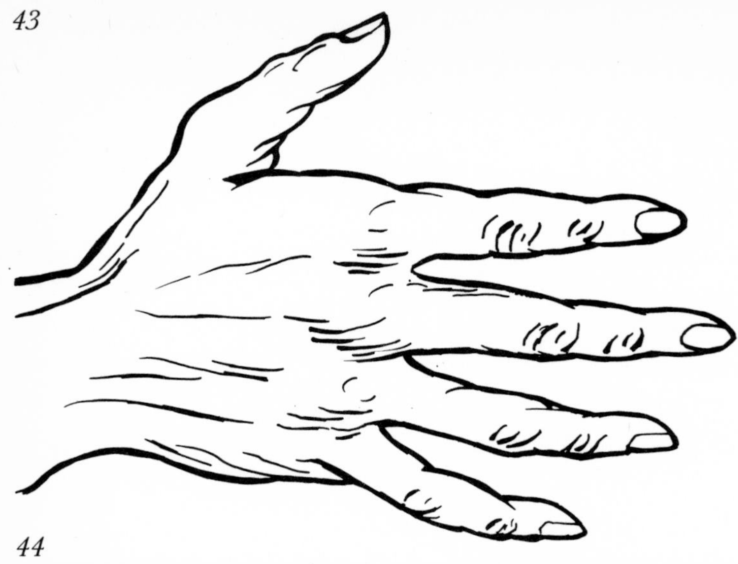

44

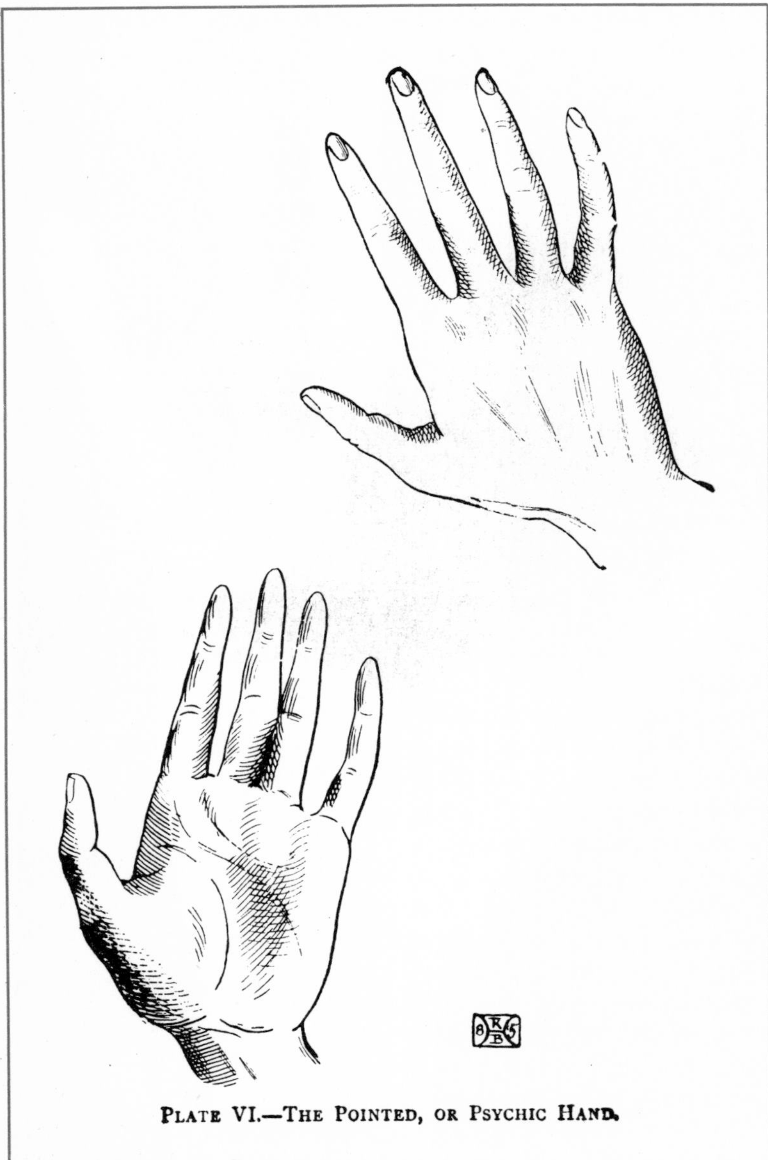

PLATE VI.—THE POINTED, OR PSYCHIC HAND.

matter, theirs the cloudland of thought, where the dreaded grub-worm of materialism dare not follow . . . (19)

The lack of respect which prevailed in the nineteenth century for the 'irrational' or 'unphilosophic' is particularly noticeable in the sixth type of hand, for Heron Allen considers it 'the most beautiful and impractical' of hands:

The Pointed, or Psychic Hand (figure 44). To these subjects belong the domains of the beautiful ideal, the land of dreams, of Utopian ideas, and of artistic fervour; they have the delicacy and true instinct of art of the conic hand, without its bad points, its sensualism, its egotism, and its worldliness. They are guided only by their idealism, by impulse, by their instinct of right in the abstract, and by their natural love and attraction for the beautiful in all things, whether mundane or celestial; bearing the same relation to the philosophic hands that the artistic bear to the useful, the relation of constract.

These hands never command, for they establish for themselves far too lofty an ideal to care about earthly domination or material interests of any kind; they are incapable of strife or struggles for glory, but, if their instincts of the ideally just are aroused, they will devote themselves even to death in defence of what they consider to be ethically right . . . They will undertake huge forlorn enterprises, but will disdain to embark upon small practicable expeditions, in quest of some material good. (2)

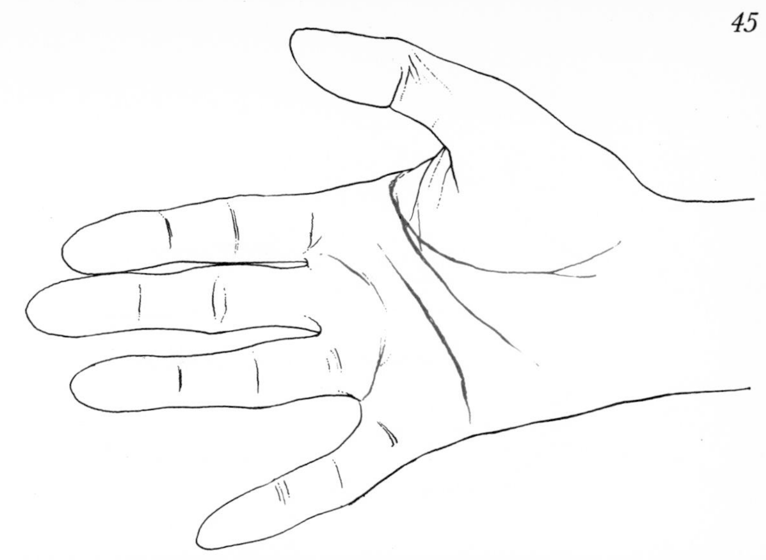

43. The back of the Psychic hand, according to 'Cheiro'.

44. The Psychic hand, according to Heron-Allen.

45. The hand of a novelist, which would appear from the system of D'Arpentigny to be of the Psychic type.

46. The 'hand of a suicide' from Cheiro's collection of prints in 'The Language of the Hand'. Again, the hand would appear to be of the Psychic type, though it would fit more convincingly into the Water type of a later classification.

Heron Allen concludes that the 'luxurious dreaming Orientals are almost exclusively of this type', (precisely the claim made by Cheiro for the Philosophic hand) and again reinforces his strange view of humanity, showing his general distaste for anything which is not practical or 'realistic':

> Among them we find spiritualists, mediums, and all the so-called 'weakminded' devotees of psychical science, who accept all that is told them without investigation or analysis, and are therefore the easy prey of 'spiritualistic' imposters. In countries where such hands predominate and hold the reins of government we find that the rule is maintained by superstition, by the priests, and by fetishism. (21)

It is surprising, in view of what he has so far said, that he can find something pleasant to say about these 'beautiful useless hands', but when he does, he labours on the sympathy of the type:

> Such subjects are ruled by heart and by soul; their feelings are acute, their nerves highly strung, and they are easily fired with a wonderous enthusiasm. Theirs are the talents which produce the most inspired poetry; their influence over the masses is extreme, from their power of communicating their enthusiasm to their fellow-men, a power whereby they appeal alike to the most refined and to the most coarse, to the most intellectual and to the most ignorant. (22)

Cheiro does not beat about the bush, and designates this 'the most beautiful but the most unfortunate of the seven':

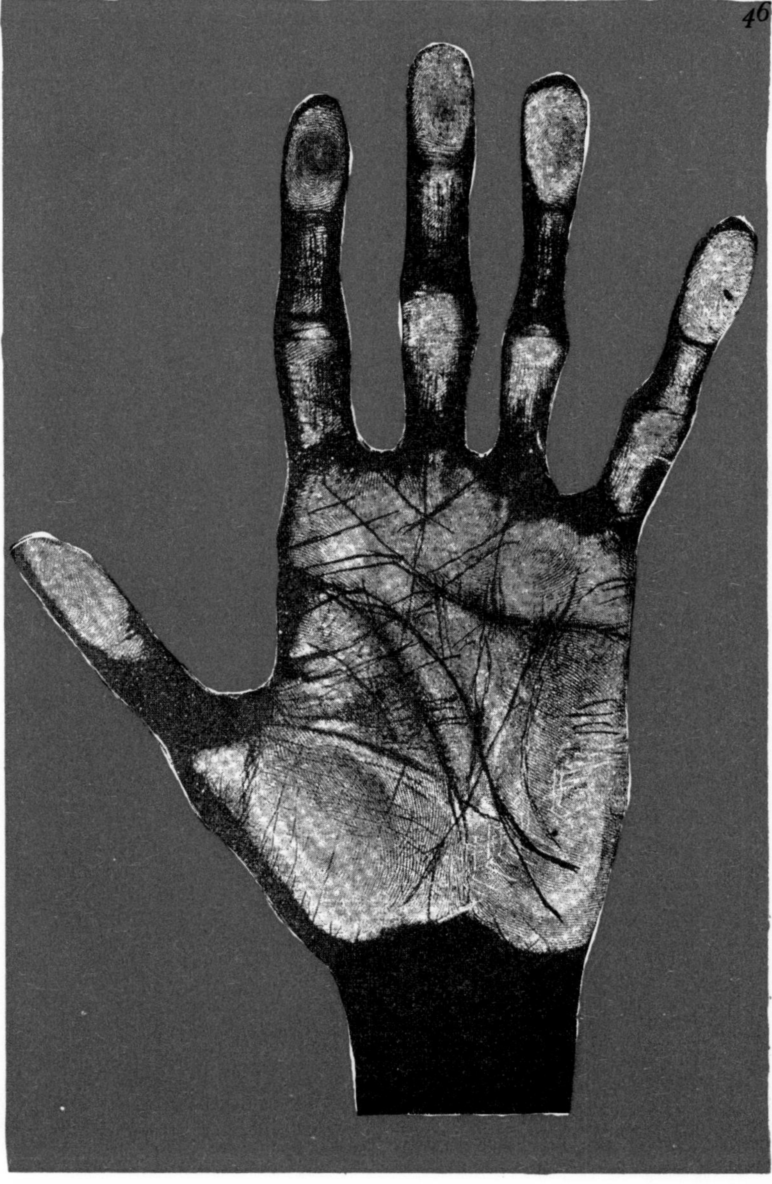

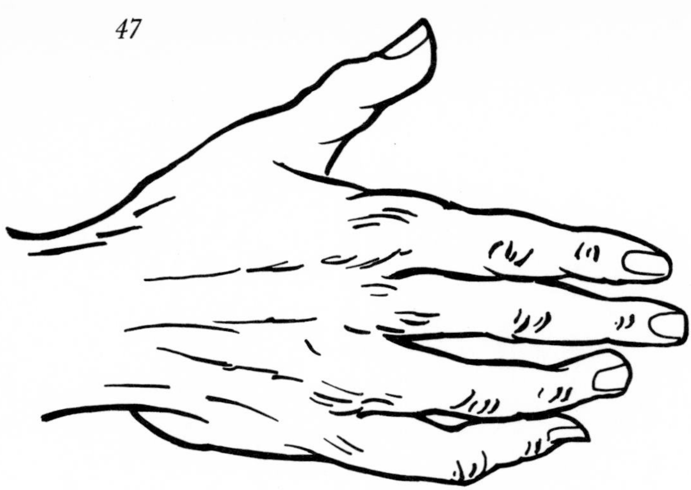

47. *The 'Mixed' hand of D'Arpentigny's seven-fold system of classification. In effect, any hand which does not fit clearly into one of the six categories reproduced on the opposite page, may be lumped under this seventh category—it is for this reason that D'Arpentigny's system is unsatisfactory.*

48. *The six main categories in D'Arpentigny's system, brought together for the purpose of comparison.*

> Possessors of these beautiful, delicate hands, the indicators of the purely sensitive nature, usually feel their position in life so keenly that they too often consider themselves useless, and become morbid and melancholy in consequence. (23)

As we have noted, the Mixed hand has been inserted to make the classification workable:

> When the seventh hand type of the classification is reached, we begin to observe some of the weaknesses of the system which has influenced so many palmists during the past century. The mixed hand is that one of which the shape is so uncertain, as to resemble, even to possibility of confusion, more than one type . . . In such cases the cheirophist must so combine, mentally, the tendencies of both types represented, as to arrive at a true analysis of the character of the subject under examination. (24)

Confusion prevails mainly because one finds that in practice almost all hands are 'mixed', all contain different elements, and it is sometimes extremely difficult to see how to distinguish which elements predominate. A combination as unlikely as the conic and the elementary would result in a strange hand, of course, and it would seem from the accompanying description provided by Heron Allen that the resultant personality would be just as hybrid:

> . . . as I have pointed out, the intelligence of art or music, and the worship of the beautiful, are the only feelings to which the true elementary hand is at all susceptible, and the artistic hand, by the exaggeration of its failings, may often degenerate into the artistico-elementary. Such a hand will betoken a vacillating, unreliable, apathetic, character without sympathy for the misfortunes, or gratification at the good luck of others. Such people are rude poets, superstitious, and very sensitive to bodily pain. Such hands denote activity by their hardness, and credulity by their pointed tips. (25)

The French palmist Desbarrolles took this question of pointed tips very seriously, and he taught that the more pointed and delicate were the fingers, the more easily would these transmit the astral energies, the 'electricity', into the human frame. He considered that the finger joints act as obstacles, and that the absence of joints produces a clear passage for the currents of animal electricity, to which he attributes the gift of prophecy and intuition. This is why 'seers, metaphysicians dreamers and poets have pointed fingers'. Such types are among the 'intermediaries between Heaven and earth, and perhaps on these grounds (certainly not after an analysis of the hands of these remarkable men), Desbarrolles affirms that Milton, Shakespeare, Schiller, Goethe, Swedenborg, Chateaubriand and Victor Hugo had such fingers. His own classification of hands into three groups was based mainly on the nature of the finger endings, since the finger tips were regarded as being kinds of receiving antennae for astral fluids. The pointed fingers gave *imagination*, the square fingers *reason*, and the spatulate fingers *action*. The threefold classification linked with the occult tradition which saw in man the combination of the three brains of emotion, reason

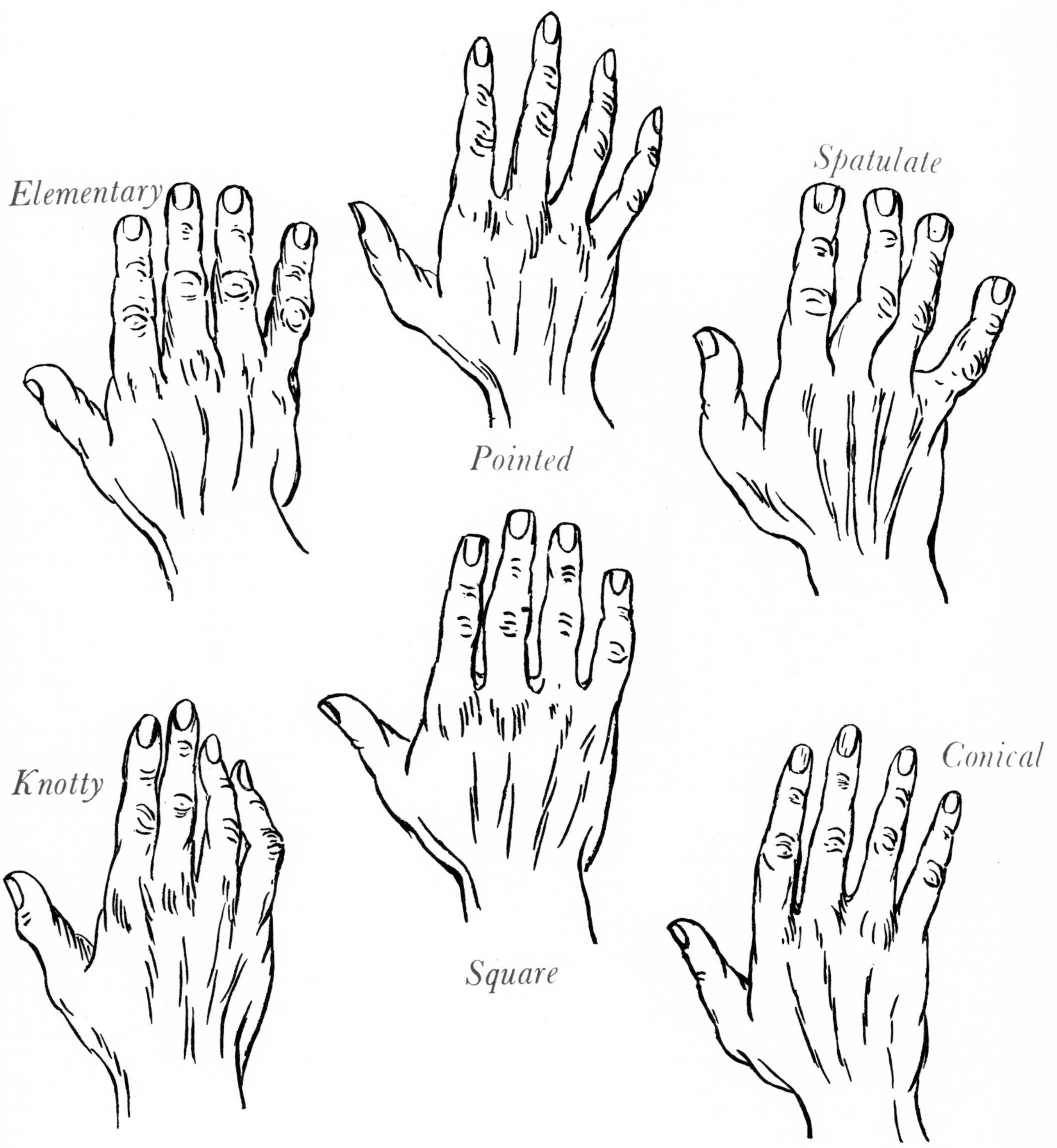
Elementary
Spatulate
Pointed
Knotty
Conical
Square

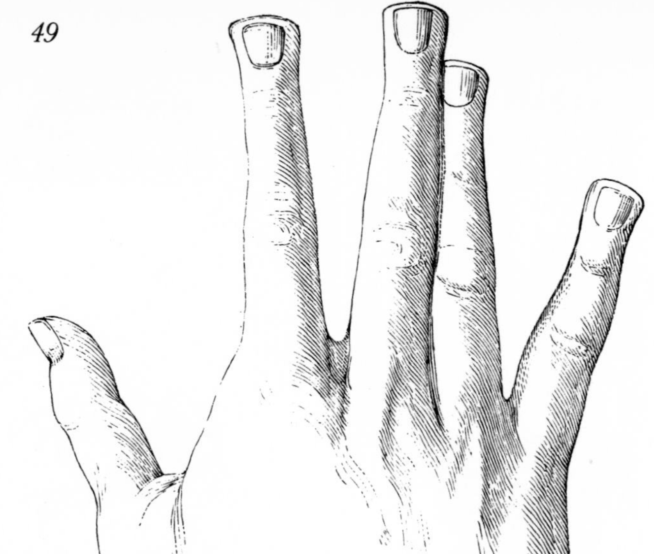

49

50

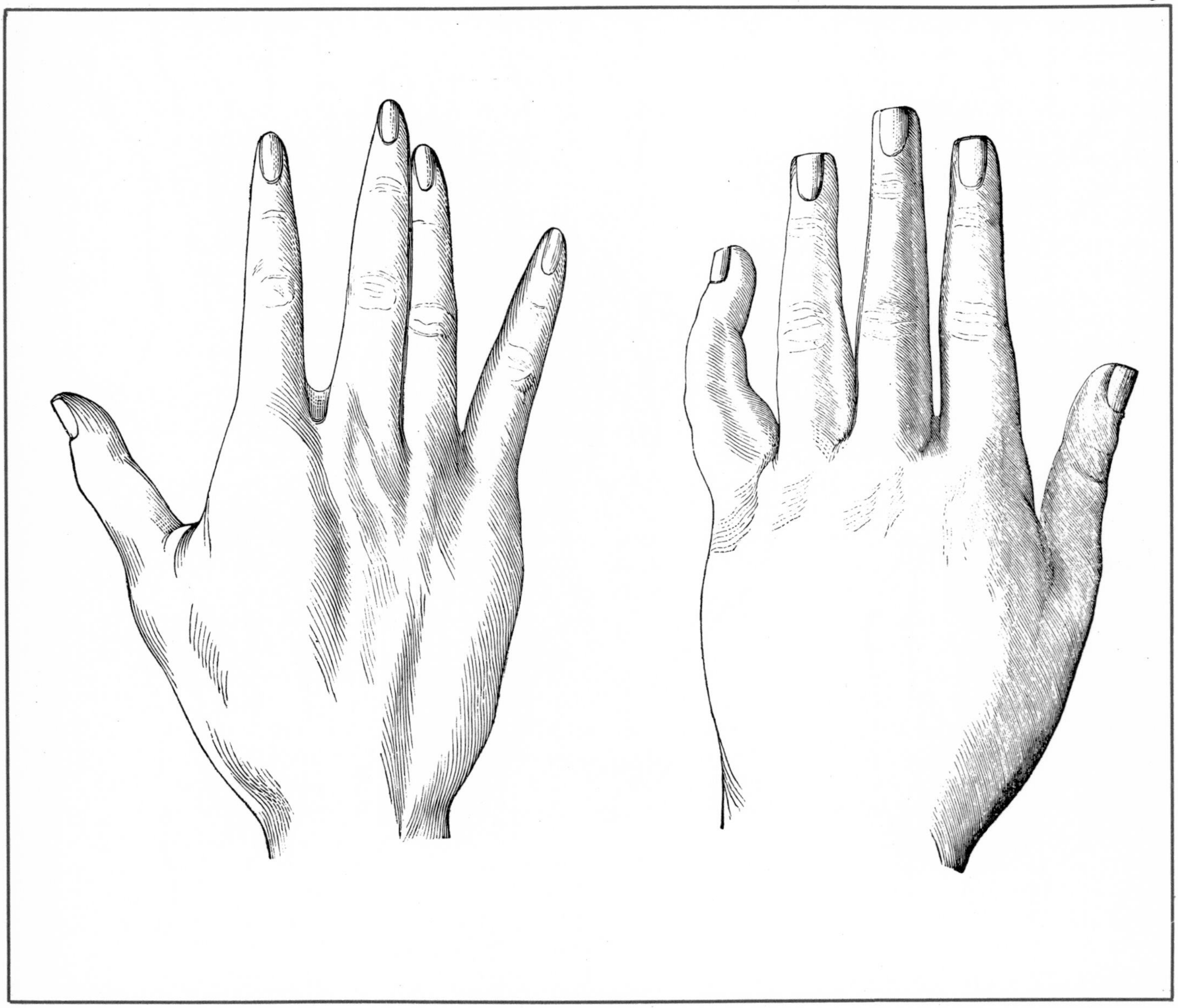

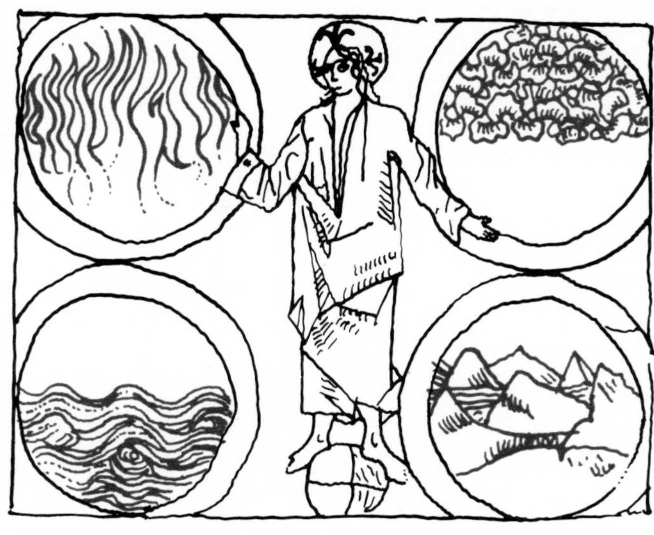

51

49. Spatulate finger ends, reproduced in Desbarrolles' 'Les Mystéres de la Main'.

50. Pointed fingers and square fingers in Desbarrolles system.

51. The four elements of the ancients—Fire, Air, Water and Earth, which form the basis of a modern system of chirognomy, of four distinctive hand types and temperaments.

and body: this tripartite relationship was established with regard to the phalanges, the first phalange relating to the divine, the second to logic, and the third to the *material instincts*. For this reason, those people with heavy or thick third phalanges (figure 131) were said to be very material, earth-bound, fond of the enjoyments of the flesh, and so on. Such theories are perhaps satisfying intellectually, in that they reduce complex hands to a system of examination which would appear to render them less complex, yet in fact they do not hold water when applied to real living hands. Hardly any hands are entirely 'pointed' or entirely 'spatulate': the tendency is for the finger of Apollo to be slightly spatulate in most hands, for the finger of Mercury to be slightly pointed in most hands, and so on. Yet the background theory is fairly reasonable, in that the finger of Mercury, whether pointed or not, relates to imagination, for this is the finger which rules over the sexual energies, and which allows an outlet for the imaginative forces which are compressed in the Mount of Moon. Again, the finger of Apollo, whether spatulate or not, relates to action, for this is the finger which rules emotional expression on a practical level, action being required to give form in the material world to emotionally held wishes and aspirations. We see, then, that there is a truth contained in these theories, and suspect that the classifications of hand types put forward by these palmists fail in many respects only because the underlying truth was not sufficiently investigated in terms of real, living hands.

The ancient tradition, revitalized by modern research, provided a much-needed key to an understanding of the hand form. From very early times it has been upheld that the basic temperaments of man may be divided into four kinds, depending upon the nature of the predominating 'humour' in the body. These four humours consist of phlegm, blood, choler and black bile, and their predominance gives rise to the temperaments called phlegmatic, sanguine, choleric and melancholic. Whilst, in theory at least, a man who had these four in balance was not subject to illness or disease, the tradition asserted that since the Fall of Man no individual has such an even balance of humours, and we were therefore all compelled towards an excess of one humour, by which we are subject to particular kinds of human weakness and 'temperament'. In other words, due to the interaction of humours, and the predominance of one particular humour, we are all imperfect, and we are all 'types' evincing particular characteristics, emotions, ideas and sense of will. Although the pervasive theory of humours has survived to a very remarkable extent in astrology, it had, by the beginning of a literary palmistic tradition in Europe, been lost to palmistry, which is perhaps surprising. In the last century, the speculation and research of several palmists suggested that a new examination of astrology might provide a key to the problems of determining which system of hand classification would be most useful towards the understanding of man. At the same time, psychologists and morphologists began to seek for the relation between hand forms and character (figures 52–55). This they did

52

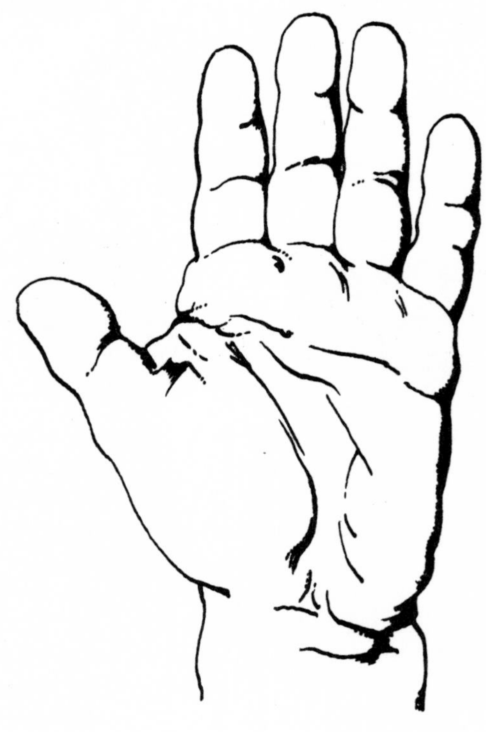

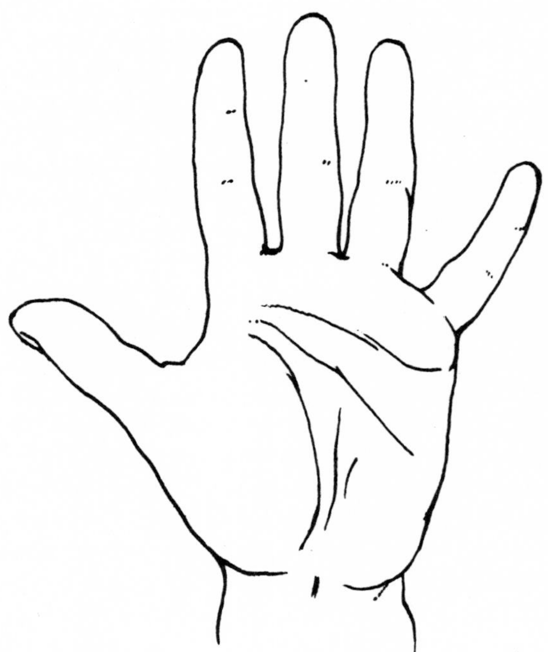

53

52. The Elementary hand according to the system of the nineteenth century German doctor and artist Carus.

53. The Sensitive hand in Carus' system.

54. The Motoric hand in Carus' system.

55. The Psychic hand in Carus' system.

mainly in accordance with normal scientific prejudice, by entirely rejecting or failing to examine the ancient traditions which explained, or sought to explain, the relationship between hand and character. The two streams of thought inherent in the Western tradition therefore separated quite clearly: on the one side there developed a series of hand-classifications in terms of 'scientific' thought—mainly of a psychological or quasi-psychological nature—so that certain doctors and psychologists originated individually systems of hand classifications which were sometimes of considerable value, especially in medical circles, for linking hand to temperament. At the same time, the more ancient system of thought, loosely termed 'occult' was also adapted by modern thinkers to the construction of hand systems. Whilst the psychologists were hampered by the fact that they had no hand classification system and no adequate classification of human beings which corresponded to any extent with the reality of the psycho-spiritual complex which is man, those involved with occult studies did at least have a system for classifying the human temperament, against which they could place the variety of hand formations with a view to understanding them. This is the main reason why the occult system of classification has proved in the long run to be most satisfactory. Another, more important reason stems from the fact that the images of the nature of man which are held by the majority of medical and psychological schools is hopelessly unreal. Only when the nature of man is rightly understood will it be possible for valid relationships between tem-

54

perament and morphology to be established.

From the studies made by occultists emerged several systems, the most immediately interesting being the fourfold classification of hand types based on the four humours and the astrological elements. The virtually obsolete 'humours' and the four elements of astrology were combined to give four basic hand types, each with a male and female designation, on the principle that the male incarnation seeks to enter matter more deeply and intimately than the female incarnation. The Water hand was predominantly of a phlegmatic disposition, extremely sensitive, and easily influenced by environment. The Air hand was predominantly of a sanguine disposition, hopeful, confident and intellectual. The Fire hand was predominantly of a choleric disposition, passionate, active, warm and intuitive. The Earth hand was predominantly of a melancholic disposition, practical, rather gloomy, and given to rhythmic expression. The first two are regarded as essentially 'feminine', the latter two as 'masculine', so that a female with a Water hand would be particularly feminine, strongly of the Water type, whilst a male with a Water hand would have a marked feminine streak in the temperament, but would not manifest so strongly the Water characteristics as would the female, The descriptions of these four hand types are of real value in the understanding of the relationship between hand and temperament, whilst the astrological tradition, being linked with the basic teaching, also throws much light on the subject. The relationship between the elements and the zodiacal signs is fundamental to palmistry.

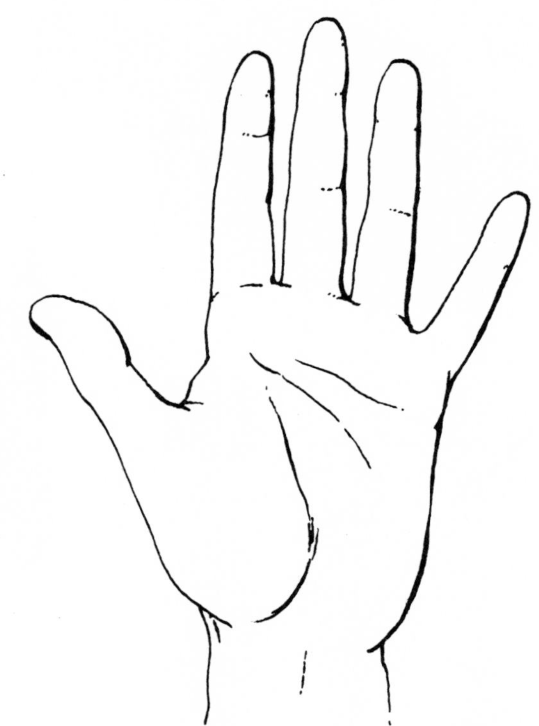

55

56

56. *The fine mesh of linear patterns characteristic of the Water hand.*

57. *The long palm and long fingers of the female Water hand.*

58. *The male Water hand.*

57

The Water Hand is a delicate hand structure–long fingers, and a long palm, with a fine mesh of linear markings (figure 57). It is called the Sensitive hand:

> A sensitive type, as his name suggests, is always impressionable: his surface moods are constantly being changed by changing conditions, and like water, he is always flowing and never constant. The feminine principle of *receptivity* is largely the cause of this constant flux of moods. It might well be argued that all types are changeable and depend on their environment for their particular manifestations, because the inability to change and to adapt can only mean an inability to life. This is true, but a Water type is particularly changeable and fluid, having none of the intellect of Air to keep him on a set course of action. (26).

With such a sensitive nature, the environment in which the type lives is of considerable importance, for the nature will tend to partake of the quality of that environment, reflecting on its surface the colours around it. Sometimes this will be to the detriment of the type, who because he is in essence insecure and emotional, is easily thrown off balance:

> The general high key to the emotions and the remarkable sensitivity to outer impressions is such that there is an unusual fluctuation in the personality for he tends to reflect the moral, emotional and physical shades of those around him. The virtues of the signs spring from the extreme sensitivity which renders him sympathetic to others. Sometimes this sensitivity leads to creativity, and

58

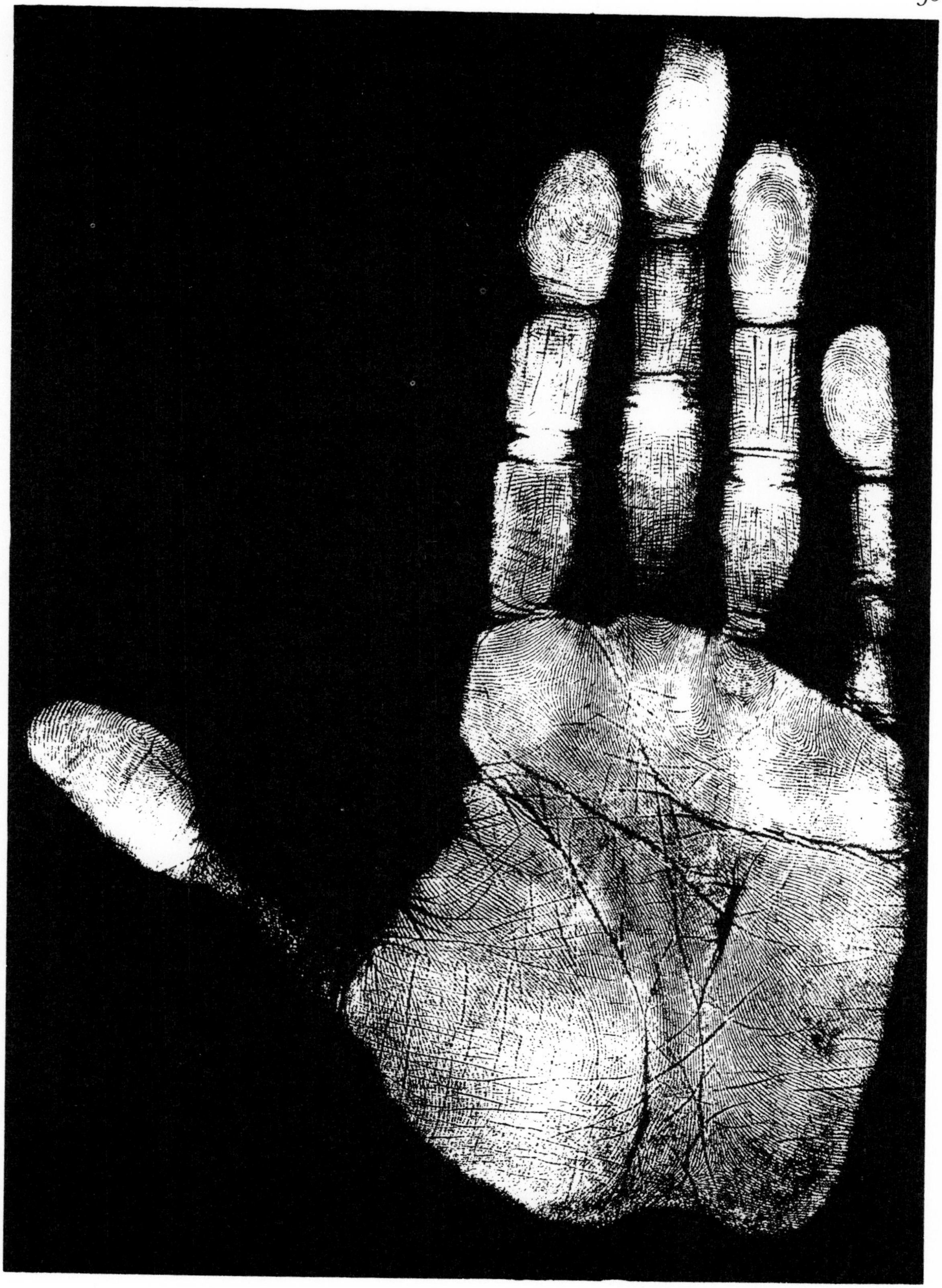

59

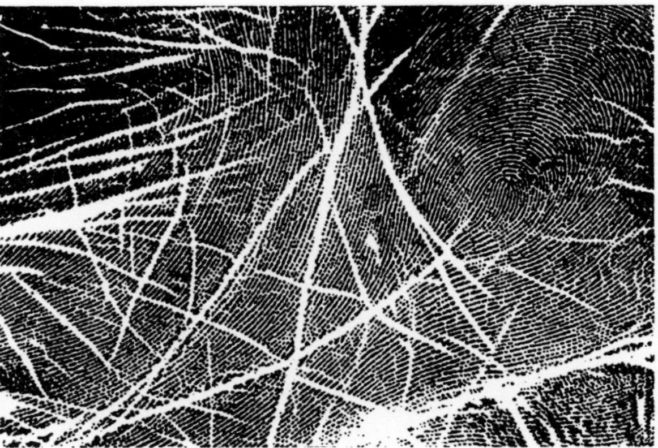

59. Characteristic line formations on an Air hand.

60. Print of a well-formed male Air hand. The outstretched fingers and general rotundity of the hand are typical.

61. The rounded 'square' of the Air palm is more easily seen in a print than in the hand itself.

then the type is not quite so emotionally lost. The faults spring from lack of practicality, and the inability to fit into normal life due to a morbid, over-imaginative or unreal grasp of life; he is secretive and tends to be withdrawn. (27)

The keywords associated with the type are summarized as follows:

> Sensitive. Withdrawn. Unstable emotionally. Requires support from others. Secretive. Receptive. Impressionable. Confused, except in field of creativity. Strictly emotional. Idealistic. Fluctuating. 'I feel' and not 'I think'. Requires direction. Likes to be alone. Perceptive within the field of emotions. (28)

In some respects, this type finds a correspondence with the lunar type described on page 56.

The Air Hand is a robust hand structure, with long fingers and a fleshy, though square palm, with a series of well-defined linear markings (figure 63). It is called the Intellectual hand:

> . . . a well-balanced, reliable type who is more intellectual than intuitive, though some Air types do have quite a brilliant intuitive sense. Judgements are arrived at quickly, but by means of a rapid intellectual effort, the conclusions being expressed clearly and with a view to informing. The dependence on intellect, as opposed to emotion, means that the type is often profoundly mistrustful of the emotional values held by others, even of his own . . . The type is generally truthful, an accurate reporter of facts, usually excellent at organising things, has a factual, discriminating mind, and generally may be trusted in most matters. (29)

The particular form of creativity found in this type springs from the urge to communicate, and this is backed by a strong wish for order:

> One great characteristic of the type is the wish for order: in every activity or situation he will attempt to establish order, which is, after all, a prelude to exact communication. In society, in the realm of politics, he will attempt to establish his own sense of order, categorizing intellectually and often making the mistake of not taking the emotions into account. His theories have a certain 'dryness' about them, and it is this dryness or abstractness which makes many of them unworkable. (30)

In general the type is companionable, though discriminating in his choice of partners: freedom loving, inquisitive and original in attitude of mind. In some respects, this type finds a correspondence with the Mercurian and Jupiterian type described on pages 63 and 66.

It is extremely difficult for the roving nature of the Air type to find inner stability alone: this is one reason why relationships play an important part in their lives. Even in relationships, however, the type tends to be fickle, changeable and sometimes unreliable, although very often these disadvantages are well worth the enduring for the lively, stimulating, humorous and intelligent exchange which arises from relationships with the type.

60

61

62

62. *Characteristic line formations in the Fire hand.*

63. *A typical Fire hand, with curiously elongated whorl patterns associated with the hand type.*

64. *The square palm and short fingers of the Earth type.*

65. *The three basic finger patterns—the arch, the loop and the whorl. The Arch is associated with Earth, the Loop with Air and Water, the Whorl with Fire.*

63

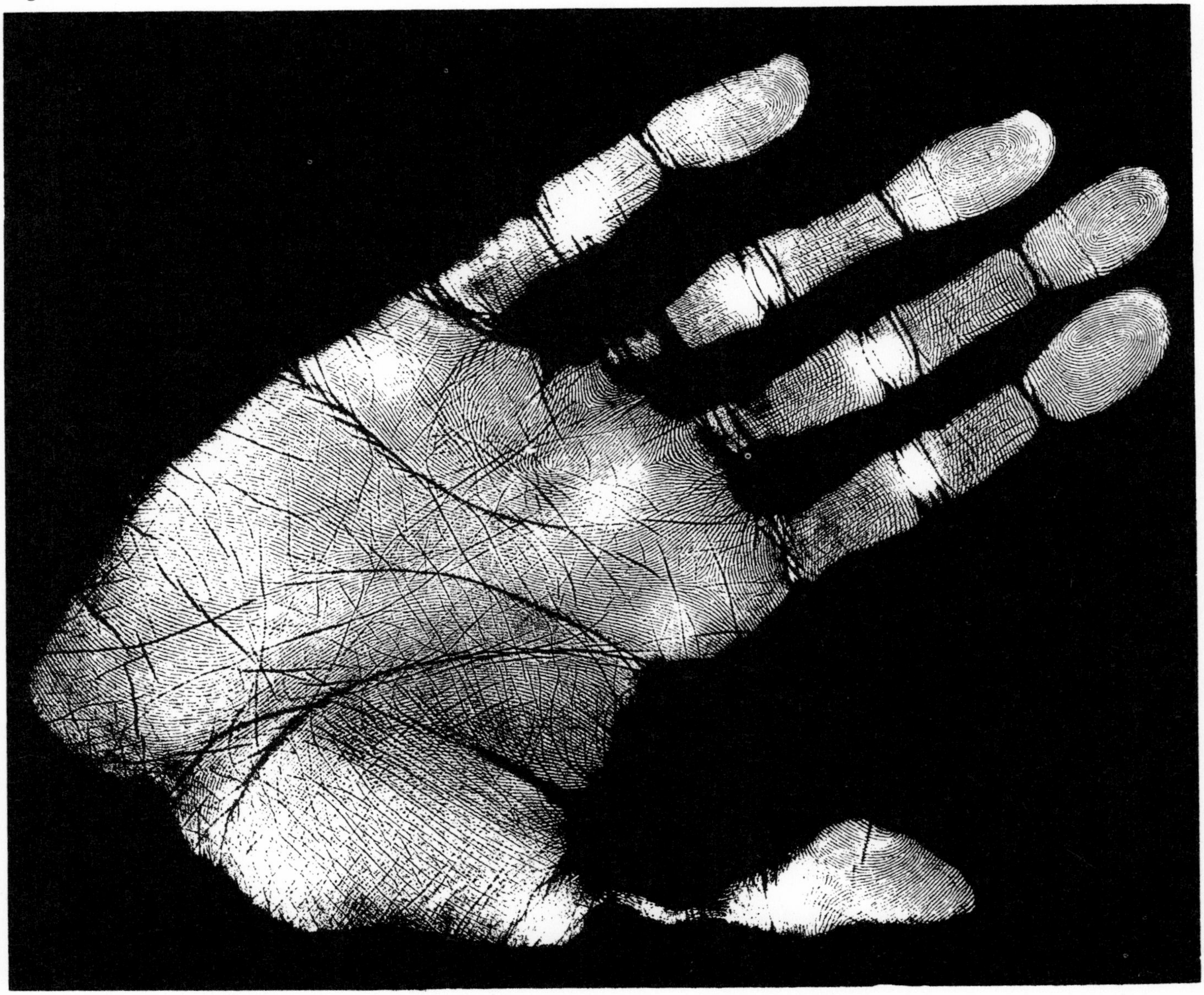

64

65

The Fire Hand is a lively structure with short fingers and a long palm, with a series of lively linear markings (figure 63). It is called the Intuitive hand:

> Here we have a somewhat dangerous combination of a fairly unbalanced emotional life, as indicated by the long palm, combining with a tendency to act freely upon decisions of an intuitive kind, as the short fingers would suggest. This is perforce a very unstable type, given to rapid judgements and equally rapid actions. Much more than the Intellectual type he is extremely extrovert by nature, but his quick emotional life makes him move towards people very rapidly, and without the conservative restraint of the Air type, with often disastrous results. (31)

In the same text we find the following keywords and phrases which express the basic nature of the 'choleric' type:

> Versatile, especially in emotional range. Warms people with his life. Full of enthusiasm. Exciting. Usually creative. Must always be active. Constantly taken up with novel ideas. Changeable. Energetic. Full of initiative. Dislikes detail. Egocentric, more than most. Intuitive rather than intellectual. Likes to be leader. Tends to be exhibitionist. Delights in self-expression. (32)

With such a strong force outwards, towards manifestation without a sense of restraint, one must of necessity find many social 'faults':

> The faults spring from excessive emotion, which may be associated with the combination of short fingers and a long palm: thus the type is impatient, sometimes exhibitionist, usually egocentric, tending to be changeable and irresponsible. He is, however, always exciting and excitable. All Fire types are impetuous, which is to say that they are capable of the throwing of themselves immediately and fully into any situation which interests them. (33)

From the above it will be evident that the main struggle with which the type has to contend in life is that of learning self-control. In many respects this type finds a correspondence with the Sun type described on page 70.

The Earth Hand is of a heavy and thick structure, with short fingers and a coarse, square palm, usually with few, though deeply incised, linear markings (figure 68). It is called the Practical hand:

> Such individuals are reliable, 'solid', one might say. Their practicality keeps their feet on the ground, they tend to dryness and like repetitive, hard, practical work in which they find pleasure in direct contact with earthly things. They are careful, guided by an innate knowledge of the rightness of things; they are trustworthy, for their natural sense of justice enables them to realize that crime does not pay. Hard work, honesty, effort and integrity of purpose combine to make the Earth type the essentially productive person in the realm of physical effort, such as building, carpentry, etc. (34)

But, alas, nothing is perfect, and, although the type is scarcely neurotic, behind the dependability and calmness there are forces which may be disruptive:

> Just as the earth is motionless, dependable

66

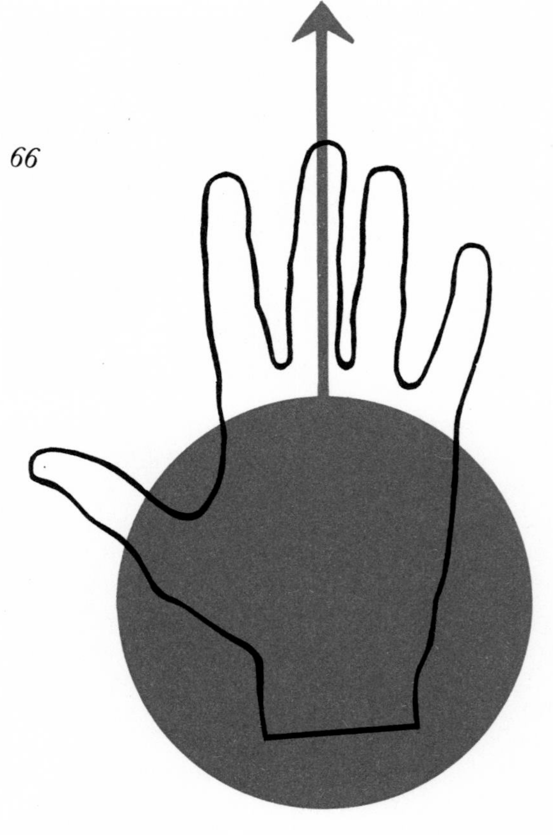

67

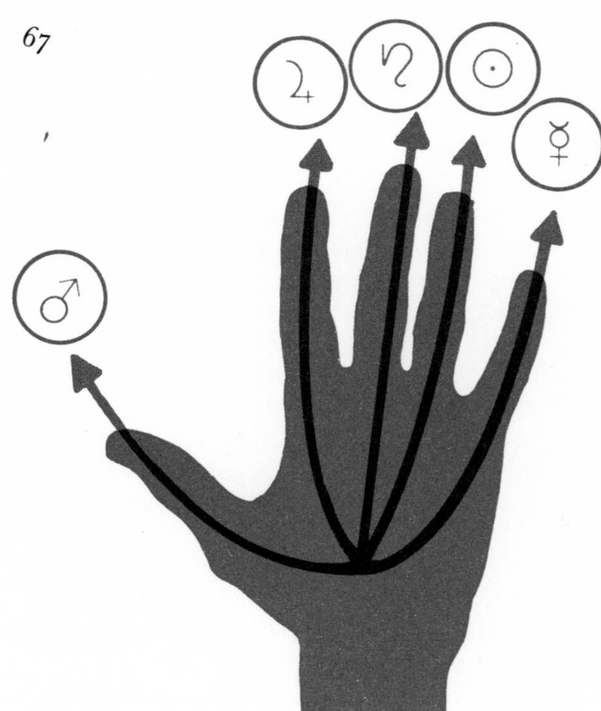

66. The palm of the hand may be regarded as a kind of reservoir of energies, which stream upwards and outwards through the various 'activities' of the finger zones.

67. Each of the fingers is related to a specific outlet or zone of experience, associated with the planets of astrology. A finger which is emphasised in a hand—through a deformity, or excessive length, or even through the wearing of a ring, lends the strength of the relevant planet to the personality.

68. A typical Earth hand, with square palm, short fingers and few lines.

and reliable on the surface, but seething like a cauldron underneath, so is the Earth type a duality. Break through his reserve, his sense of justice and his adherence to rhythms, and destructive energies may be released. (35)

Such energies are not always destructive, however, for under certain circumstances the Earth type may be creative in the widest sense of the word, though always there will be a vitality, adherence to rhythms or repetitions, which gives the creativity a particular stamp of Earth. The more ordinary characteristics may be described in the following keywords and phrases:

Practical. Gifted with the hands. Reliable. Has his 'feet on the ground'. His love for rhythm. Delights in physical action. Tends to be possessive. Steadfast. Conservative. Reserved. Critical and suspicious. Utilitarian. Impatient of detail except where a craft is concerned. Penchant for out-of-door work. (36)

It is through the traditional association with Melancholia that we touch upon the inner core of the Earth type, for this points to the dejection, the periodic cycle of depression and gloom to which the type is subjected. In some respects, this type finds a correspondence with the Earth type described on page 73.

When the type is caught up in such depression, he becomes very isolated from his surroundings, extremely involved with self to the exclusion of others, and this earth "mood" will weigh upon him for some time, in marked contrast to his more normal open-hearted dealings with others.

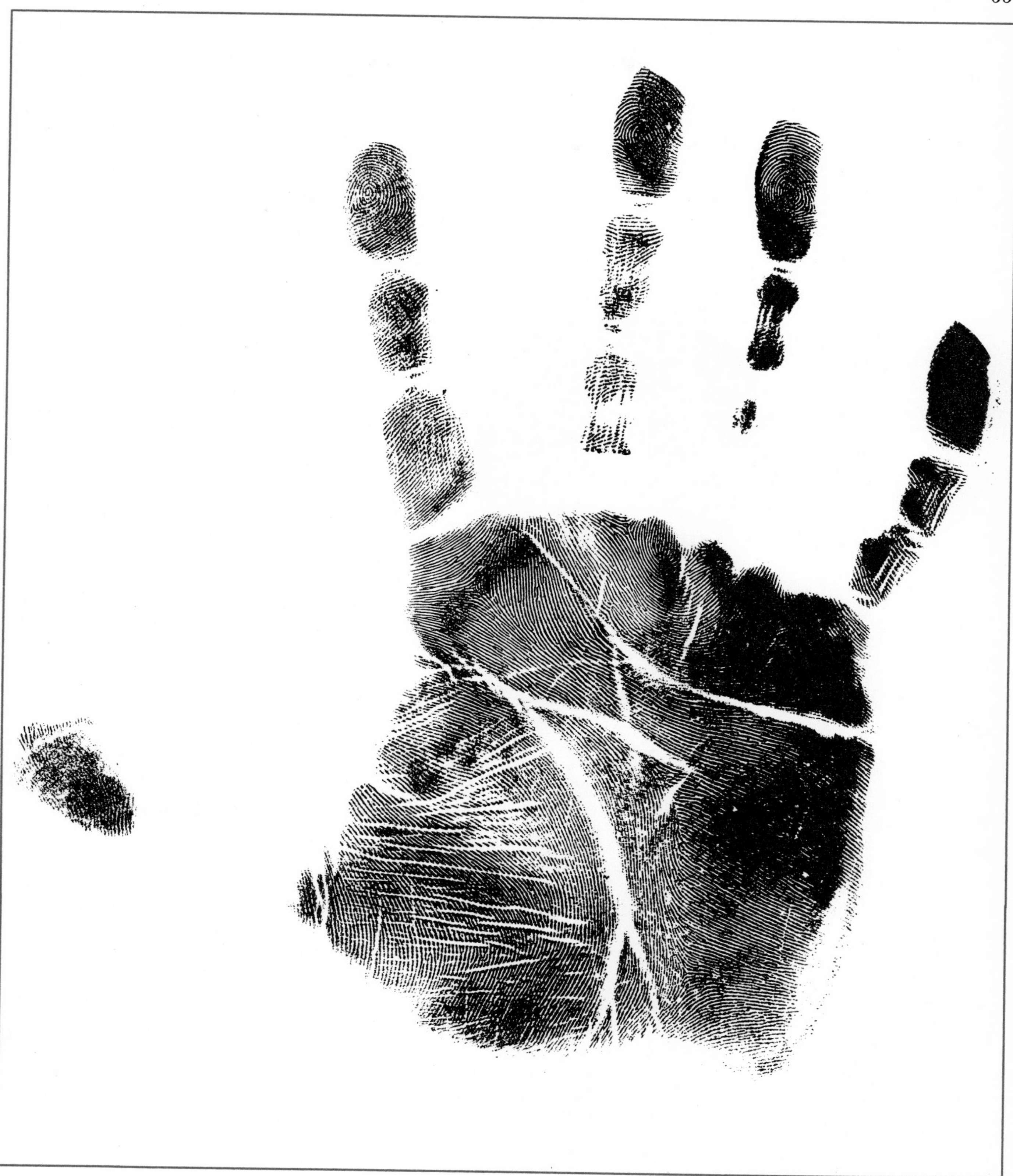

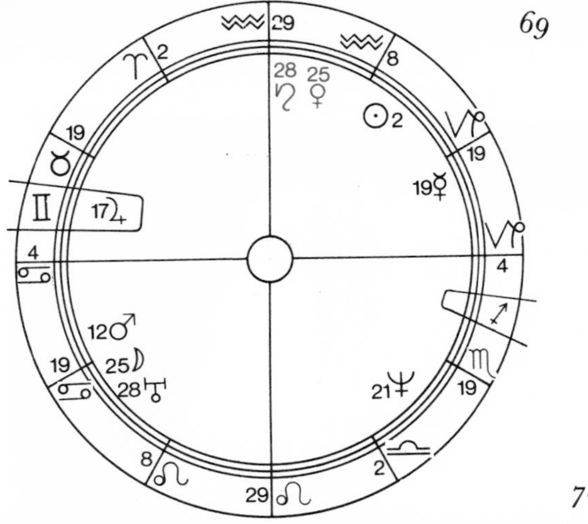

69

70

69. In the present century many attempts have been made to
70. relate hand form and linear structure with astrological doctrine. In this example the conjunction between Venus and Saturn (in colour), may be seen manifesting in the very long line of Saturn.

71. The Italian chiromancer Barthelemy Cocles reading palms.

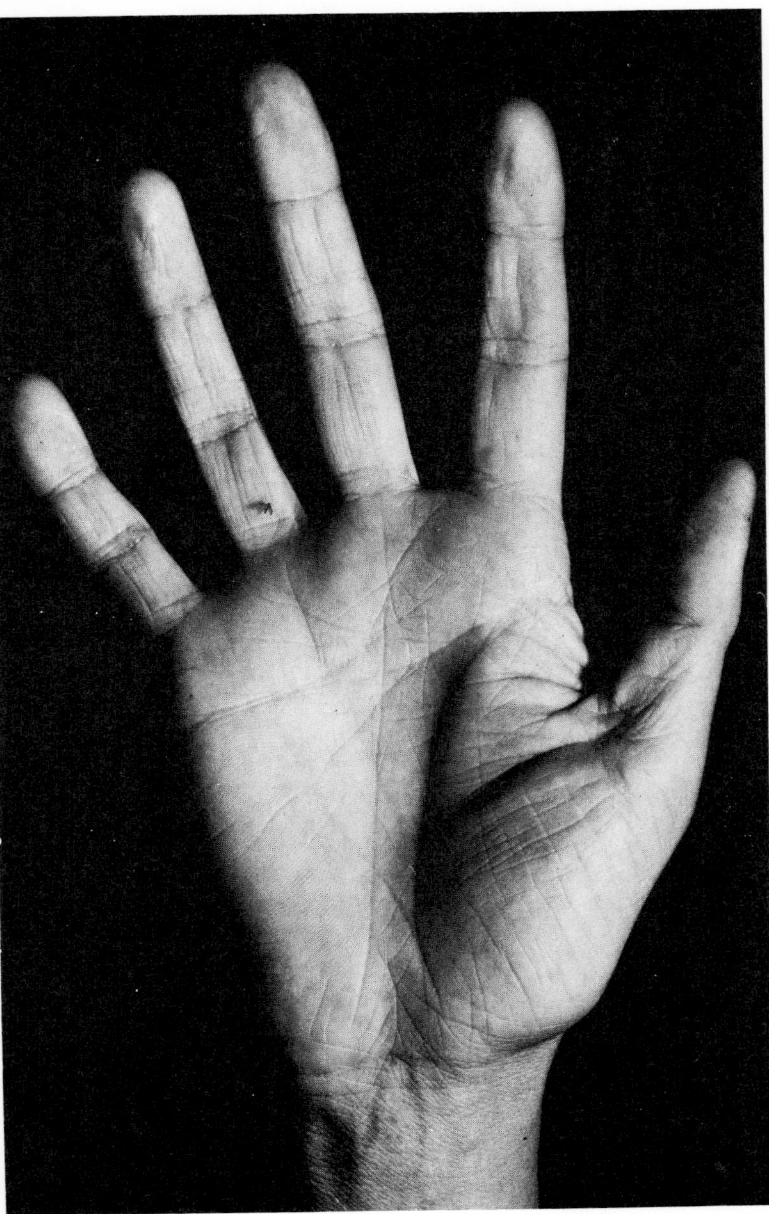

Yet another system of hand classification which has emerged from the attempt to link astrology with palmistry is that put forward by the French astrologer and palmist Georges Muchery. In this system, a series of eight hand forms have been described named after the traditional astrological planets and associated with distinctive characteristics which are usually linked with the influence of the planets. The system presumes that a particular planet will have dominance over a subject, and that this will inevitably show in the hand, a presumption which is in no way contradicted by occult theory. Perhaps the major difficulty with the system is that one frequently finds hands which do not fit easily within the classification. However, the eight hand types are themselves very distinctive, as are the characteristics and temperaments associated with them.

Before we examine these, it will be of value to note that the system of Muchery is modern in its basic approach, in that it attempts to link directly the two apparently divergent systems of chiromancy and chirognomy. For example, when the Solar hand, the hand of Apollo (figure 79), is being discussed, Muchery points out that in this hand the traditional 'ring of Solomon', or indeed any rays across the area below the finger of Jupiter (figure 79), indicate that the subject

> . . . will not have a happy home life, or at least that he will not find a marriage which will respond absolutely to his own requirements. One might say that this is the type which gives rise to most divorces in both sexes. (37)

71

72

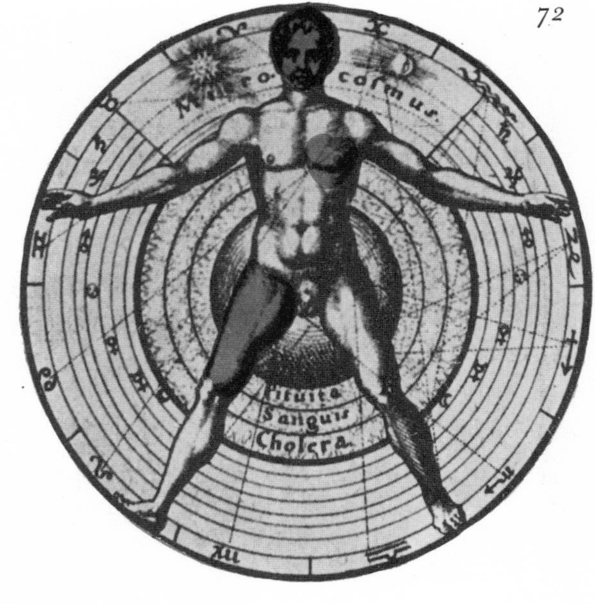

72 *Cosmic man, with the three Fire elements, as manifest in Aries, Leo, and Sagittarius, with their associations with parts of the body.*

73 *The corresponding three Fire elements as seen in the hand, relating to Moving, Thinking and Feeling.*

74 *Astrological diagram linking zodiacal man with the parts of the body, and with parts of t e hand, based on the evidence in 'The Hand and the Horoscope'. (See bibliography at p. 142).*

73

MOVING

FEELING

THINKING

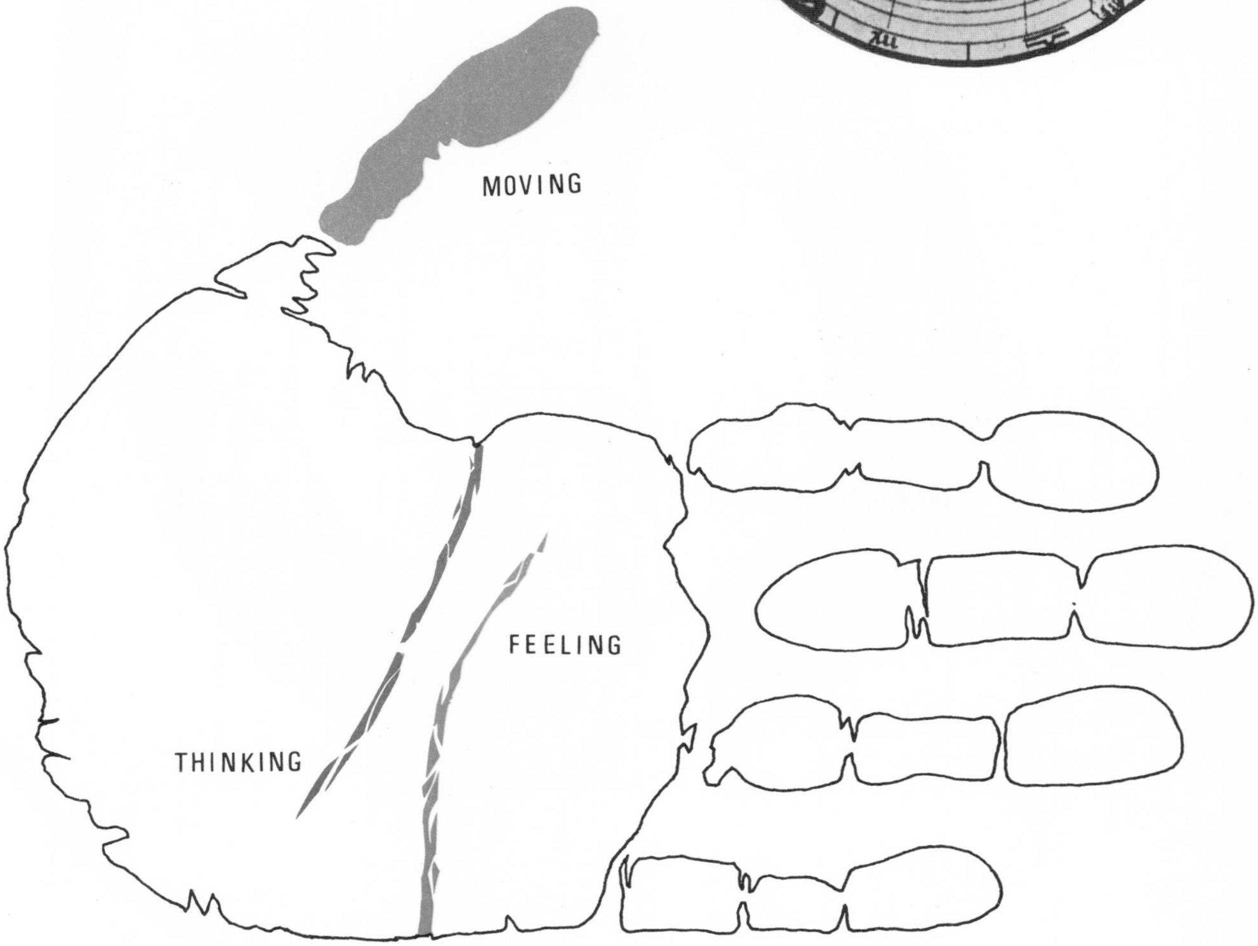

74

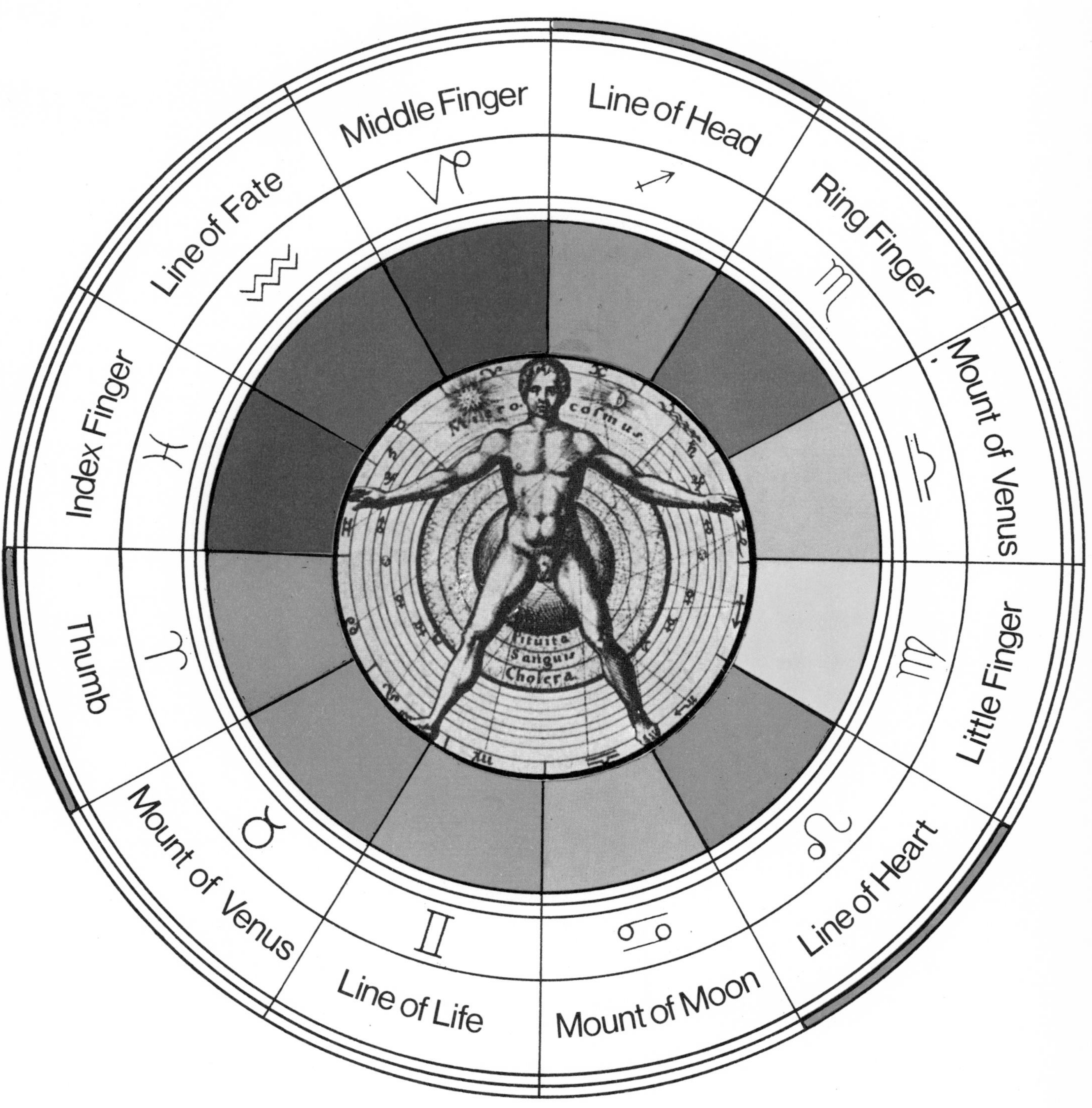
Middle Finger
Line of Head
Ring Finger
Mount of Venus
Little Finger
Line of Heart
Mount of Moon
Line of Life
Mount of Venus
Thumb
Index Finger
Line of Fate
Pituita
Sanguis
Cholera

75

75. *The Earth hand, based on Muchery's system of astrological classification.*

76. *The Lunar hand according to Muchery.*

77. *The planetary Saturn devouring his own child, symbolizing the destructive power of time. Saturn rules over the temporal order of things—that which structures life through sequence.*

78. *Saturn driving monsters with his levelling scythe. Here the god is pictured as the ruler over limitation and restriction.*

Muchery's system insists that the line structures should not be interpreted *in vacuo*, as was the practice with earlier forms of palmistry, even late into the nineteenth century: the line formations must be related to the basic temperament as represented by the hand formation.

The eightfold system may best be represented by actual examples which approximate to those described by Muchery. There are according to Muchery several peculiarities which distinguish the eight hands, in addition to the general shape and qualities represented in the examples:

The hand of Saturn (figure 79) has a line which runs from the line of Life, across the Hand and upwards towards the middle finger. The fingers themselves bend inwards towards Saturn. The Mount of Saturn is strongly rayed with lines, whilst the finger of Saturn is long.

The Lunar hand (figure 76) has a spiral on the Mount of Moon, which is itself very strongly rayed and low-set. It is a very soft hand. The lines are weak, superficial, numerous and meshed. The line of Fate originates from the Mount of Moon.

The Venusian hand (figure 79) has a strong Girdle of Venus, whilst the mount of Venus is raised, bowl shaped, and strongly rayed in the centre. The line of Saturn commences from the Mount of Venus. The thumb is short and thick, whilst the hand itself is small in relation to the size of the subject.

The Martian hand (figure 79) has a cross in the centre of the hand, the traditional 'plain of Mars'. The thumb is particularly noticeable, the first phalange being very strong and thick. The lines are deeply graven, and tend to be short.

The Mercurial hand (figure 79) has a longish finger of Mercury as well as a marked line of Intuition, leading towards the Mount of Mercury, which is in the form of a well-rayed protuberance. The fingers tend to orientate towards the thumb, whilst the lower phalanges of the fingers are large (though not necessarily thick).

The Jupiterian hand (figure 79) has particularly thick and heavy third phalanges, such that on a print one is able to inscribe them in a circle. The hand is quite large, thick and relatively soft.

The Solar hand (figure 79) has a palm noticeably longer than the fingers (which links with the Fire type of the preceeding classifications), the fingers being knotty. The first phalange of the thumb is long; the finger of Apollo is longer than that of Jupiter, whilst the line of Apollo is naturally well in evidence.

The Earth hand (figure 75) is easily recognisable from its thickness and firmness, by the deep incisions of the lines. The thumb is square. A line of Head which terminates on or towards Mercury indicates an earth influx, whilst closely joined lines of Life and Head also points to an earthly nature.

The temperaments accompanying such hand formations, are linked, as we might well imagine, with the natures of the ruling planets in terms of appearance, disposition and general psyche. The more obvious of such characteristics may be gleaned from quotations taken from the work of the American palmist William Benham, who describes the planetary

76

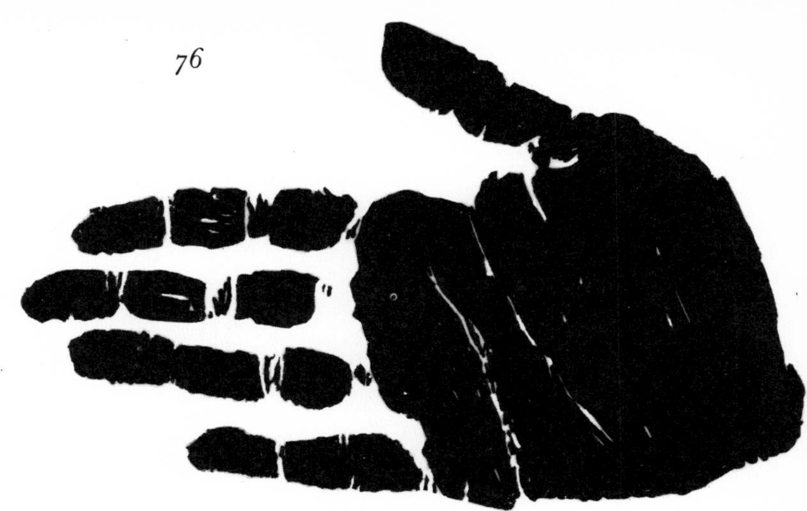

77

78

types in the traditional manner–white being very white, and black being exceeding black. Common sense tells us that the world consists of shades, however. The traditional black and white images are useful in that they enable us to fix in our minds the qualities of the important planetary forces which lie behind the occult explanations of the nature of man. In practice we are compelled to observe that *everyone* has something of every planetary force in his makeup–the truth is that certain planetary and zodiacal influences are given particular emphasis in our beings, and the practice of astrology revolves around attempting to determine the nature of such emphasis which produces the individuality. Thus, the 'ideal planetary types', no more than the 'ideal planetary hands' do not find an existence in the material world–the approximations which we find do, however, express tendencies which are observable in everyone to one degree or another. For this reason alone a study of the planetary types is important.

Saturn is the planet which rules over the sense of restriction and limitation in the personality–it is therefore well said that Saturn indicates the fears which dominate the native, though Saturn is also the force which supports the spiritual life by providing a vehicle or structure by which such spiritual energies may manifest on earth. A strong Saturn lends an element of practicality and material values, as well as inducing a sense of justice into the outlook–the Saturnian feels that everything must be paid for. Associated with this we find an amazing perseverance, an

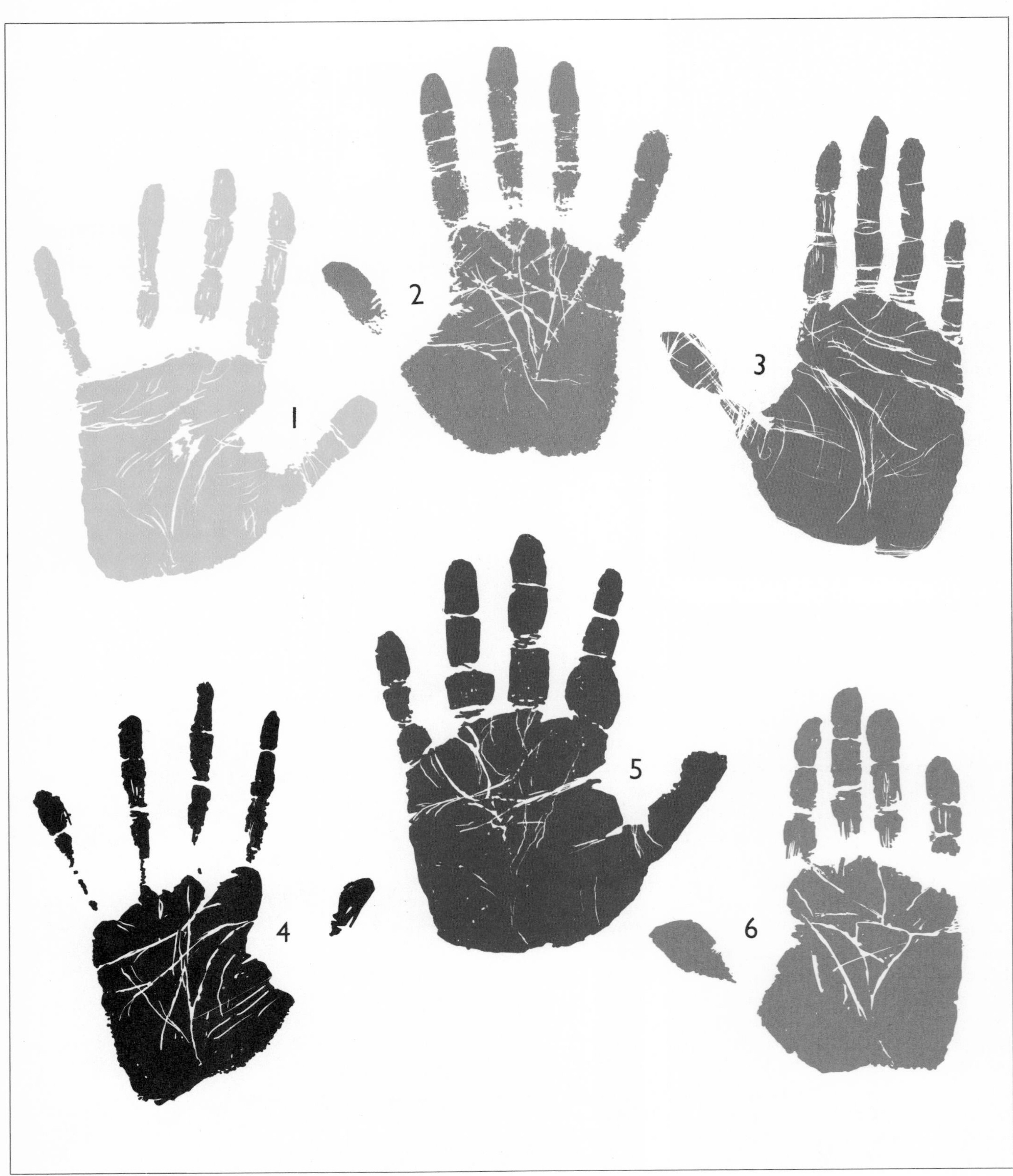
1
2
3
4
5
6

80

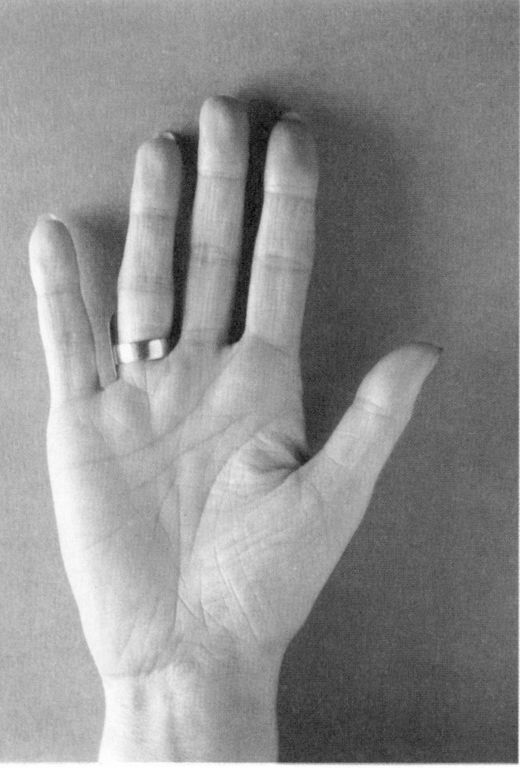

79. *Six hands based on Muchery's system. 1, Mercury. 2, Solar. 3, Venus. 4, Saturn. 5, Jupiter. 6, Mars.*

80. *The palmistic tradition rightly infers that a longish hand*
81. *(87) will be found on a more nervous and erratic personality, whilst a thick and fleshy hand will be found on a more stable and responsible personality.*

82. *A fifteenth century hand schema, from a manuscript in the Bodleian Library, Oxford.*

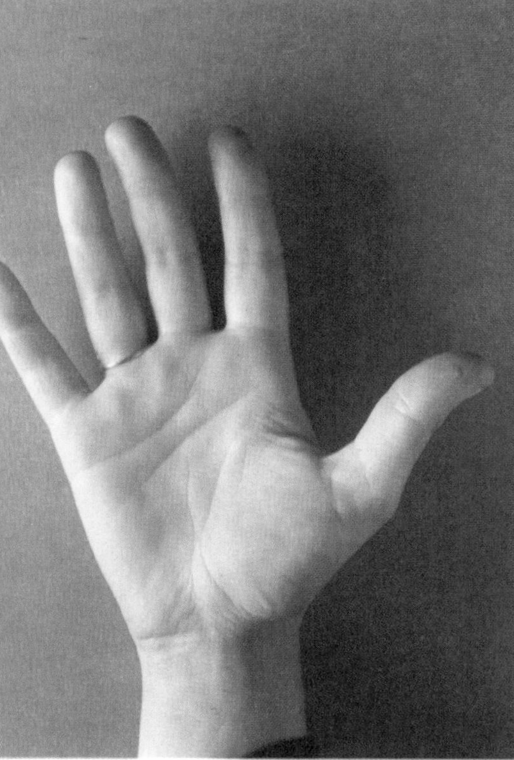

81

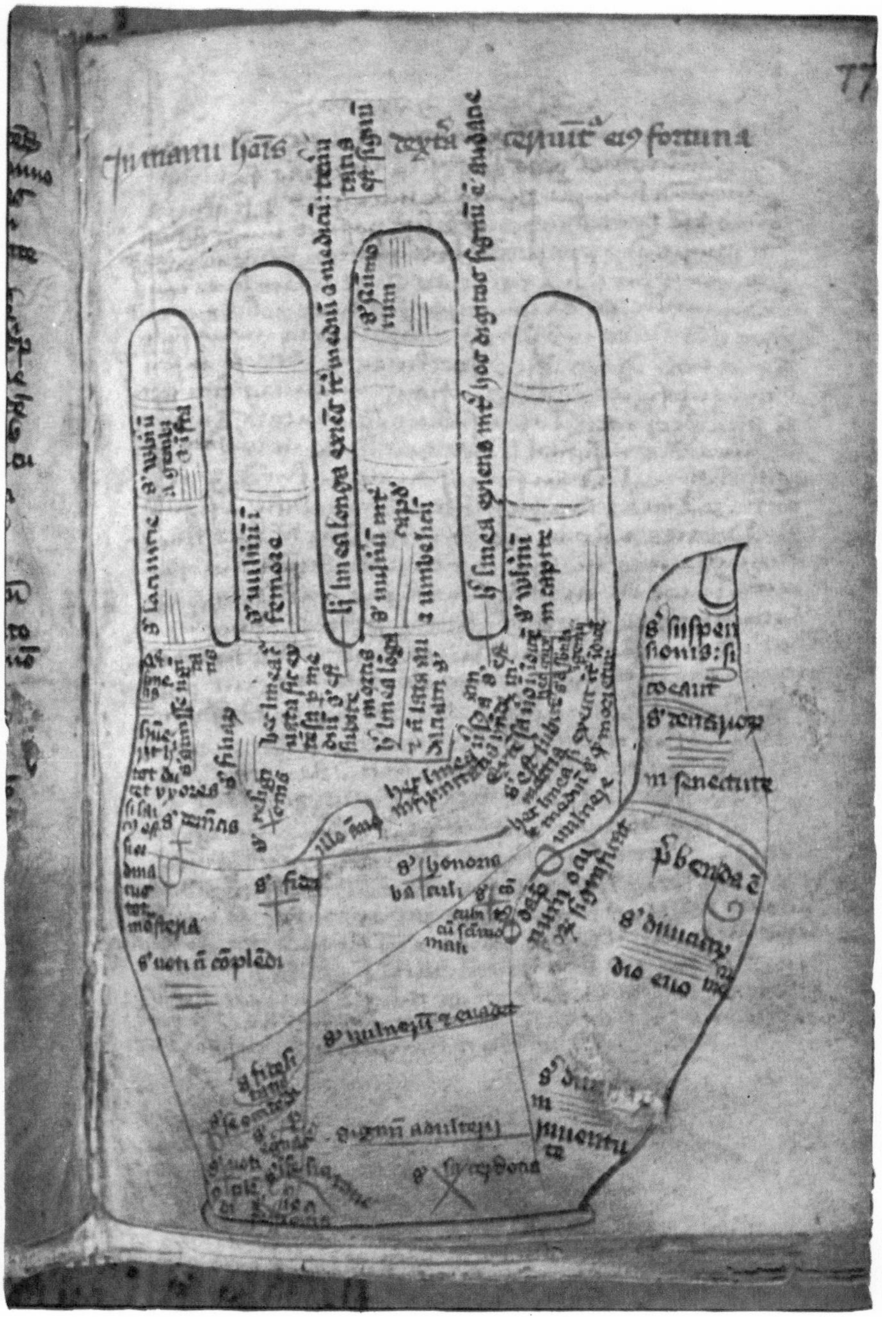

82

83

ability for concentration, hard work, and a strain of parsimony. In excess, the influence of Saturn hardens the subject, who will become limited in his ability to deal with world, since he is easily isolated from the life-giving spiritual forces: he will be over-cautious, brittle, conservative, narrow, and stingy, especially subject to the melancholia for which the planet is famous. Such qualities as these are certainly linked with the Saturnian hand, and to a certain extent with the Earth hand (page 45). Within the hand itself we find that the finger of Saturn, the middle finger, may be associated with such qualities and energies, as may the line of Fate, which runs up the centre of the hand. Attempts to link astrology with palmistic theory have shown that the finger of Saturn is to be associated with the more humane Aquarius, over which this planet had rule in traditional astrology.

> *Saturn* The whole appearance of the Saturnian impresses you with its lack of nourishment lack of healthy blood supply, and its lean gawkiness; the dark, sad eyes, stiff, black hair, narrow chest, sloping shoulders, and shuffling gait all combine to bear this out. He is a man to whom a bright side of life does not often appear, one whose life is lightened by no joy of exuberant spirits, filled with no animal vitality, no heat, warmth, and magnetism . . . Instead of seeking the society of others he avoids it, and his tendency is to withdraw himself from the social world. He prefers the country to the city, is often a student, and chooses agricultural pursuits, chemistry, and other laboratory occupations, which do not require him to come in contact with people . . . He is eminently cautious and prudent. He is superstitious of both the fidelity and honesty of his fellows, and does not readily go into business enterprises with them . . . His prudence gives him another quality–he is saving and even stingy and miserly. The Saturnian loves music . . . He writes well, produces histories, fine treatises on scientific and occult subjects . . . He is opinionated, does not like to be contradicted, is independent, and dislikes restraint. (38)

The Moon is the 'planet' which rules over the personality, the feminine vehicle, or mask, through which the selfhood of the Sun mediates with the world. A strong Moon makes the subject highly imaginative and receptive, subject to shyness and changeability, though sometimes it introduces a strong element of shrewdness and practical ability into the life of the subject. In excess it tends to create over-impressionable states, intense emotionalism and strong moods, which militate against a harmonious relationship with the material world. Such qualities as these are certainly linked with the Lunar hand, as with the Water hand (page 40), and within the hand itself we find that the Mount of Moon may be associated with such qualities and energies. The part of the hand is also associated with the zodiacal sign Cancer, which is ruled over by the Moon.

> *The Lunarian* The Lunarian is controlled by imagination, consequently he is dreamy, fanciful and idealistic. He is one who builds castles, plans great enterprises, which are

83. The planetary Lunar, ruler over Cancer, surrounded by clouds and various symbols of femininity.

84. The Moon ruling the lower, inner part of the hand, is traditionally the seat of the imaginative faculties.

85. The hand of the Theosophist Annie Besant, from 'Cheiro's collection of prints.

84

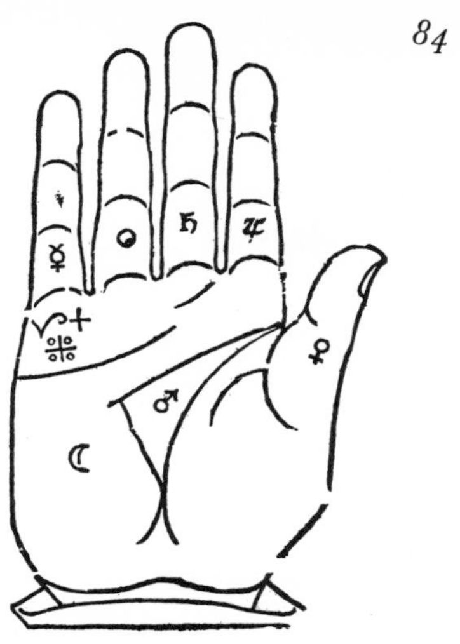

85

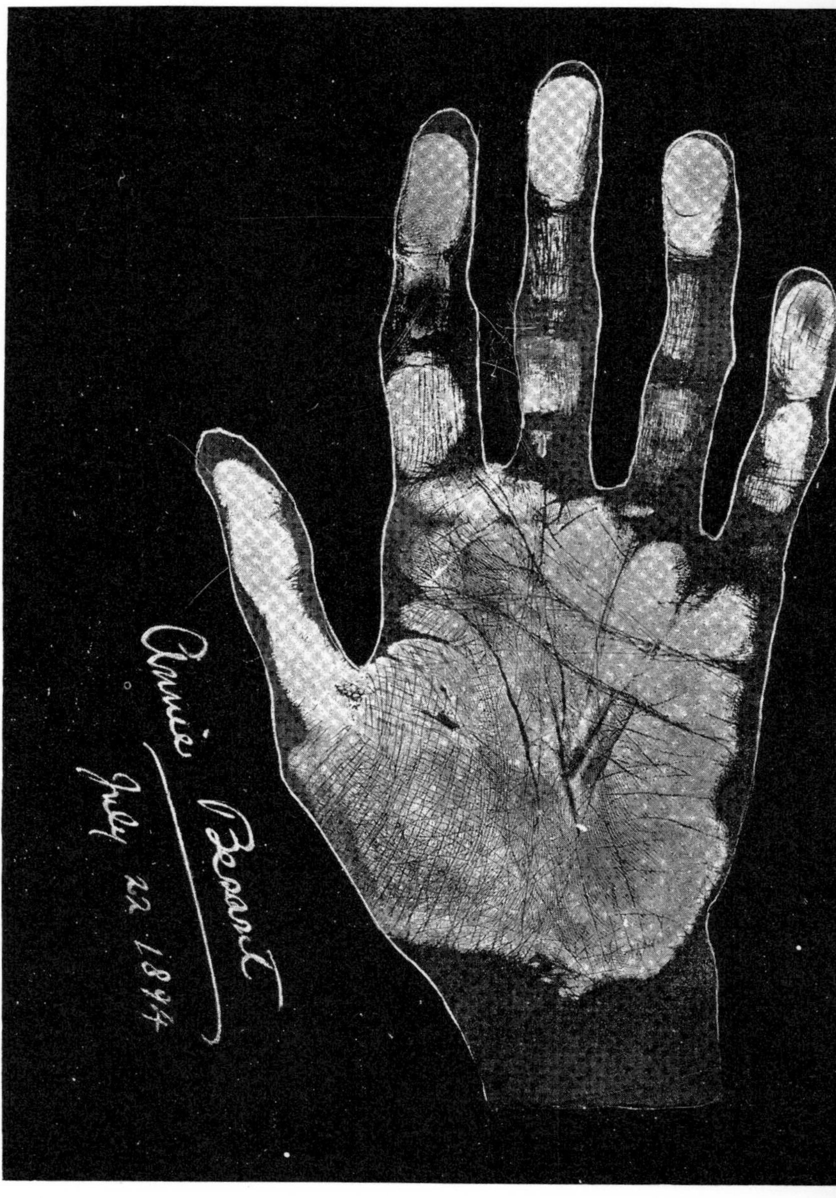

never put into operation because they generally have no practical value.

From the flabby, spongy character of his hand and muscular development, he is lazy in the extreme, preferring to live in cloudland rather than to dwell in an abode upon earth. He is constantly a prey to his imaginings, thinks he is ill, and has divers ailments, is fickle, restless, and changeable. It is hard for him to settle down to humdrum life, for he is always yearning for things beyond his reach. Therefore he is never satisfied long in one place, but desires a constant change of location and scene. This restless disposition leads him to spend his last dollar for travel, and often the Lunarian becomes a great traveller . . . He is lazy physically and lazy mentally. He loves to dream dreams, and work, which means either mental or physical exertion, is extremely distasteful to him. He is dreamy in look, his eyes have an uncanny expression, and their light blue or gray colour speaks of coldness and dreaminess. Thus he becomes mystical, often melancholy, and grows superstitious. He believes in signs and omens, and has wonderful visions and hallucinations which grow to be real to him and influence him greatly. He is slow in his movements, phlegmatic in disposition, and extremely sensitive. He imagines slights when none are intended, and shrinks into himself and away from company. He does not love or seek society. He realizes that he is different from other people, so retires to the woods or secluded places where he can enjoy himself by

86

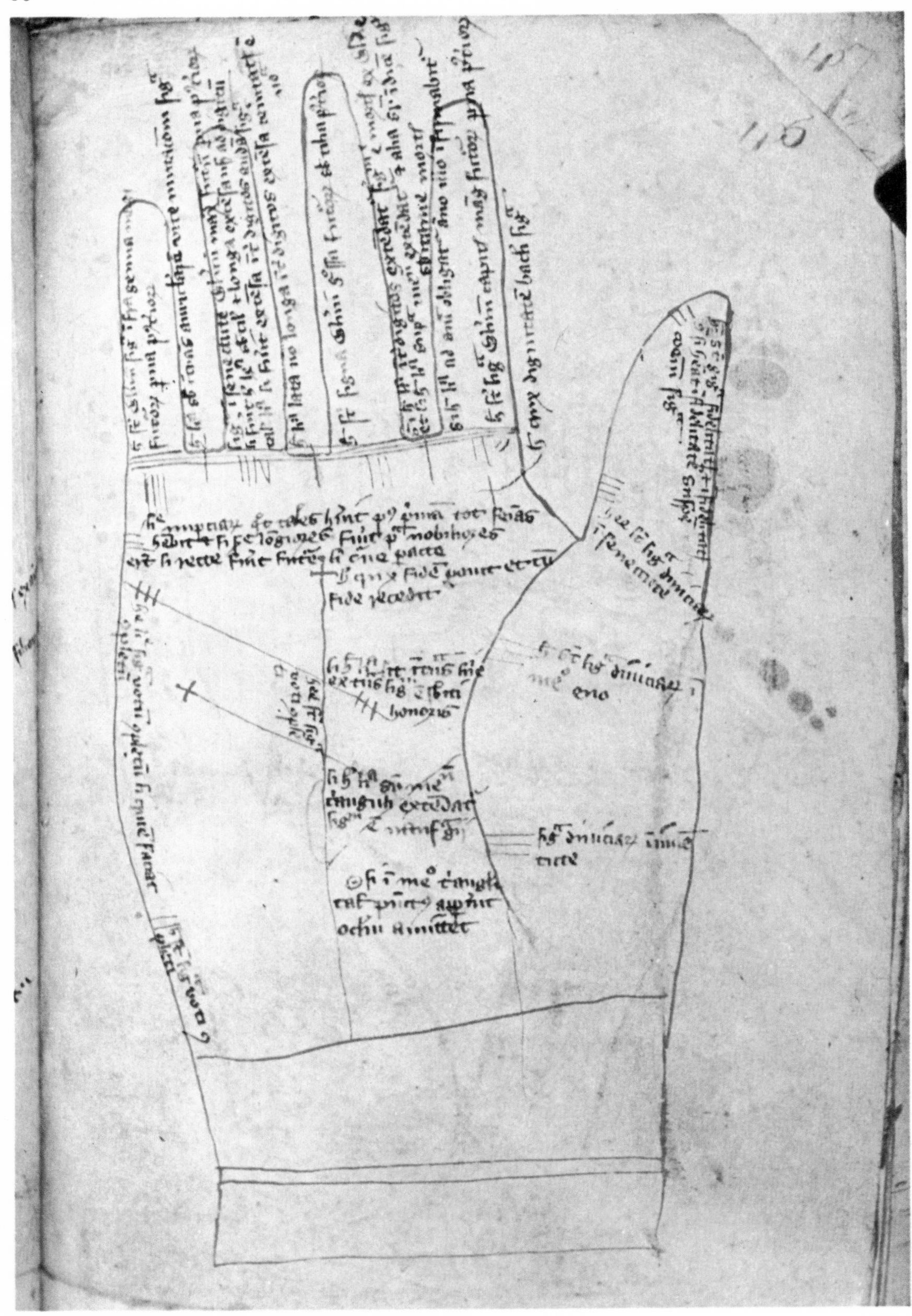

86. *Palmistry of the fixed-symbol type, from a mediaeval manuscript in the Bodleian Library, Oxford.*

87. The 'triad of palmistry'. The Jupiter of Pisces lifts up the personality into spirituality, whilst the Venus of Taurus pulls it down into materiality. Caught between the two is the activity of Mars, which represents the self of Aries. This is why the thumb is such a useful index of personality.

87

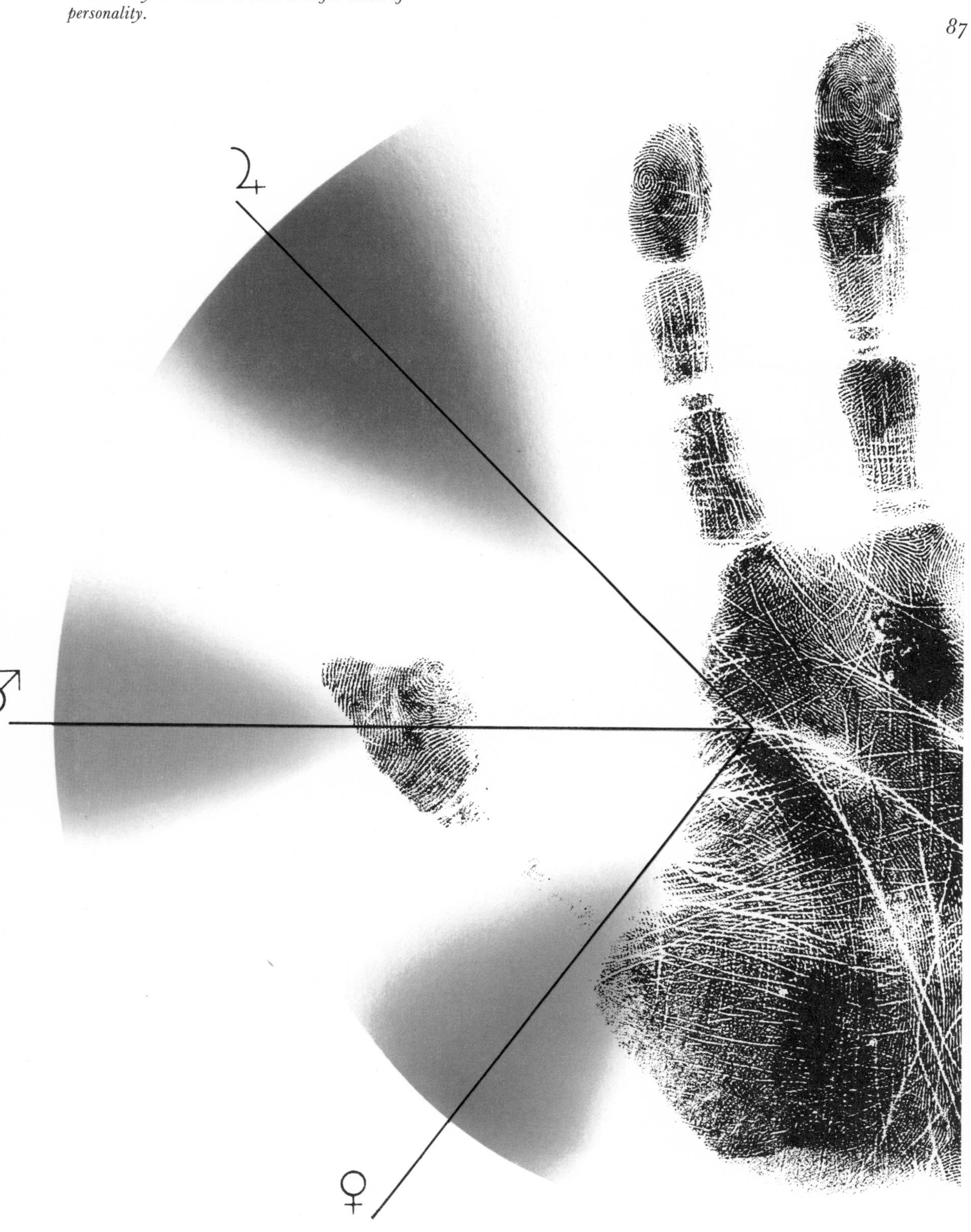

88

himself. He loves nature, birds, flowers and all things which elevate the senses and excite the imagination, and to such surroundings he goes when out of touch with the world and its inhabitants . . . He is never generous; to him selfishness is innate. He is a big eater, though not sensual nor amorous. In his case the sexual appetites are excited by imagination, and not by physical heat. The Lunarian is lacking in self-confidence, and feels his unfitness for the active pursuits of life. He also lacks energy and perseverance, consequently he is unsuccessful in the business world. If he is of a common type he has a hard time to get along. If of a high type he becomes a good writer of romance or fiction, and even of history . . . Thus we see in the Lunarian a peculiar subject, in whom imagination and fancy are always the dominating motives. (39)

Venus is the planet which governs the sympathies and underlying harmonies within the subject, and it is linked with the abilities to be receptive to emotional impressions, in particular to artistic impressions: it is directly associated with feminine sexuality. A strong Venus makes the subject idealistic, warm, expressive, well-balanced, refined and agreeable. In excess it tends to emphasise the Venusian urge to avoid contact with the material condition, with the result that the subject may become lethargic and lacking in enterprise or self-confidence. Such qualities as these are certainly linked with the Venusian hand, as well as with the Air hand (page 42) in a feminine subject whilst within the hand itself we find that the ball of the thumb, the Mount of Venus, traditionally ruled by this planet, is an indicator of such qualities and energies, along with the girdle of Venus (page 132). These two Venusian influxes in the hand may be associated respectively with Taurus and Libra, both ruled by the harmonious Venus.

The Venusian Standing as it does for love, sympathy, and generosity, the Venusian type is a good one, and, as one of its greatest qualifications is attraction for its fellows, it necessarily needs warmth and heat, for heat attracts and cold repels. This Venusian heat means a plentiful supply of good-quality blood, and a strong heart to pump it, consequently the Venusian is a healthy type and a handsome one, for good health begets good looks, producing not always rounded, doll-like beauty, but freshness and attractiveness. We find each type endowed with whatever accompaniments of health and characteristics are necessary to best fit it to bring forward the elementary forces which it represents, so the Venusian, being created to emphasise love, is given health, warmth, and physical attractiveness, that, wherever he appears, love may be inspired. There is about the Venusian no hint of gloom, biliousness, coldness, or selfishness–all is warmth, life, beauty, and attraction; consequently the Venusian is beset with many temptations, is constantly attracted to the opposite sex, has strong physical passion, and needs a fine Head line (self-control and judgement) and a large thumb (determination) to keep him in the

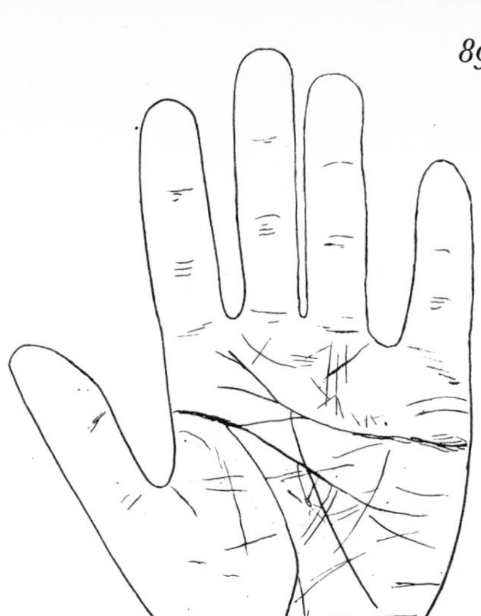

88. The Venus of astrology, ruler over Taurus and Libra, hailed by the blindfolded Cupid, and winged hearts. (from Indagine)

89. A drawing of the hand of Beerbohm Tree, as reproduced in the nineteenth century magazine 'The Palmist'.

straight and narrow path . . . When a Venusian development is found strong in a woman's hand, it will not speak of such profligacy as the same development would in the hand of a man. In a man, a strong Venusian Mount either makes him somewhat feminine in his characteristics, especially if smooth fingers, conic tips, and soft consistency are present; or else it makes him fiery and heated in his passions, and if the hand be hard this subject will indulge these desires, not restraining them as will a woman with the same development . . . The Venusian is essentially an affectionate subject. He is instinctively drawn towards his fellow-man by feelings of kinship and human sympathy, and these feelings easily ripen into love, which is his primary and typical attribute. With the Venusian there is no such feeling of repellance, or a desire to retire from the haunts of mankind, as we find with the Saturnian. Neither has he the Saturnian's instinctive hatred of his fellows. He is rather attracted toward them, seeks their society, is agreeable, kind, sympathetic, lovable, and popular. Never will you find a Venusian who turns a deaf ear to the sufferings or appeals of any human being, and never will you find a Venusian with a stiff thumb. Supple thumbs are always present, and their generosity and liberality extends to all who appeal for help. Thus the Venusian is besieged by those who have a tale of woe, for all are sure to find heartfelt sympathy in their misfortunes, and they know that whatever aid is possible will be given. In hours of affliction or despair the Venusian never deserts a friend, but with open hand and all the tenderness of his warm heart he relieves distress and suffering wherever found. Thus the Venusian attracts all who come to him by the bond of humanity, which seems to link him to mankind in general. He is often the victim of rogues, who, knowing his sympathetic nature and generosity, impose upon him with ease . . . Everything is bright to him, and this brightness he sheds upon his more serious-minded fellows, attracting and helping them through the world. This is why he is popular and loved, and from the exuberance of goodness in his heart he returns this love in abundant measure. He is fond of all amusements, dancing, society, gallantry, and forms of gaiety. His lack of seriousness is often carried too far, for he will pursue pleasure to the exclusion of business, and therefore does not grow wealthy. He does not value riches, nor assume responsibility yet such a one as he always gets along in some way, so he is careless, and improvident–but happy. He is entirely unselfish. When distress is present he sinks self entirely, and his first thought and effort are for others. He is bright, sparkling, vivacious, spontaneous, and genial, and the life of every company in which he may be. He is not profoundly studious, nor very ambitious, but is content to enjoy life. He is a great lover of the beautiful. Dress, home, surroundings, flowers, pictures, and art in every form attract, and in all of these he loves harmony, taste, and beauty. To him it is more essential that things should be

90

90. *Mercury, the ruler over Gemini and Virgo, holding the caduceus, a theurgic symbol.*

91. *The traditional Plain of Mars and the mount of Mars, combine to draw a swathe across the palm. This has considerable importance in the development of palmistic theory.*

92. *The system of dating events on the Life line, as used by Desbarrolles. There is much disagreement among palmists as to how events should be dated.*

91

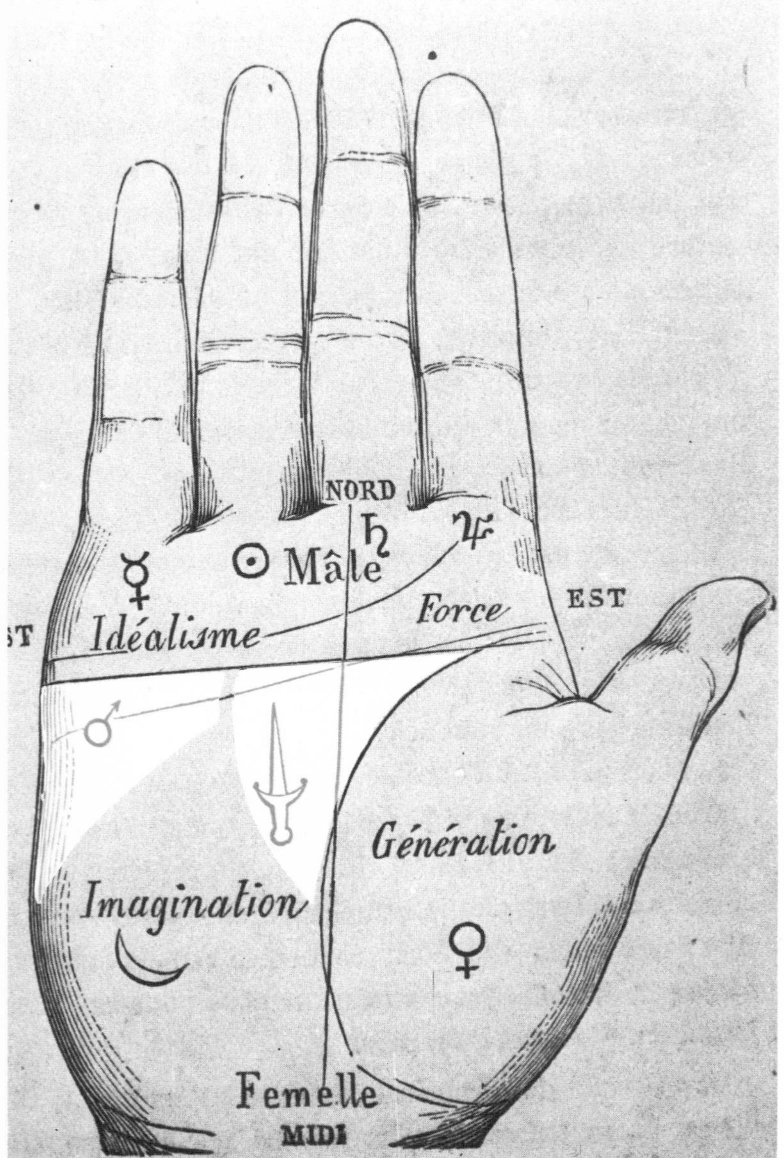

beautiful and enjoyable than that they should be useful. (40)

Mars is the planet which governs the energy of the subject, and it is linked with the ability to endure conflict with the material world, conveying as it does the spirit of selfhood into the physical world: it is directly linked with masculine sexuality. A strong Mars makes the subject active, energetic, courageous, restless and opinionated. In excess it tends to be extremist in action, inducing an element of cruelty into the personality, as well as burning away human refinement to the extent that the subject will appear cocky and brash. Such qualities as these are certainly linked with the Martian hand, whilst within the hand itself we find that the thumb, traditionally ruled by Mars, is indicative of such qualities and energies. The finger of Apollo has been suggested as the reservoir of Martian energies, rather than of solar energies, though these are the so-called 'negative' energies of Mars, associated with the zodiacal sign Scorpio.

The Martian His vigorous constitution fills him with the desire to accomplish whatever he sets out to do, and his energy makes him put forward the utmost effort to gain success. He is exceedingly generous in the use of his money, caring for wealth only for what it will buy for him. He is the one who loves to have friends and admirers, and generally succeeds in gaining them. He is exceedingly devoted to these friends and will fight for them, as well as spend his money freely with them and on their behalf. He is not always refined and delicate in his

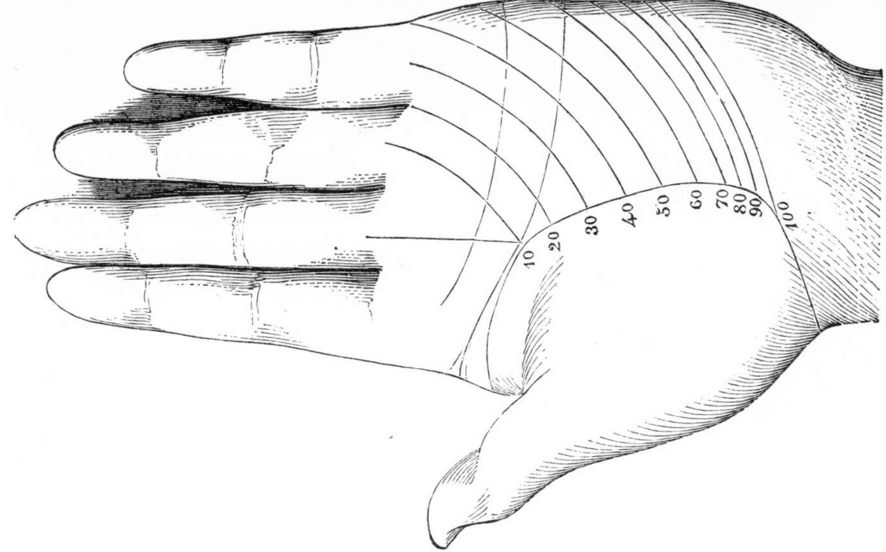

92

ways, but is often brusque and lacking in tact . . . The Martian can be reasoned with and coaxed, but never driven, and he is exceedingly amorous. His strong blood current and big muscular development speak of an exuberance of health, and fill him with the fire of passion, and the opposite sex becomes very attractive. When he falls in love it is with all the intensity of his strong nature, and he simply proceeds to storm the heart of his charmer, as he does the works of an enemy, using his Martian fire and dash to astound the object of his love so that she is apt to surrender to the assault. No sickly sentimentality takes part in his wooing; it is audacity and vigour from the start to finish . . . His is a big nature, he is not narrow in his views, and in all games of sport he wants absolute fairness to rule and the best man to win. He is primarily an active type, so those things which are accomplished by daring and energy seem to him the real things. The student and philosopher appear to him small and insignificant. The achievements accomplished before the eyes of the world are what appeal to him. The Martian is found in every walk of life. His strong characteristics are daily felt in the mental world, the business community, the army, the church, the state–everywhere. He must be put into occupations and surroundings where he can work off his surplus energy either in pushing his affairs or fighting the field. To put a Martian where he must be under restraint would be like stopping the safety-valve on a boiler . . . (41)

Mercury is the planet which rules over the communicative faculties in the subject; in some respects, therefore, it may be linked with speech and with hand gestures, as well as with writing. Whilst Jupiter rules the quality of mentality, Mercury governs the way in which the mentality is expressed. A strong Mercury makes the subject quick, volatile, changeable, inquiring, ingenious and often remarkably persuasive. In excess the subject tends to exaggeration, and often becomes too quick for less volatile types, in which case he may be opportunist or exaggerated in speech or persuasive ability. Such qualities as these are certainly linked with the Mercurial hand, whilst within the hand itself we find that the finger of Mercury, as well as the line of Intuition, may be associated with such qualities and energies. The little finger is concerned with Virgo, in which sign the planet manifests strongly. Attempts to associate the zodiac with the hand have suggested that Mercury should be regarded also as having rule over the line of Life, which is connected with the Air sign of Gemini.

The Mercurian is the quickest and most active of all the types and this activity is not confined to his physical agility but applies to the mental as well. He is like a flash in his intuitive faculty, and enjoys everything in which he can use his quickness to wither a mental or physical test. He is the personification of grace in his movements and is skilful in everything he undertakes. In all games he is proficient, and he plays with his head as well as his hands, winning because he plans his moves, and shrewdly estimates the ability of his opponent. In all athletic sports

93

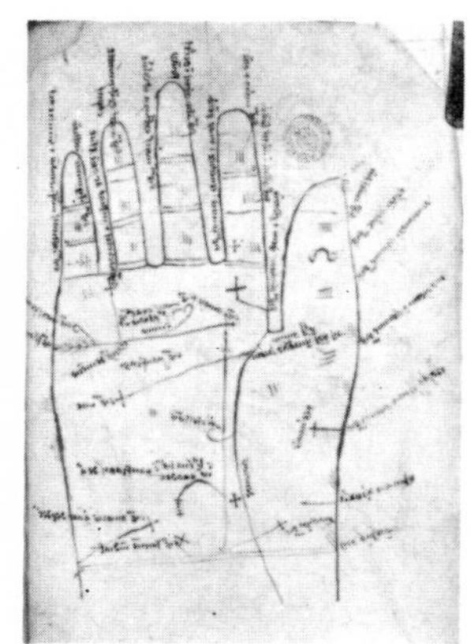

94

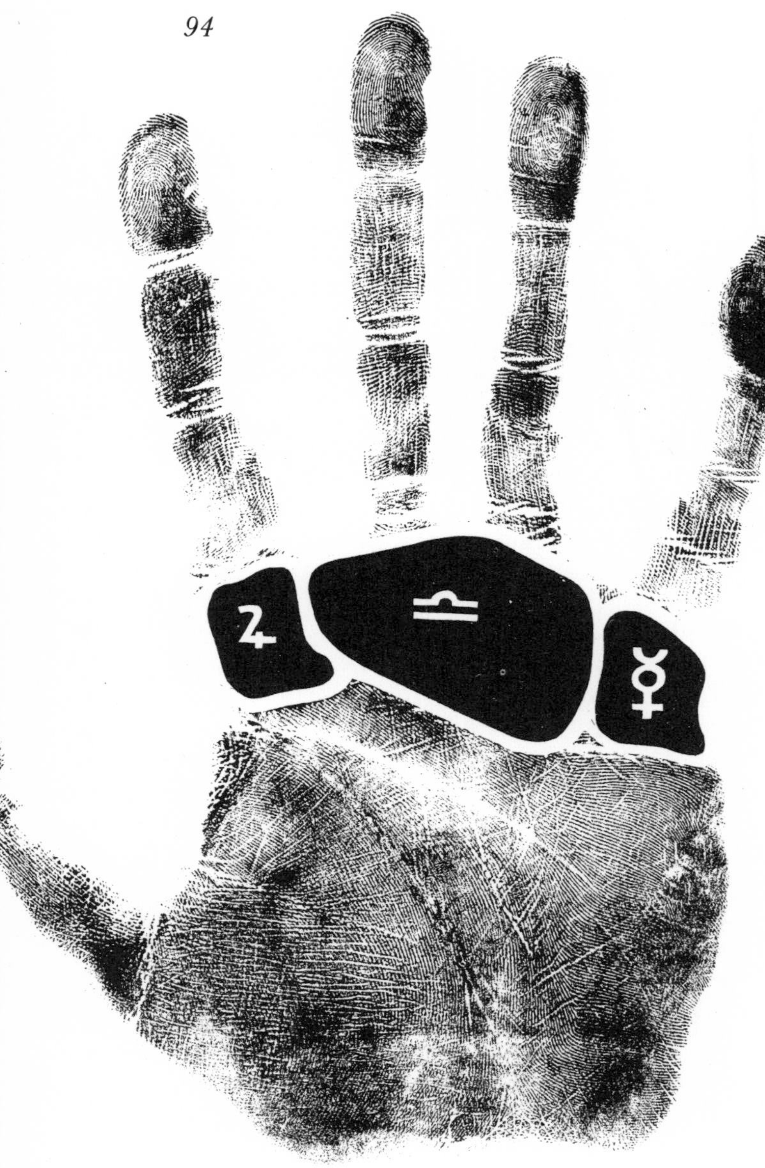

93. Palmistry of the fixed symbol type, from a mediaeval manuscript in the Bodleian Library, Oxford.

94. The girdle of Venus and the line of Apollo are merged, in some systems of palmistry, to form the mount of Libra, separating the mount of Jupiter from the mount of Mercury. The rationale behind this merging of Venus and Sun may be understood in astrological terms.

95. The small lines running over the percussion, under Mercury, are popularly called 'marriage lines', but they have nothing to do with marriage, or indeed with relationships.

96. An example from the nineteenth century 'Palmist' of how the so-called 'marriage lines' were interpreted.

where dexterity and skill, rather than brute strength, are needed, he is the victor. In argument he is at home, for no one has greater facility of expression than he. This, added to the quickness with which he can grasp and turn an opportunity to his account, brings him out ahead, if his side of the question has even a semblance of validity. He is especially fond of oratory, and eloquence in any line strongly moves him. With his keenness and the power of expressing himself well, he is very tactful and adroit, thus making many friends by saying the right thing at the right time. As an after dinner speaker he is a success, and in a battle of words or badinage is an opponent hard to overcome.

One of the chief elements of the Mercurian's success is his ability to judge human nature and character. He mentally estimates everyone whom he meets, and uses his quick mind and tactful way to make a friend and accomplish what he wishes. He is adroit, crafty, and a constant schemer, using all his powers of shrewdness, intuition, and oratory to get himself through the world . . . Of all the types, none is stronger in the business world than the Mercurian. He has shrewdness, diplomacy, tact, management, influence over people, judgement of human nature, energy, and the power of expressing himself, all of which are the very strongest elements one could have for a successful business career. No better illustration of the success of the Mercurian in the business world can be given than to point to the standing of the Hebrew race in mercantile

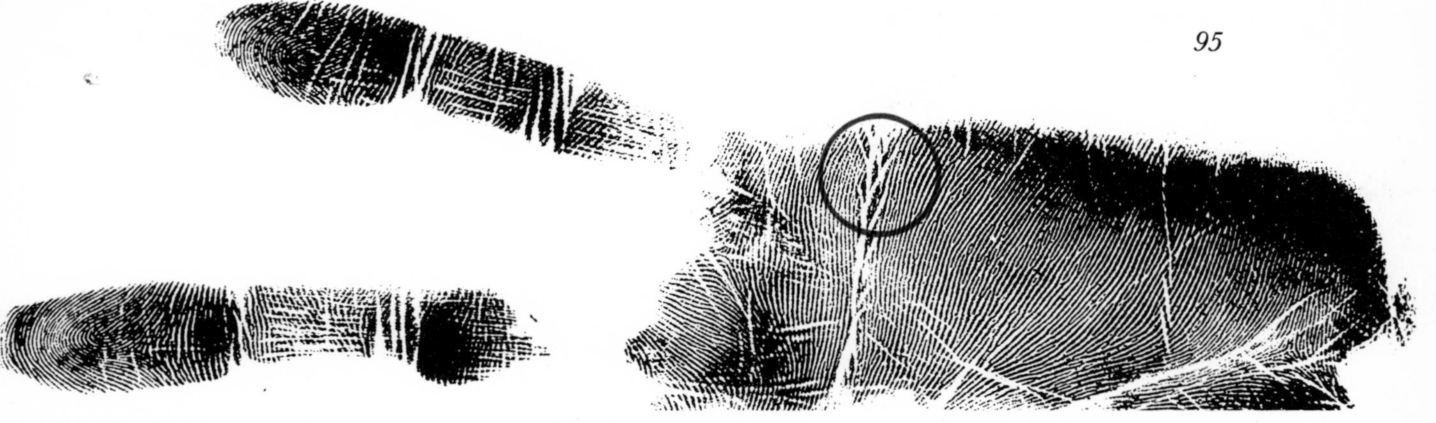

95

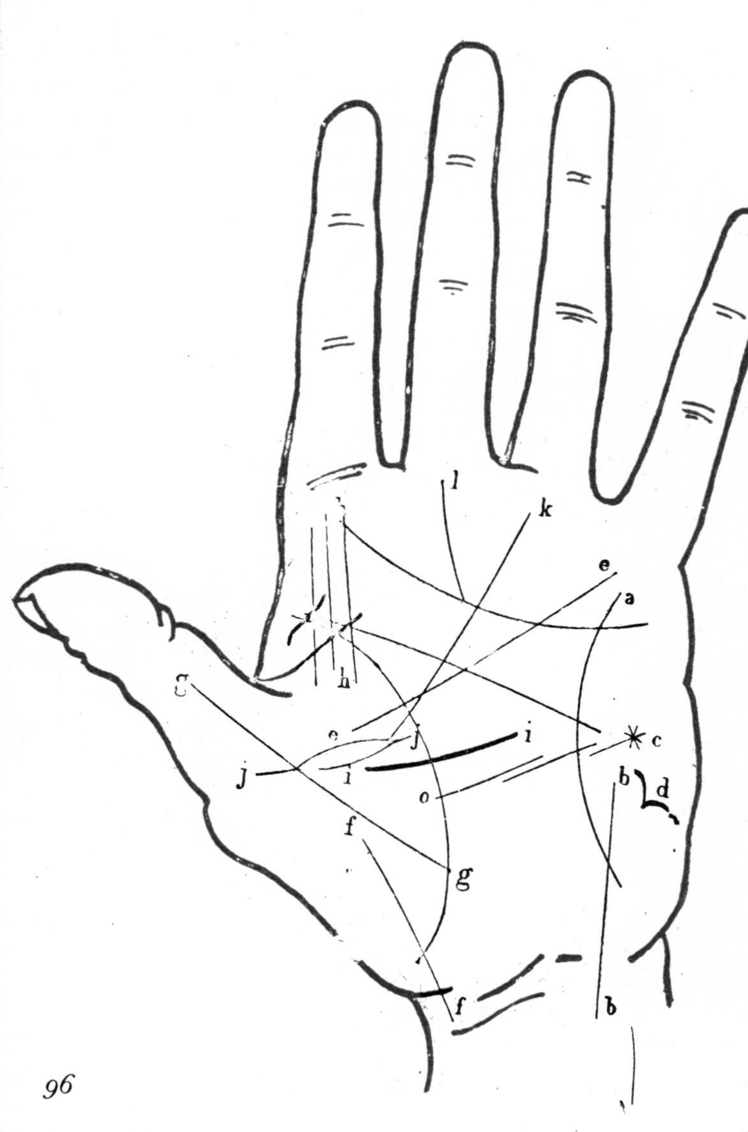

96

216 CHEIROMANCY.

cheiromants have affirmed that a woman having this mount well rayed is sure to marry a doctor, or, at any rate, a man of science. If the lines on the mount merely take the form of little flecks and dashes, it is a practically sure indication of a babbling, chattering disposition.

Lines on the percussion—*i.e.*, on the edge of the hand, between the base of the little finger and the line of heart—indicate *liaisons*, or serious affairs of the heart if horizontal, [*i.e.*, parallel with the line of the heart,] each line denoting a separate *liaison* or love affair, a single deep line denoting one strong and lasting affection.[116] If vertical they denote, almost invariably, the number of children which the subject has had. De Peruchio lays down the rule that if they are strong they denote boys, if faint, girls; and if they are short or indistinct the children are either dead or not yet born. Several vertical lines on the percussion, crossed by a line which starts from a star upon the mount, betrays sterility, whilst a marriage line, ending abruptly by a star, indicates a marriage or *liaison* of short duration, terminated by death.

The mount quite smooth and unlined indicates a cool, determined, and constant condition of mind. A grille upon the mount is a dangerous prognostic of a violent death, a circle also placed upon the mount indicating that it will be by water. A spot upon the mount indicates an error or misfortune in business.

If the mount is high, and the hand contain a long line of Apollo, the commercial instinct will work itself out in speculation rather than in recognized and persevering commerce.

97

98

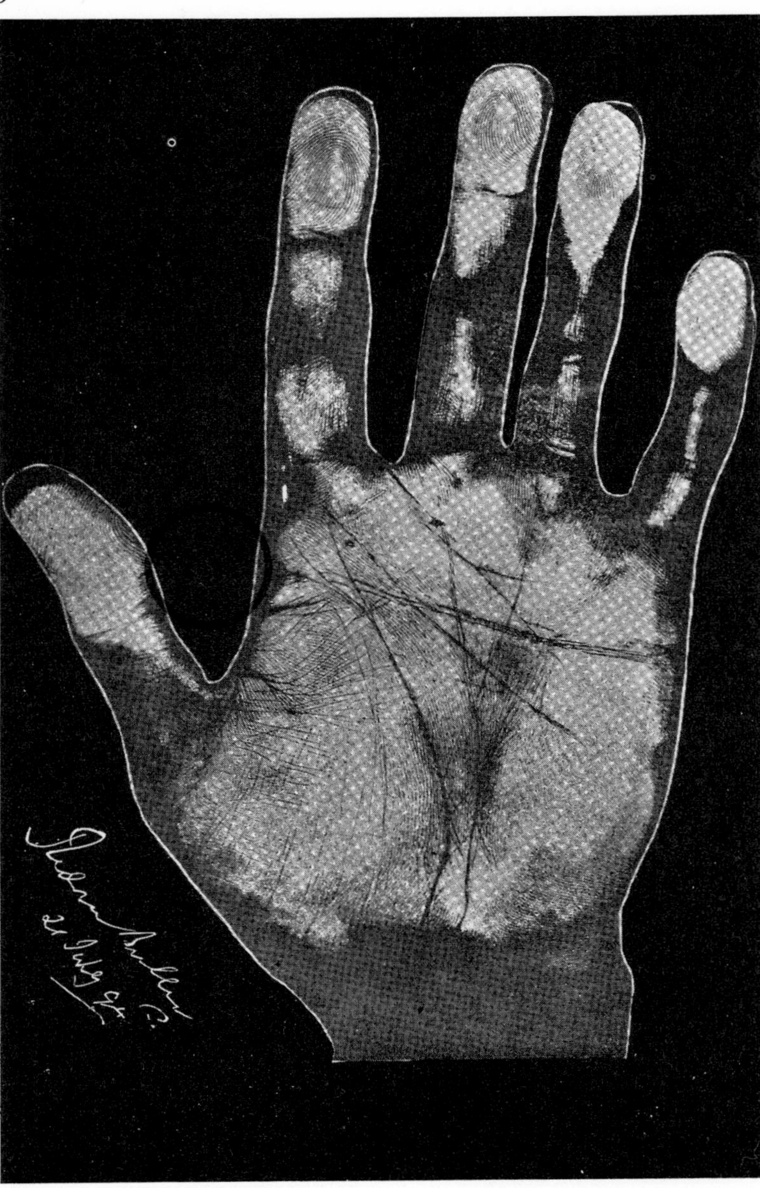

97. Jupiter, ruler over Sagittarius and Pisces, receiving adulation, as is his wont.

98. The hand of General Buller, from 'Cheiro's' collection. The line encircled under Jupiter is a line of Ambition.

99. The hands of two modern 'pop' singers, the top female, the bottom male.

circles today, and to state that a very large percentage of these people are Mercurians. They are ingenious in their ways of planning new schemes to make money, and original in their manner of putting them into operation. Mercurians are great imitators, and so clever that they can steal some other man's idea and pass it as their own. They make good actors and their powers of mimicry and study of nature enable them to create on the stage lifelike and realistic characters. They make excellent lawyers, having the keenness, the faculty of seeing a question from its many sides, as well as a knowledge of the failings of humanity. To this add oratory, and it completes an excellent combination of qualities to make a good lawyer. They are excellent teachers, for their grasp of scientific knowledge, backed by an ability to say what they mean, gives them a mastery in this field, and being judges of human nature, they know how best to reach each and every pupil. (42)

Jupiter is the planet which rules over the expansive nature of the personality, over those gentle, sympathetic and humane qualities found within most people. A strong Jupiter induces a strong moral nature, making the subject generous, warm, loyal, helpful, stable emotionally, wide in his interests, and expansive in mental outlook. In excess the subject will become over-expansive, self-indulgent, prone to speculation and self-assertive. Such qualities as these are certainly linked with the Jupiterian hand, as with the Air hand (page 42), particularly in a masculine subject. Within the hand itself we find that the finger

100

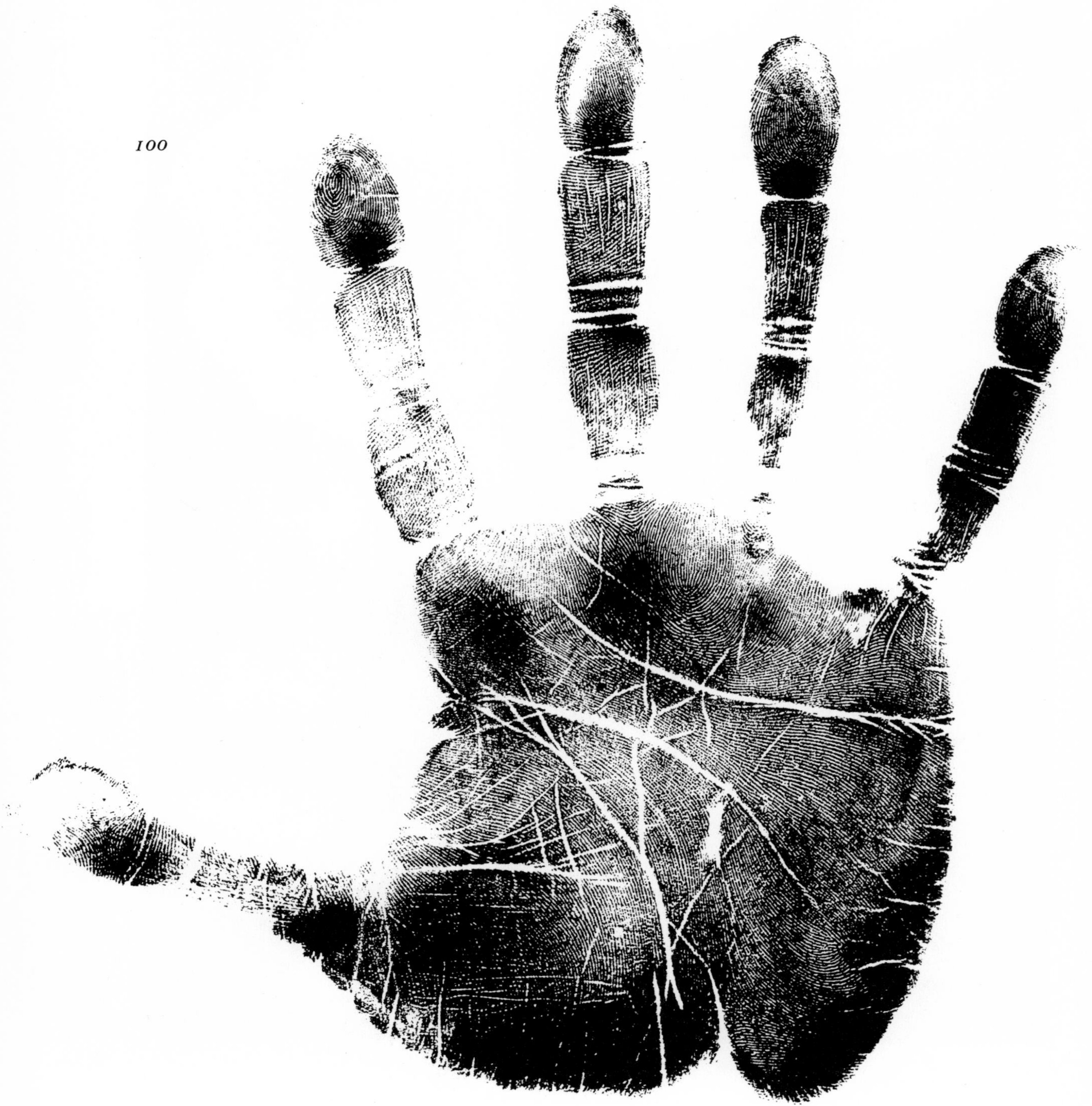

101

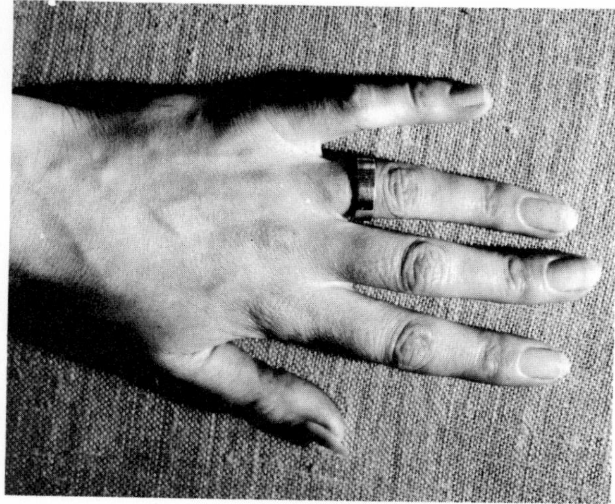

100. A Jupiterian hand, large and fleshy. In the astrological system, this would be an Air hand.

101. A finger of Jupiter which is noticeably longer than the finger of Apollo generally adds a degree of Jupiterian characteristic to the personality. This is why a long finger of Jupiter is often taken as a sign of 'strong ambition' or 'a domineering nature'.

102. An example of a short finger of Jupiter, which implies deficient Jupiterian qualities—often interpreted as 'inferiority complex'.

of Jupiter is also associated with such forces, though these are of a more spiritualized nature. Attempts to link astrology with the hand have suggested that the Jupiter of Pisces should have direct rule over the finger of Jupiter, whilst the head line, indicator of the intellectual expansiveness and mental directness associated with Jupiter, should be associated with the Jupiter of Sagittarius.

The Jupiterian They are conscious of their strength, and this gives them reliance in their ability. They depend upon themselves, work out their own plans, and thus do not have the habit of asking advice. They are inclined to bluster and talk loudly, not in a quarrelsome way, it is true, but in a manner full of self-confidence and self-assertion. They are aware of the influence they exert, and it naturally makes them vain. This vanity knows the power of the rich, musical voice in swaying men, and they like to hear the sound of this voice as well as to see it shaping the views of others. Leadership is always uppermost in their minds.

With all his vanity the Jupiterian is warm-hearted. He has a fellow-feeling for humanity that exhibits itself in practical ways. A word of comfort from so strong a person to one in distress does a world of good, and the kindly spirit he shows to all who appeal to him binds closer the following he attracts. Nor is his kindness confined to words, for he gives as well, and is generous and charitable. This Jupiterian beneficence is dispensed in a manly, openhearted way that makes the recipients feel that the donor is glad to give. Here again his nature

102

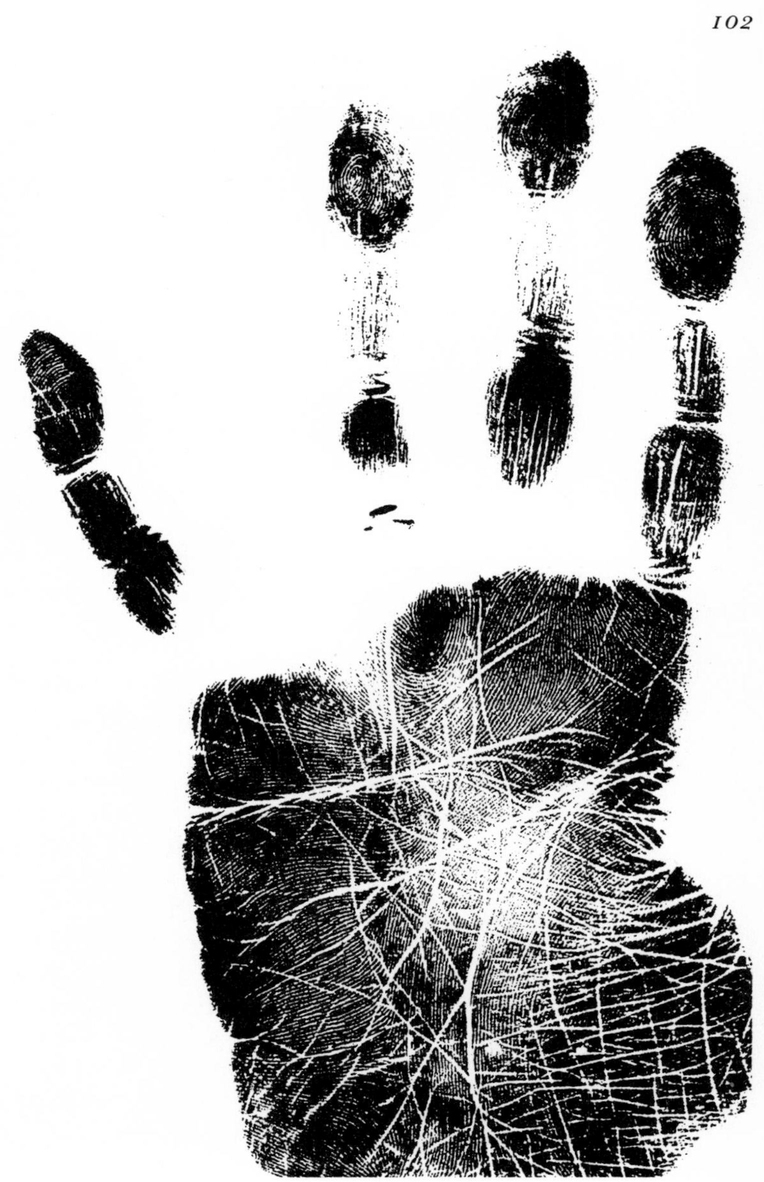

103. The Sun, ruler over Leo, seated in splendour.

104. The fingers of Saturn, Apollo and Mercury with fire whorls, lend a very strong solar force to a hand which in other respects may be quite un-Fire like.

105. The hand of Sarah Bernhardt, preserved (and perhaps even added to) by 'Cheiro'. Observe the extremely well developed line of Apollo, which is always a sign of creativity.

furnishes him to help carry out the things he was created to do, viz., to attract and lead. The Jupiterian, in his capacity as a leader, would, if unjust inflict harm in many ways upon his fellows. With his big, manly way of looking at things he is eminently just, and strives to encourage and support fairness and business honesty. He is a dashing fellow, one who has much attraction for the opposite sex, and will always be found gallant and courteous. He is extravagant. To him power and rule mean more than money, and while he obtains large sums from his enterprises, he does not hoard it, and has a contempt for anything resembling small dealing or miserliness. He is inherently religious. . . He is honest, and in all things despises cheating and fraud, honor being one of his leading attributes. He believes in right and independence, and his counsel and support are always with the oppressed. This faculty of insisting that common people have their due makes him, despite his aristocratic tendencies, the idol of the multitude. He is not hard to get along with, is easily pleased, especially with attentions to himself, and has a faculty for keeping friends. Jupiterians are, if any type may claim this distinction, lucky, for they have so many desirable and attractive qualities that they are pushed forward by their friends into successful careers, because they are general favorites. There is another factor in their composition that enables them to rise over every obstacle. They are ambitious, and with this tremendous force behind them, urging on the strong qualities they possess, the Jupiterian is one of the most invincible of all the types. Ambition is powerful as a moving force in human success, and the Jupiterian is the embodiment of ambition. He has pride as well, for no man could possess his aristocratic, dignified, ambitious qualities without also having pride in himself and his achievements. This pride is but natural; it is not a fault, and for its possession he should not be blamed. (43)

The Sun is the 'planet. which rules over the self, the masculine principle of domination, and is linked with the conscious aim of the subject, with the direction in which his will is exercised. A strong Sun makes the subject dignified, brilliant, self-confident and self-reliant, magnanimous, generous and creative in outlook. In excess it tends to manifest itself through egocentricity, bombast and incompetence. Such qualities as these are certainly linked with the Sun hand, as with the Fire hand (page 45), and within the hand itself we find that the line of Apollo and the finger of Apollo are linked with such qualities and energies. The line of Heart is also linked with solar energies, since this line is associated with the zodiacal sign Leo, which is ruled over by the Sun.

The Sun type The Apollonian is highly intuitive. He sees through things more quickly than other people and especially is this perceptive faculty strong in his art and literature. He does not labor to learn, as does his companion, the Saturnian, neither is he as profound and deep. But the Apollonian, no matter how little he may really

104

know, will make a brilliant show of it, and in any company, from the seeming depth of his knowledge and research, is a surprise. This arises from the wonderful versatility of his nature, and the quick way he has of grasping a small idea and making a great deal out of it. He is inventive as well as an umitator, and can put old things in new ways. Thus he often gets credit for knowing a great deal more than he really does. He is always the centre of attraction in whatever company he may be found, and will adapt himself to circumstances and people. He can be thrown with scientists and will cope with them in whatever field of rearch they are working. He will, with equal facility and without thought or preparation, join a body of socialists, artists, anarchists, doctors, lawyers, or any profession or class, and will astonish those present with his seeming mastery of the particular subject. His adaptability and versatility are astonishing, and 'brilliant' is the only word that fitly describes him.

He fairly sparkles with intuition, and seems to learn without study. This makes him sought by all classes of people. He is the life of the drawing-room, the hero of the athletic field, the daring and successful plunger either in the stock market or at the gaming table. In any and all walks of life he is found, full of dash, brilliancy, versatility. For him the beautiful in nature, women, home decorations, and dress, have always a fascination. Anything that lacks beauty is repulsive. With this strong passion in him he is the artist always in everything. He may

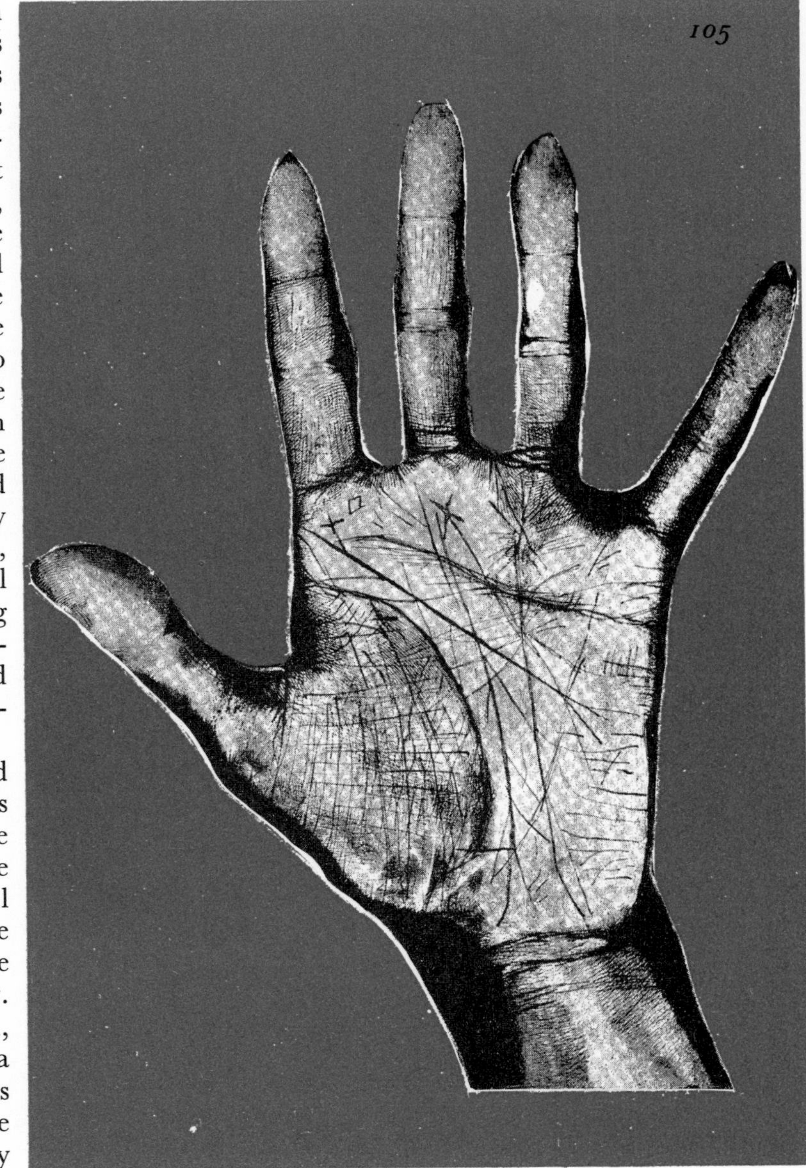
105

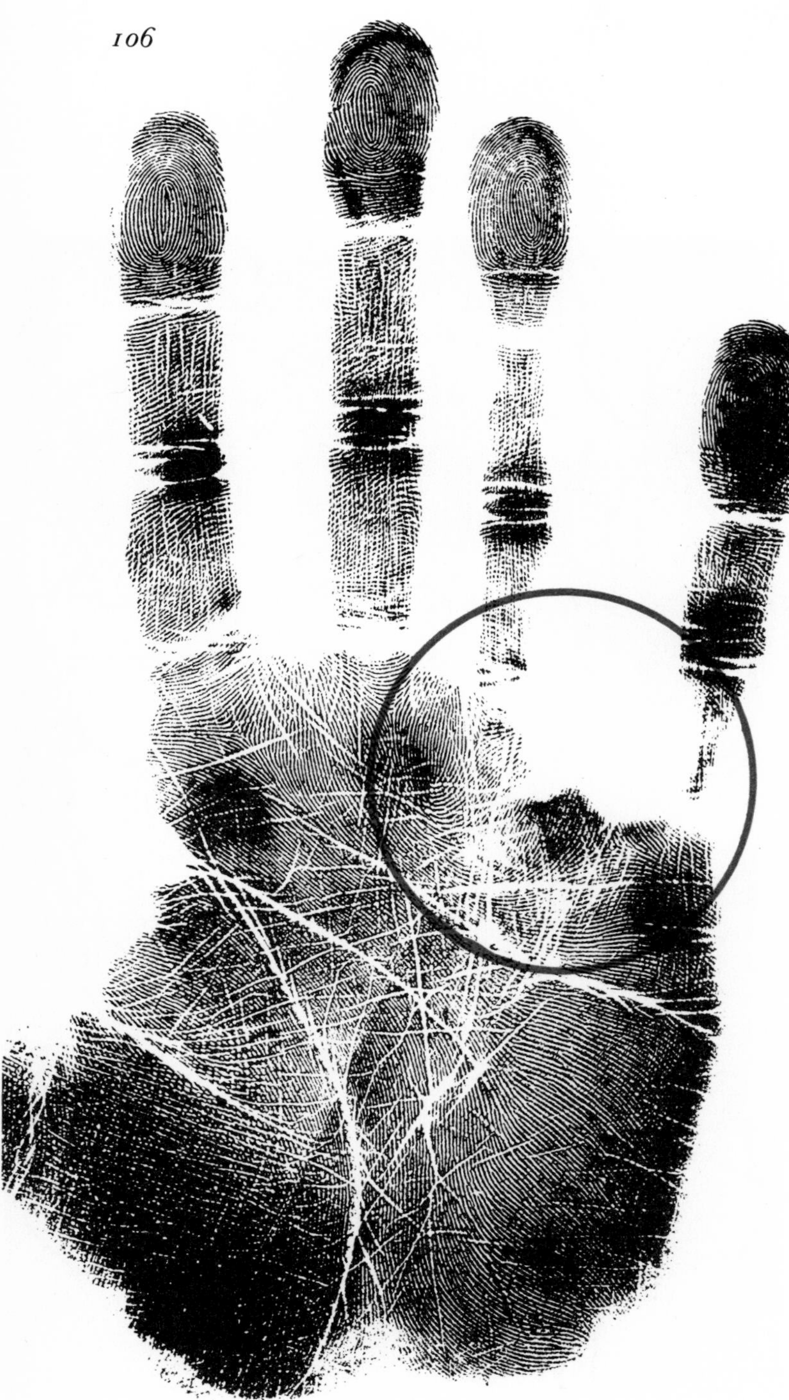

not be the great painter, but if he has short nails, surely he is the critic. He adores art in every form, and owing to his versatility, he is always a dabbler in it. He loves fine clothes, luxurious home surroundings, and jewels . . . Being brilliant, he makes enemies often become bitter and envious rivals. His brain is clear, and in all matters of business, religion, art, or literature he sees things from a logical point of view. He has a great facility for expression, and while not always deep, is easy to understand. To him success is natural, and it comes by the very force of circumstance. Friends and the world like him and gladly do much to forward his interests, and he is thus pushed by his admirers into many advantageous enterprises. He attains high positions and is a great money-maker. He is never economical and does not rely on putting away a part of his earnings, but by brilliant and successful spurts forges ahead. His tastes are luxurious and his expenditure follows them, but he makes so much that the expenses seem little . . . Among his other accomplishments, he is proficient in occult sciences, and does some wonderful things. He cannot explain how, but knows it is not from deep study. It is in reality his highly intuitive faculties that make him proficient here. He is cheerful, happy, and bright, and though he is subject to bursts of quick temper which are fierce while they last, it is only a momentary flash, and he holds no resentment. He does not harbor grudges and has the ability to win over his worst enemy to at least a seeming friendship. He does not make lasting friends,

106. A strong line of Apollo on the hand of an artist.

107. Detail from 106 to show how the line under the Apollo finger is often of a multiple nature, indicating versatility.

108. A sixteenth century version of the kind of lines found in plate 106. (after Taisnier

109. Portrait of Taisnier from his 'Popus Mathematicus' a comprehensive tabulation of chiromantical lore of the sixteenth century.

IOANNIS TAISNIER

but by his brilliance temporarily attracts and enslaves. He himself is not a lasting friend; consequently he does not inspire true friendship in others. (44)

The Earth type Benham follows the tradition to the extent that he does not describe the Earth type. The tradition tends to regard Saturn as the most Earthy of the types, for it is the force of Saturn which governs the physical form, the weight of materiality, the structure of our vehicle, which weighs down the spirit, and induces an element of melancholia into the being. To a certain extent the Saturnine force is found manifesting in the personalities of those possessed of an Earth hand, though it must be observed that there is considerable difference between the Earth hand of Muchery and that described in the system on page 45. The main thing which the two types possess in common is a certain lack of lightness, a serious and moody outlook which precludes the immediate expression of emotions–typical Saturnine characteristics. The Earth type is, however, in no way as austere and miserable as the textbook descriptions of Saturn would have us believe! The temperament and personality which may be associated with this hand has to a certain extent been described already on page 45 in the fourfold classification. Muchery is content to describe the type as 'concrete', though positive, solid, ponderous and essentially practical, and given more to obeying than commanding.

Something of the variety of palmistic systems may be grasped if we examine an ancient Chinese system, and compare this with the traditional Western system. In order that we

110

110. The mount of Moon, seat of imagination.

111. Taisnier's account of lines on the mount of Venus, now called 'worry lines'.

112. The mount of Venus.

might make this comparison we shall have to examine in a little more detail certain of the traditions concerning Western palmistry.

The Mount of Moon is traditionally the source of imagination, so that a low-set or much-lined mount is supposed to indicate an extremely sensitive, imaginative nature. Lines running from this mount to other parts of the hand are supposed to be carrying this highly-charged, imaginative energy into those domains: a strong mount gives a rather dreamy, restless personality:

> Such subjects are generally capricious and changeable, egoists, and inclined to be idle: their imagination often makes them hypochondriacal, and their abstraction often causes them to develop the faculty of presentiment, giving them intuition, prophetic instincts, and dreams. They are fond of voyages by reason of their restlessness, they are more mystic than religious, phlegmatic in habit, fantastic, and given to romance in matters of art and literature. (45)

It is as though this lunar influence drives the subject away from the body into the world of dreams. On the other side of the hand is the equally important mount of Venus, which has the effect of driving the personality further into the material world. A prominent mount tends to give sensuality:

> These subjects are great lovers of pleasure and society: they are fond of applause, but more from their love of giving pleasure to others than for its own sake. They hate any form of quarrel or strife, and are essentially gay, though they are less noisily gay, as a rule. (46)

111

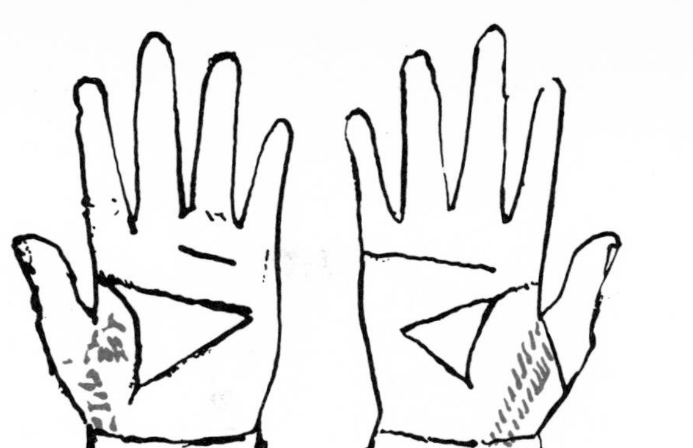

II *Lineæ quædam à rascetta ad pollicem vergentes, in ultima*

112

All very innocent, you might say, except:

> An excess of the mount will betray debauchery, effrontery, licence, inconstancy, vanity, flirtation, and levity. (47)

This is the other face of Venus, the goddess who is at once the patron of the art, demure of aspect, and yet also the ruler over sexuality and love.

Above these two mounts we find the wedge of flesh which marks the centre of the hand. This area was accorded the rulership of Mars in the early forms of palmistry, and was called the Plain of Mars. For various reasons this central portion of the hand is rarely accorded a meaning nowadays, and in modern palmistry the rulership is virtually ignored–possibly because it was difficult to see how a 'mount', which is in fact a depression, could be particularly emphatic or 'raised' in a hand and possibly also because there was some conflict in a system which accorded a Martian rulership to another, quite unrelated, part of the hand: namely the thumb. Some palmists visualised a 'mount' of Mars, underneath the mount of Mercury (figure 117), with the plain of Mars in the centre.

> The main characteristics indicated by a development of the Mount of Mars are courage, calmness, *sang froid* in moments of emergency, resignation in misfortune, pride, resolution, resistance, and devotion, with a strong capacity to command . . .
>
> An excessive development of this mount . . . will indicate brusquerie, fury, injustice of mind, and defiance of manner. Lines on the mount always denote hot temper. This excessive development generally betrays

113

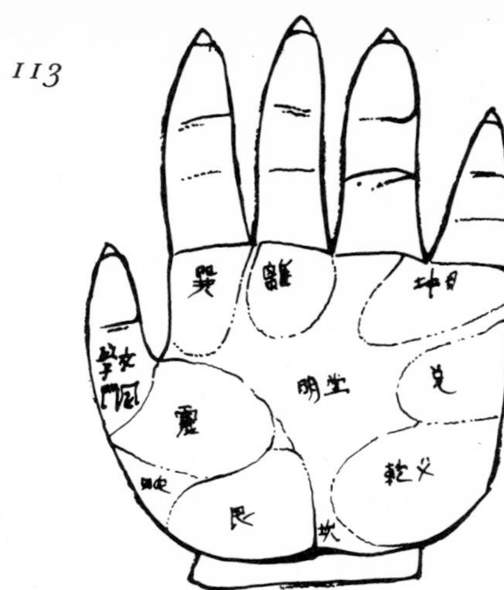

113. The traditional Chinese hand system, based on the ancient I Ching predictive method.

114. The I Ching *is a Chinese text which is consulted with the aid of sticks. The basic symbolizm of the text has been appropriated for use in palmistry, as well as in astrology.*

115. The four elemental areas of the hand, relating to the Western astrological tradition.

116. The four temperamental types, linked with the four elements. From a fifteenth century manuscript in the British Museum.

114

lasciviousness, and exaggeration in speech.

The Plain of Mars highly developed or covered with lines indicates a love of contest, struggle, and war, especially if the nails be short and a cross be found in the plain. This network of little lines in the Plain of Mars always indicates obstacles in the way of good fortune. (48)

We know already, of course, that the mounts under the fingers are ruled by the planetary forces from which they receive their names. If we take into account the rulership of these zones, and link them with the four main lines, we do in fact find that the hand itself is a miniature zodiac. Naturally, if we compare this zodiacal hand with the Chinese hand, in which the zodiac is not so important, we should find interesting relationships between the areas, though a quite different system. This is especially noticeable, for just as astrology has always influenced occult Western thought, and is therefore deeply embedded in palmistic theory, the predictive method of the *I Ching* (figure 114) has always influenced occult Chinese thought, and is therefore deeply embedded in palmistic theory in China.

When we turn to Chinese palmistry, we may well be impressed initially that this system of hand classification is also based on the concept of basic elements; unfortunately, however, any attempt to link these with the four elements of the West proves unrewarding. For a start, the Chinese system is based on *five* elements, which are Fire, Earth, Water (as in our own system) but with the addition of Metal and Wood, and the absence of Air.

115

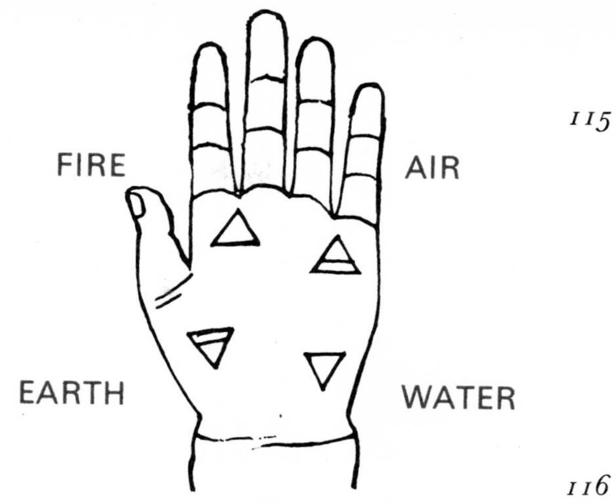

116

There appears to be no logical division by which one may recognise the hand types; only the Earth hand, which is short, thick and heavy, and which shows 'small success, often with great labour', is like the Earth hand of our own classification. The five types are in fact linked with planetary forces, Earth being the Saturn hand, Fire the Mars hand, Water the Mercury hand, Metal the Venus hand, with Wood the Jupiter hand. The Chinese hand system would appear to be very little, then, which may link with the Western tradition, save through the planetary influences, yet when we turn to the system of interpreting character from the surface of the hand, we do find, in fact, very many correspondencies.

The system at figure 113 is based on a Chinese palmistic diagram which is reputed to be well over two thousand years old. The hand is divided into eight basic areas or 'palaces', each of which corresponds to the eight trigrams of the famous Chinese *I Ching*, which is a graphic philosophical machine, (figure 119) commonly used for predicting the future. If one superimposes these Palaces over the zones and mounts of the traditional European system, then very interesting relationships may be established. The associations attached to the eight trigrams are extremely complex, but the following brief accounts, abstracted from the *I Ching* itself will indicate certain relationships between hand and character in a remarkably similar way:

SUN approximates to the mount of Jupiter, it is a strong and pervasive force, associated

117. *By the late nineteenth century the three areas of Mars drew a wide zone across the hand. The traditional plane of Mars was encased in the lower Mars (above the mount of Venus) and upper Mars. See, for example, Benham's diagram at figure 30.*

118. *The Chinese system, and its nomenclature.*

119. *Schema linking the parts of the hand in the Chinese system to the eight trigrams of the* I Ching, *with the romanized names. See text opposite.*

117

with the idea of a moving wind, which is refreshing to the world over which it blows, yet which is itself unaffected by material things, since it can 'go round' them without losing its energy or direction. For this reason it is likened to the human intellect which follows the material world, without of necessity being either perverted or injured by it: the fundamental idea behind *Sun* is that of human Intellect. It implies man's ability to think, to reason, and to operate in the physical world. There is an obvious connexion here with the expansive Jupiter, which rules over mentality.

LI approximates to the mount of Saturn, yet the Chinese character itself suggests quite a different concept to this cold body, for it means 'flame' or brightness. We do however, see something of the connexion with Saturn when realize that the Chinese associate the area with the fame and glory of 'official position', which very often requires the subject to live 'away from home' in a foreign province. Thus the area is linked with 'position' or 'social standing' and separation as well as with career, all Saturnian concepts. *Li* itself is associated with perception, with the dispersal of consciousness.

K'UN is the female principle, and literally means 'earth'. It is located beneath the fingers of Apollo and Mercury, and both in localization and nomenclature might superficially suggest a deep rift between the Chinese and Western systems. The connexion between sexuality and receptivity, and indeed, the astrological connexion between the little finger and Virgo (figure 61) do however,

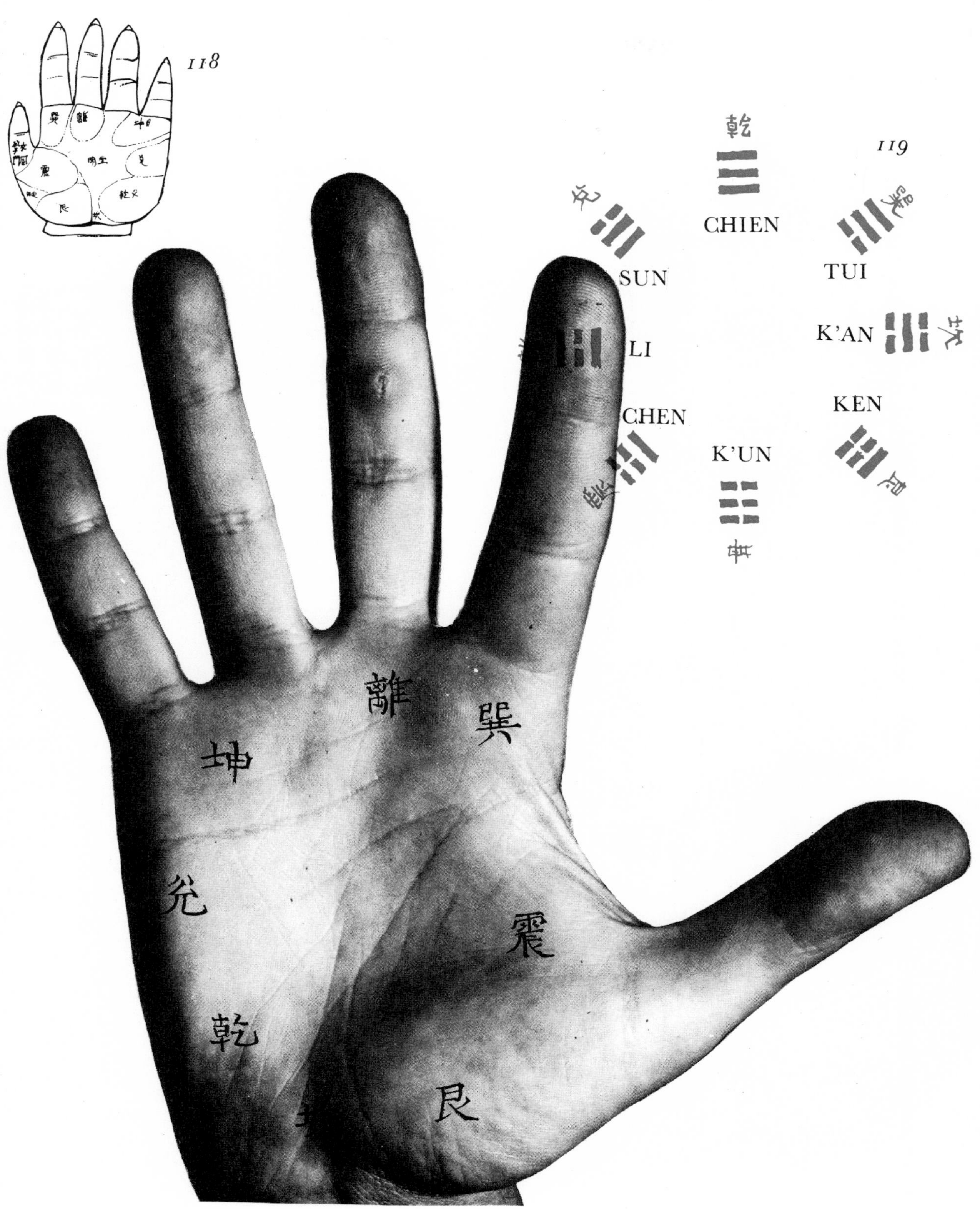
118
119
乾
CHIEN
SUN
TUI
LI
K'AN
CHEN
KEN
K'UN
離
巽
坤
兌
震
乾
艮

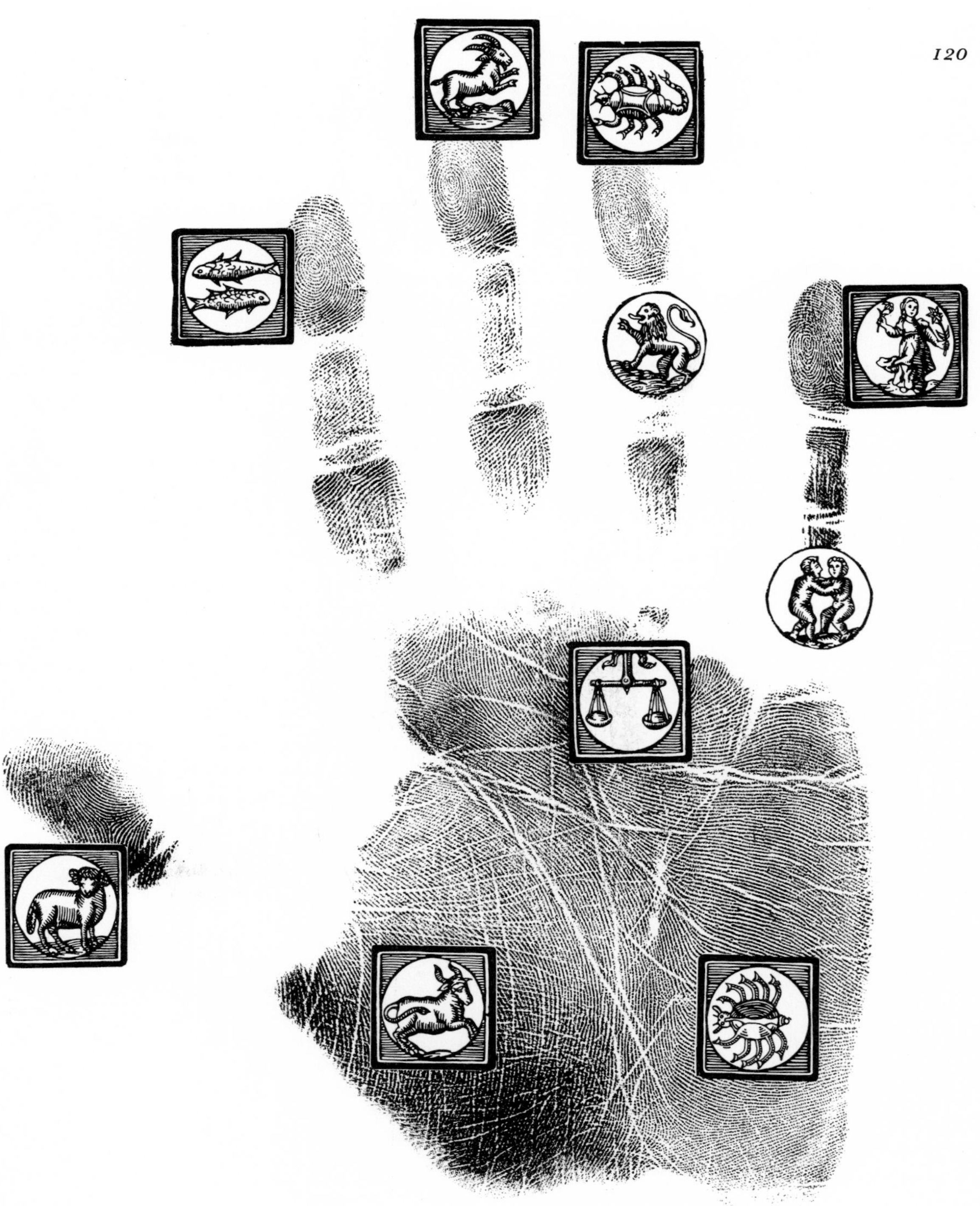

120

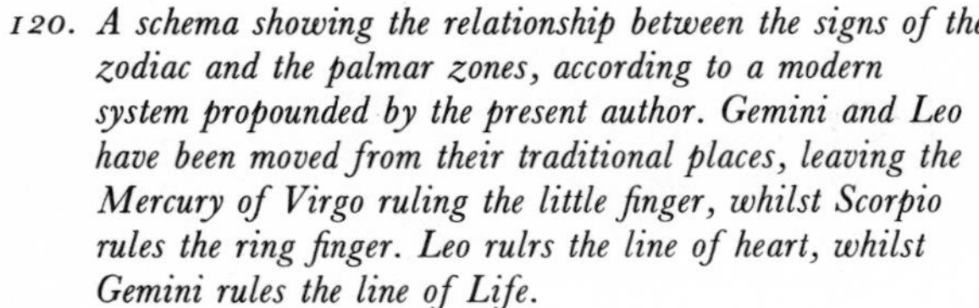

120. A schema showing the relationship between the signs of the zodiac and the palmar zones, according to a modern system propounded by the present author. Gemini and Leo have been moved from their traditional places, leaving the Mercury of Virgo ruling the little finger, whilst Scorpio rules the ring finger. Leo rulrs the line of heart, whilst Gemini rules the line of Life.

121. In the early forms of palmistry, the lines on the thumb were regarded as being of very great importance, since the thumb represented the activity of Mars, and the selfhood.

121

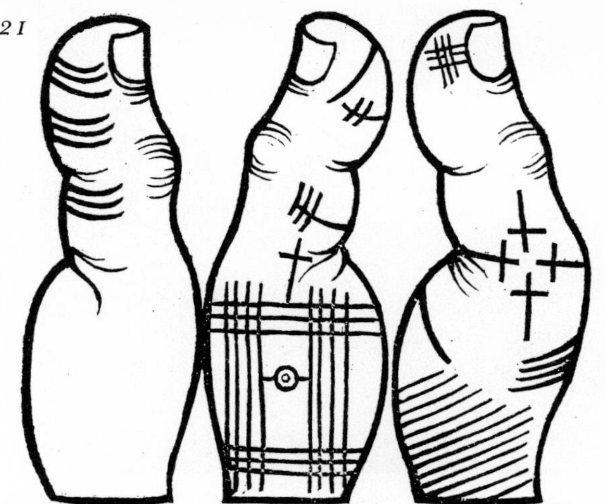

suggest that the relationship is worth close study, especially as the connexion with creativity (Apollo) has been hinted at:

> The Fundamental thoughts are connected with the compliance and the subordination of the *yin* aspect of the Creative Spirit–with the qualities to the production of substance and to the moulding of substance into form. (48)

The *yin* referred to is the basic material and receptive element in the material world, and is linked with the idea of 'giving'. This is one reason why the Palace of *K'un* was called, in less fortunate or more fortunate days, depending upon how one looks at it, 'the palace of servants and slaves'.

TUI is located in the upper part of the mount of Moon, and is the palace which is linked with wives, favourites and children, though more in the sense that the palmist will evaluate from this Palace the degree to which satisfaction will be gained from these things. It is the zone of desire in regard to generation, and we therefore still find an interesting correspondence with the mount of Moon. The trigram *Tui* is linked with the idea of joy, and is in the Chinese imagery shown as a body of water, 'a joyous lake', reminding one of the watery nature of the Moon is astrology.

CHIEN is located in the lower part of the mount of Moon, and is the Palace which is indicative of the protective instincts of the father, and is further associated with the idea of education. *Chien* means literally 'Heaven', and being of a strictly masculine nature, we find it difficult to link this Palace with anything in the Western tradition of the lunar nature of this mount. None the less, the Chinese name does imply that the zone relates to strongly spiritualized qualities, and *Chien* is highly creative in application.

K'AN is localized between the bottom of the lunar mount, and the line of Life. The name of the trigram implies great danger, or a difficulty to be overcome: it also means 'defile' or 'abyss', and is therefore appropriately placed in the abyss between the mounts of Moon and Venus–or, in the Chinese tradition, between the skies of the heavenly *Chien* and the mountains of *Ken*. The area which in the occult tradition must be linked with the idea of rebirth is claimed to be 'a repository of the benefits of hereditary virtue'. The main idea is that before incarnation the spirit chooses the family line, and through these, certain hereditary characteristics, which it will work upon during the course of life, to produce characteristics, which will serve its own purpose. We may, in the light of this tradition, see a connexion between this Palace, and the line of Saturn, which springs from this area, and which is associated with destiny.

KEN is localized in the lower part of the Mount of Venus. The word in Chinese means 'limits' or 'hard' or 'obstinate', though it is more commonly imaged as being a mountain:

> Mountains are always obstacles, yet at the same time they are protection against invaders. The height of the mount will indicate the measure in which the entourage will be an obstacle or a protection. (49)

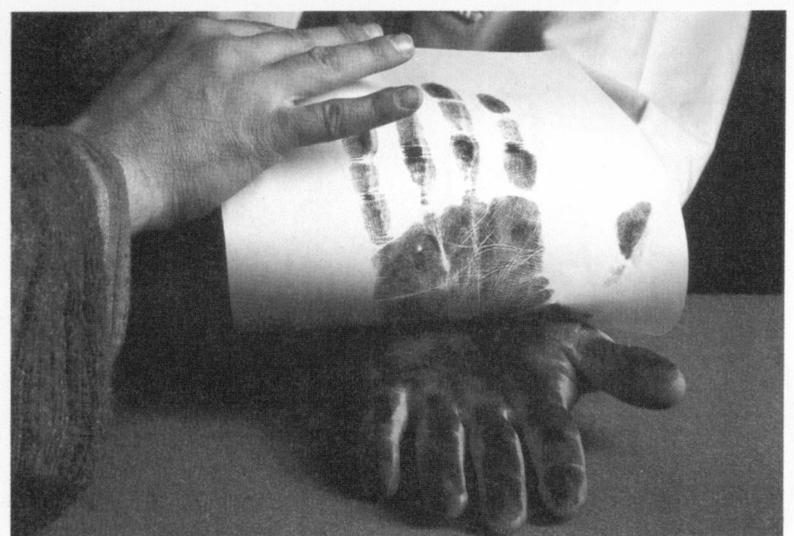

122

122. *The making of hand prints nowadays is much simpler than the practice adhered to in the nineteenth century and before. In earlier times, it was more practical to make drawings, or to print by pressing the hand into a soot deposit (which is why Cheiro's collection shows white hands against a black background). Today prints are made by rolling the hand with lion-ink, and pressing paper onto the hand in order to receive a print.*

123. *A magnifying glass is useful for examining the tiny details of the hand—especially of malformations on the papillary ridges, which so often predict coming illnesses.*

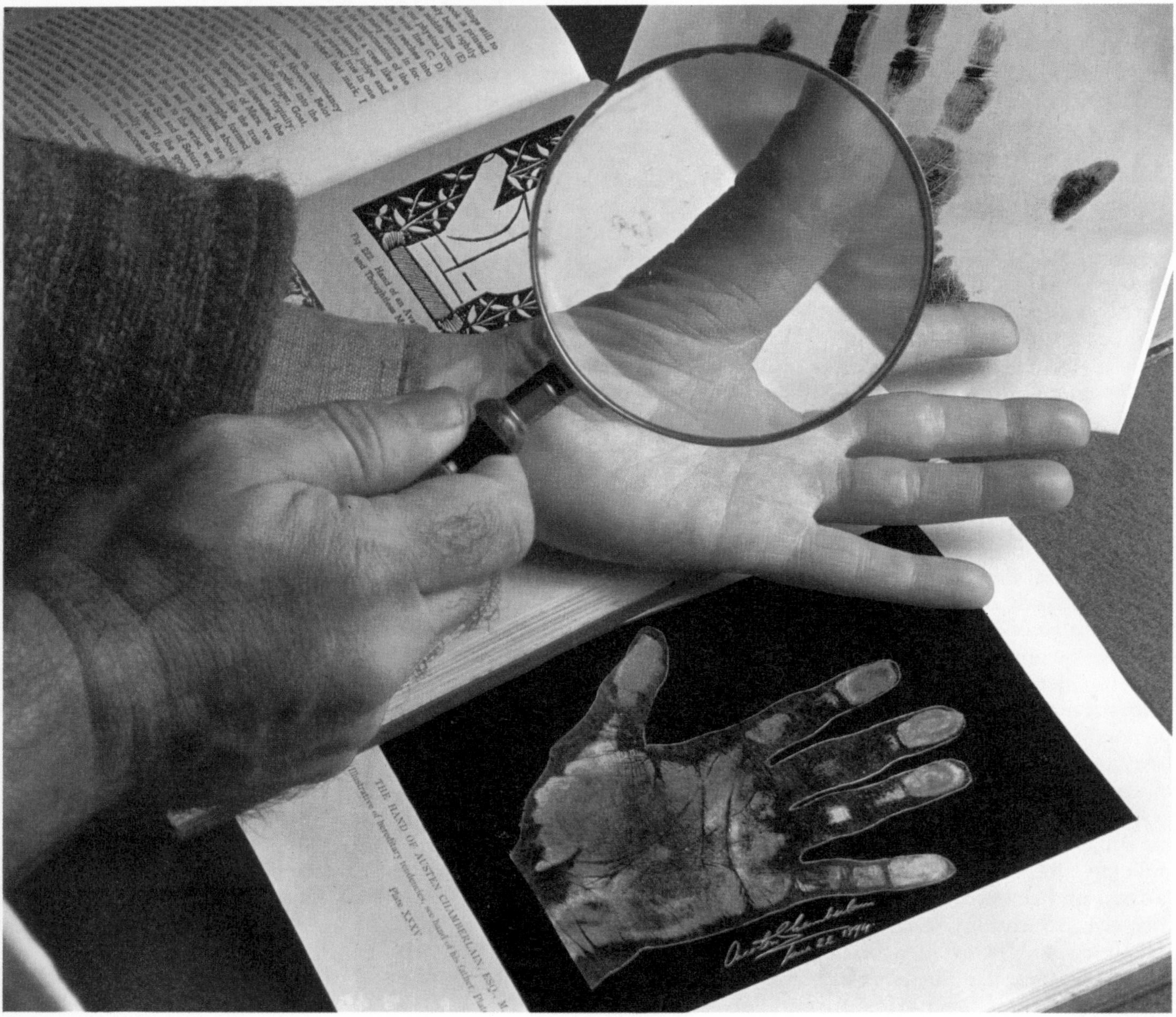

123

124. A schema showing the traditional relationship of planets with the more modern localization of the four elements with the hand. Jupiter and Mars are 'warm' planets, localized in the Fire area of the fingers. Sun and Mercury are 'active' planets, localized in the Air area of the fingers. Venus is a 'material and physical' planet, localized in the Earth part of the palm, whilst the Moon is a 'sensitive' planet, localized in that part of the hand associated with the waters of the subconscious.

124

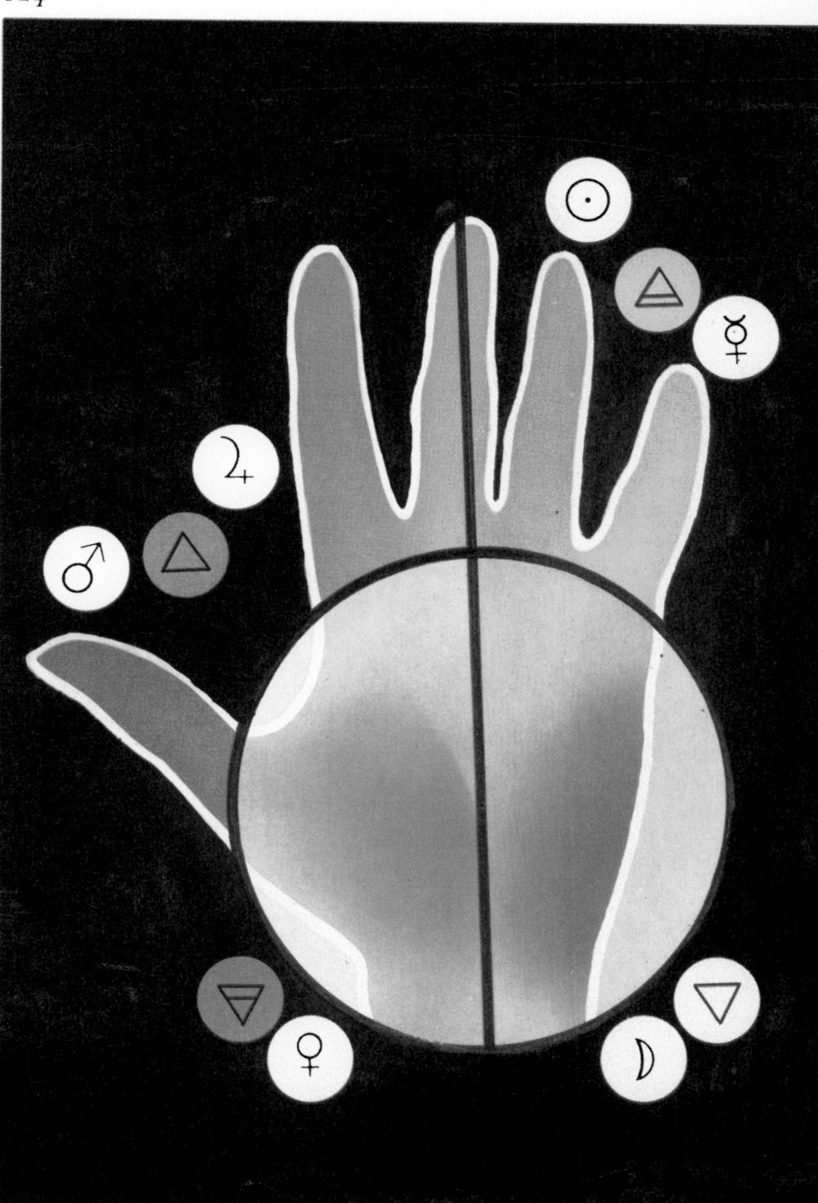

Ken also means 'keeping still' and is therefore associated with meditation as well as with the idea of deliberation. Taken in isolation, therefore, it is difficult to see the connexion between this and the European mount of Venus, though when one sees that above it is the Palace of *Chen* of the 'Lightning flash', then we may see a connexion in the idea of static earth being stimulated into action through the disturbance of the spirit. Venus is associated with Earth, and is at the same time a vibrant force, linked with arts, music and beauty.

CHEN occupies the upper part of the Mount of Venus, and may find its real significance in its relationship with *Ken*. The Chinese character is usually translated as meaning 'lightning', though it does connote more the idea of 'a quickening force' or an 'exciting force'. As a vivifying element, therefore, we do see some connexion with the Mount of Venus, and even more so when we note that the Chinese palmists read into the height of this mount the measure and quality of the energy of the subject as it is expressed through work or love.

Just as we have seen something of the relationship of these last two Palaces to Venus through considering their interaction, so may we grasp the more complex relationship which *Tui*, *Chein* and *K'an* hold to the mount of Moon by studying their interaction, for here we see creative potential hemmed in by danger and joyful expression–in strict Chinese imagery, we see the heavenly force hemmed between the stagnant waters of *K'an* and the joyful waters of *Tui*.

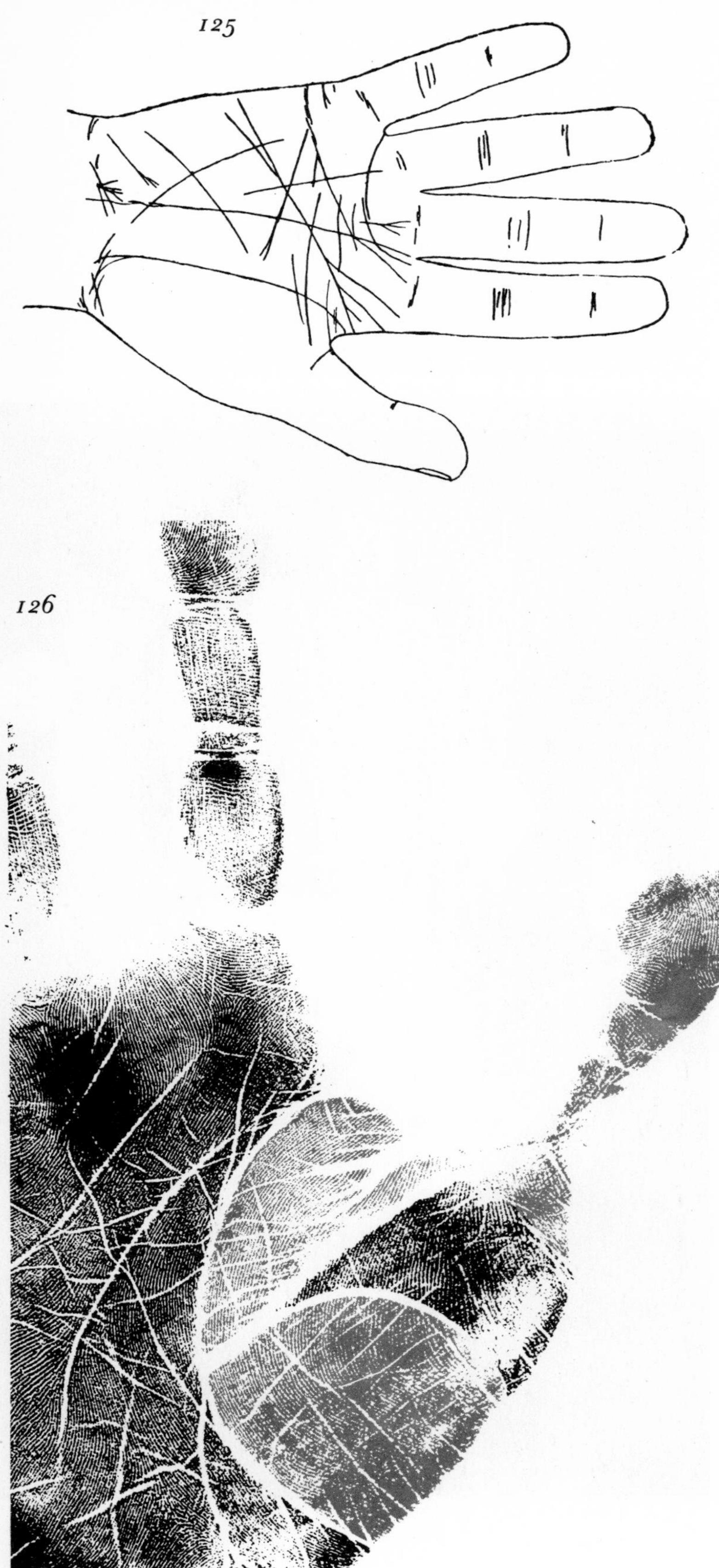

125. A chirological reconstruction of the hand of Queen Elizabeth I, made from 'The Palmist' of 1894. The Chirmomancer admits that the lines are 'entirely imaginary'—this superficial approach to palmistry is unfortunately typical of the time.

126. The area of T'ien, *below the thumb. See text below.*

127. The relationship between the Plaine of Mars and the Chinese Ming T'ang *is remarkable. The glyph for Mars is essentially a drawing of the conflict between Earth and Sun (cross and circle), whilst the character for* Ming *is a drawing of the meeting of the lunar and solar forces.*

128. The Ming T'ang *in the centre of the hand. See text below.*

The Chinese in any case do not think of the trigrammatic forces as static elements, but as forces in continual movement and interchange, so that it may be as well for us to think of the basic palmistic diagram as running in circular motion. A commentary from the *I Ching* serves to capture something of the vitality underlying this diagram:

> Thunder (*Chen*) gives motion to things. Wind (*Sun*) scatters things for a while. Rain (*K'an*) enriches things through moisture, whilst the sun (Li) makes things brilliant. *Ken* keeps things steady, whilst *Tui* enables them to take pleasure. *Chien* makes them superior, whilst *K'un* conceals them . . . (50)

There are two other palmar areas in the Chinese tradition, one of which fails to find much correspondence with the modern European tradition. Between the palaces of *Chen* and *Ken* (figure 126) we find the small *T'ien*, an area which is supposed to indicate the subject's acquisitive urges and abilities on the material plane—which is presumably why it is named after the two fundamentals of materiality, land and property, or literally 'fields and houses'.

In the centre of the palm, roughly corresponding to the traditional plain of Mars, we find the *Ming T'ang*, which has been translated as 'audience room', but which has a much more complex meaning than any single phrase may convey. The term was used during the *Chou* dynasty in connexion with sacrifice, and in this respect it was meant to apply to a room in which only high dignitaries met. The term also has a special connotation in acupuncture and in *feng shui*, the Chinese system of using lay lines and telluric forces.* In addition to

* The usual translation for *Feng shui* is 'geomancy', but geomancy, a European and Arabic system of divination, bears no relationship whatsoever to *feng shui*.

127

♂ = ♁ = + ☉ = ⊕ ☉

明 日 ☉ 月 ☽ = ☉☽ = ◐ ☉

128

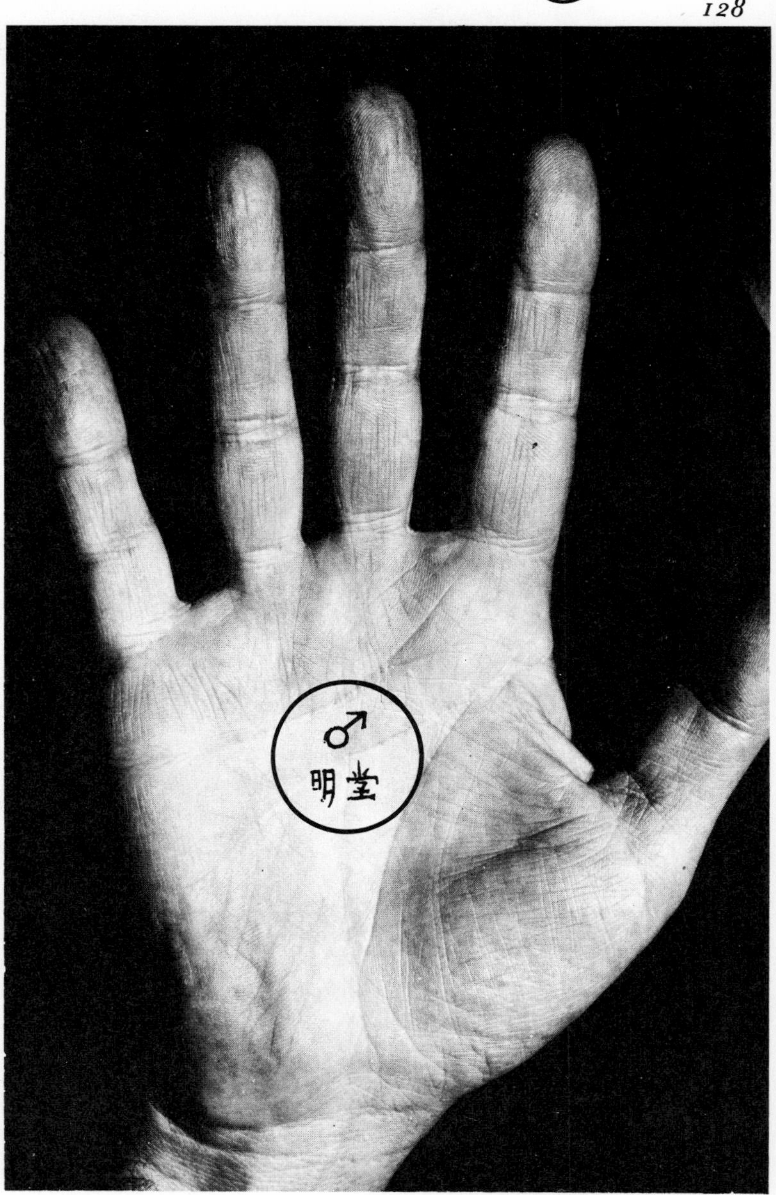

these meanings, we may also interpret it as 'the central courtyard of a dwelling', as well as 'an open level space of great brilliance'. In the Chinese palmistic system this is the area from which the subject surveys and directs his life: the palmist estimates from it the good fortune and respectability of the subject, as well as the strength of his judgement and self discipline. Clearly there is a strong link here with the Mars of our European tradition.

Within the European tradition Mars is a centripetal force: it is the force within human beings which seeks to pull the outer world into the inner world of self. Mars literally seeks to 'devour' the world. It is for this reason that a strong Mars is a sign of aggression, especially when it is under pressure, and it is for this reason that a strong Mars, either in the horoscope or in the hand, is the most obvious index of the degree of power which a subject may exert within his environment. The rule of Mars over the thumb reminds us more of the Chinese *Chen,* which 'gives motion to things', but in its more obvious centripetal effect we cannot help observing that the European Mars is certainly the measure of the relationship between the outer and the inner world of man, and may therefore usefully be associated with *Ming T'ang*.

The difference between this ancient oriental system and the Western systems is sufficient to demonstrate that quite separate traditions are involved–yet, at the same time, the similarities are such as to convince any thoughtful mind that the theories of palmistry must be based on something more than mere imagination.

129

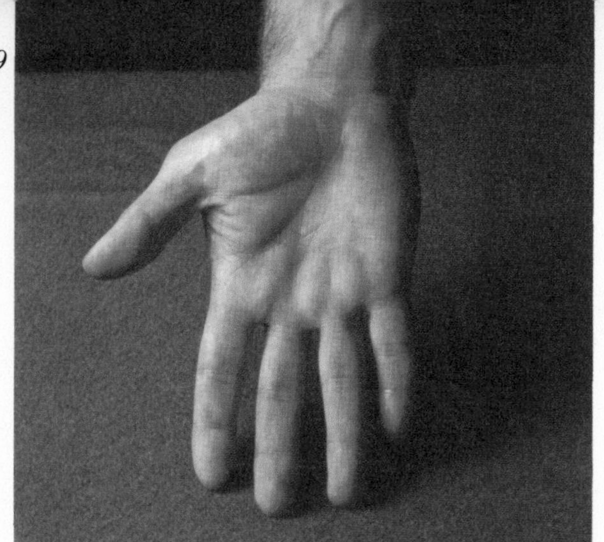

130

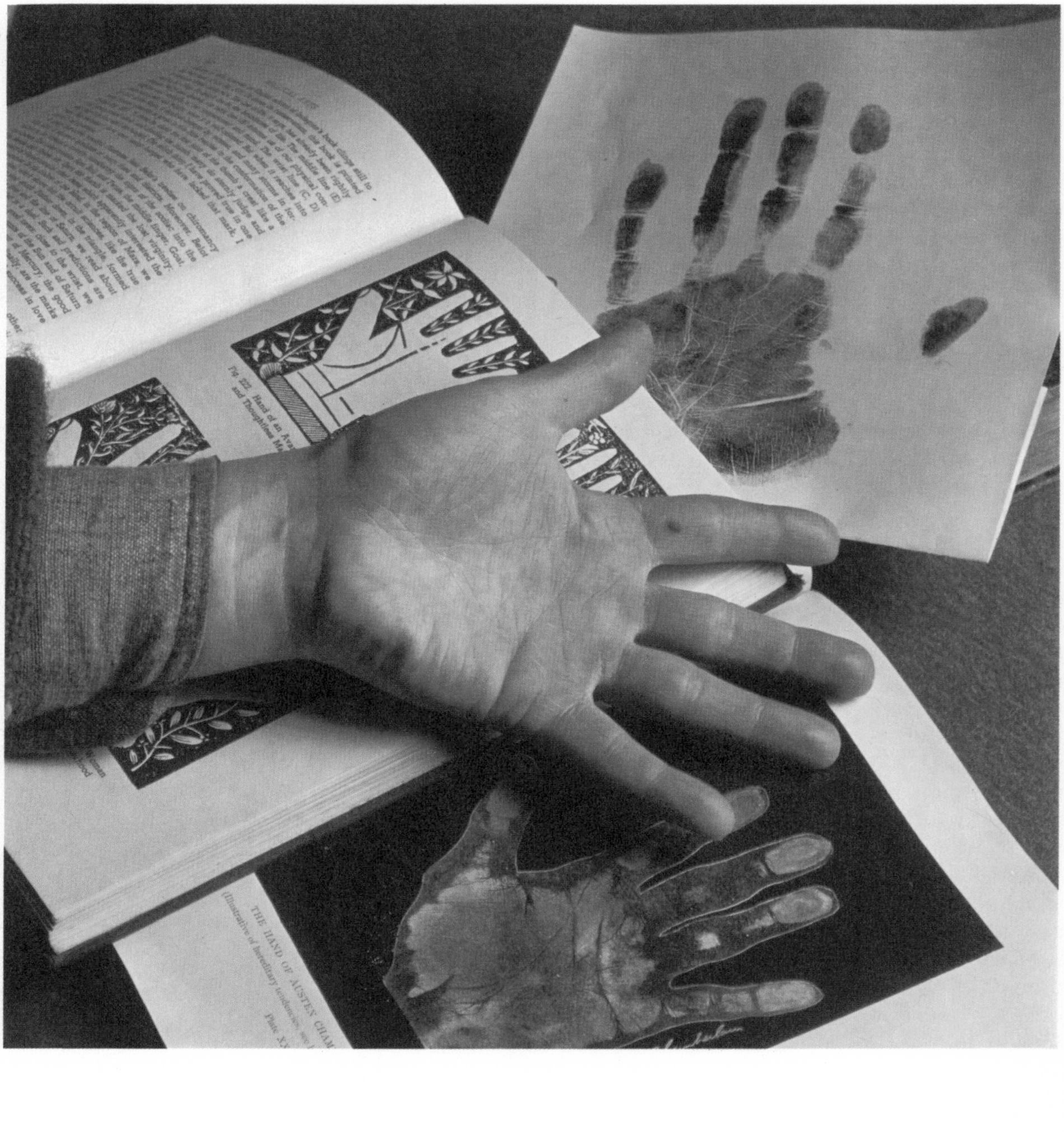

129. The tradition of mount interpretation was in its most advanced stage highly complex, involved with localizing the centre of a mount (three being clearly visible in this photograph), and then determining how far the centres deviated from the central axis of the relevant finger. The method has been largely rejected by modern palmists.

130. The problem of 'left hand, right hand' is widely discussed among amateur palmists, but professionals examine the hand used by the subject when they wish to establish a basic reading for him.

131. The thick basal phalange on the finger of Jupiter is traditionally supposed to indicate great materiality, for it brings to Earth the force of Jupiter. The ring on Mercury has the opposite effect, for it restricts materiality in the field of relationships with others—for this reason it is often a sign of difficulties in relationships, especially sexual ones.

131

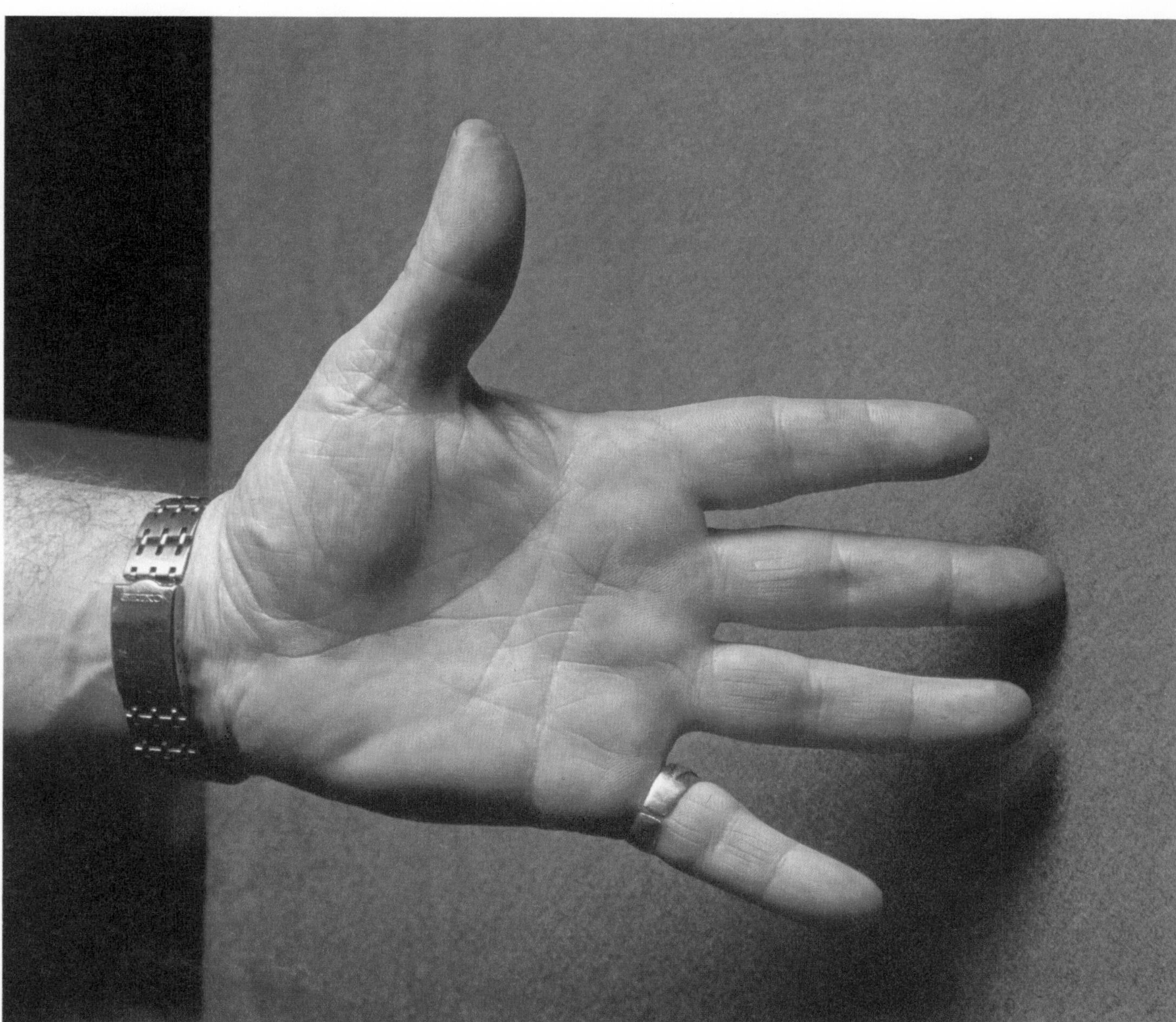

132. *An example of a triple-rayed Girdle of Venus, sweeping over the termination of the line of Head, itself turns down towards the line of Head.*

133. *In this hand the broken rays of the Girdle mingle freely with the line of Head.*

134. *A sixteenth century hand schema, which serves to simplify the hand structure to such an extent that a student of palmistry may well be confused when turning to a living hand in order to identify the lines.*

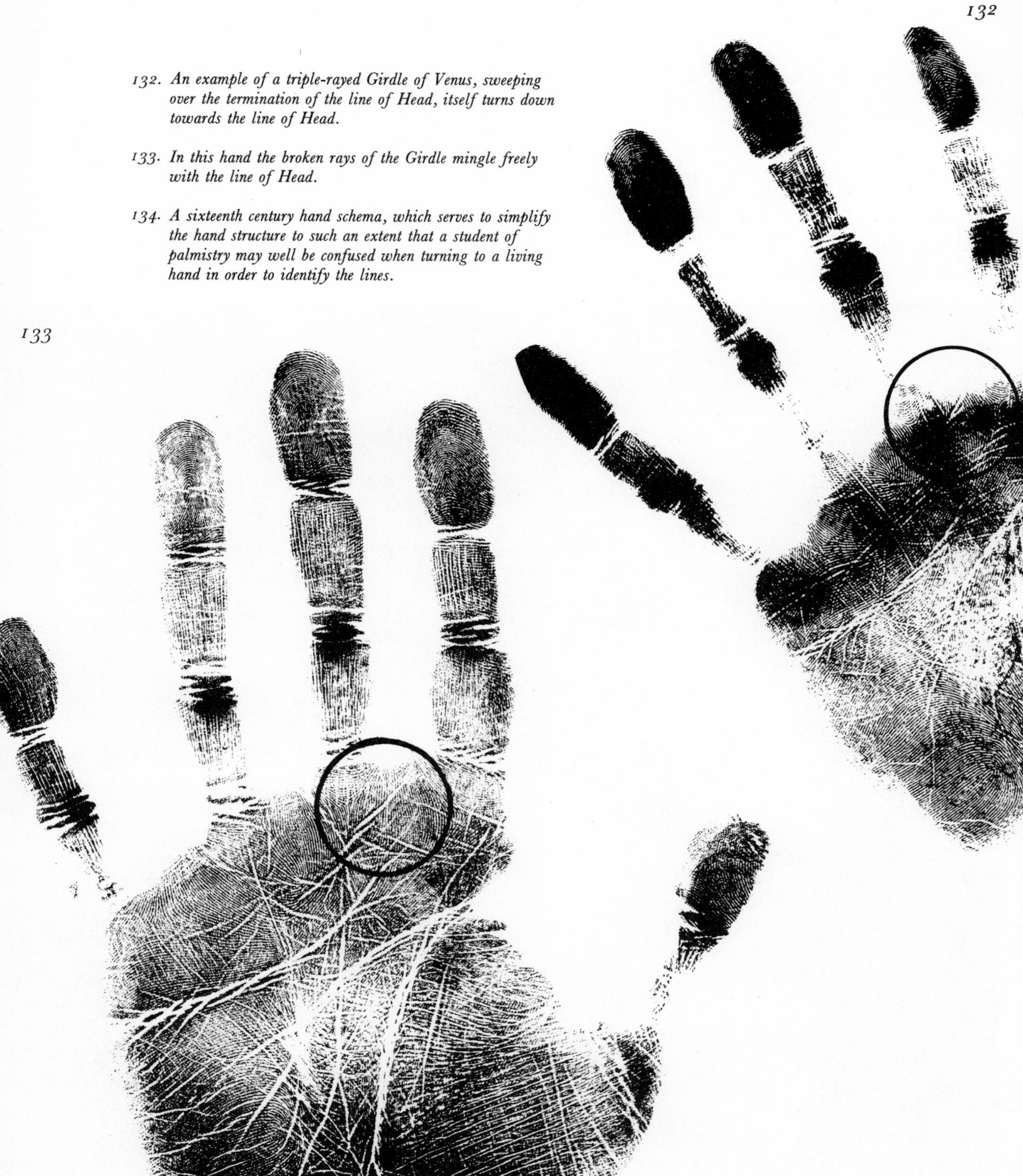

The lines of the hand

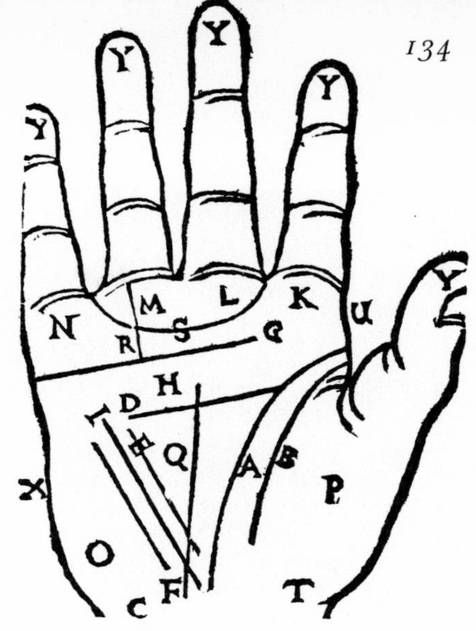

134

The study of the lines of the hand, has, until comparatively recent times, been regarded as quite a separate activity from the study of the form of the hand. Very few serious attempts have been made to codify the lines, and to set out in a systematic manner how the different line formations, qualities, and courses are related to the human temperament. The result is that the main body of palmistic tradition consists of a series of personal, and often unrelated teachings concerning how individual symbols within the hand may be interpreted. This is in curious contrast with the traditional teachings concerning the importance which the structure of the hand bears to the interpretation of character, teachings which, although usually very simple, were on the whole reasonably accurate. The very earliest palmistic documents tend to agree about the form of the hand, but disagree violently about how the lines and symbols should be interpreted. There are many sources from which we may give examples of the difference between what we call now *chirognomy* and *chiromancy*, and it is mainly out of an antiquarian interest that we choose the teaching ineptly attributed to Aristotle, which is merely on a par with the earliest palmistic systems found in Europe in the fourteenth and fifteenth centuries:

> . . . if the Hand be soft and long, and lean withal, it denotes the Person of a good Understanding, a Lover of Peace and Honesty, discreet, serviceable, and good Neighbour, a Lover of Learning. He whose Hands are very thick, and very short, is thereby signified to be faithful, strong and labourious, and one that cannot long retain his Anger. He whose Hands are full of Hairs, and those Hairs thick, and great ones, if his Fingers withal be crooked, is thereby denoted to be luxurious, vain, false, of a dull Understanding and Disposition, and more foolish than wise. He whose Hands and Fingers do bend upwards, is commonly a Man liberal, serviceable, a Keeper of Secrets, and apt to his Power (for he is seldom fortunate) to do any Man a Courtesie. He whose Hands are stiff, and will not bend at the upper Joynts near to his Finger is always a wretched, miserable Person, covetous, obstinate, incredulous, and one that will believe nothing that contradicts his own private Interest. (51)

Everything is black and white in this not too generous world, and yet we do at least find a certain accuracy of observation which disappears entirely when we turn to the study of the lines. It is one of the mysteries attached to the history of palmistry that the pragmatic side of chrognomy, which so clearly has always depended upon a simple examination of the hand, should have been swamped by the more dubious business of interpretation of the lines, and this strictly in terms of fixed symbols. Thus, we see in this same text the darker side of the Girdle of Venus developed:

> The *Line* of *Venus,* if it happens to be cut or divided near the Fore-finger, threatens Ruin to the party, and that it shall befall him by means of lacivious Women, and bad Company: Two crosses upon this Line, one being on the Fore-finger, and the other bending towards the little Finger,

135

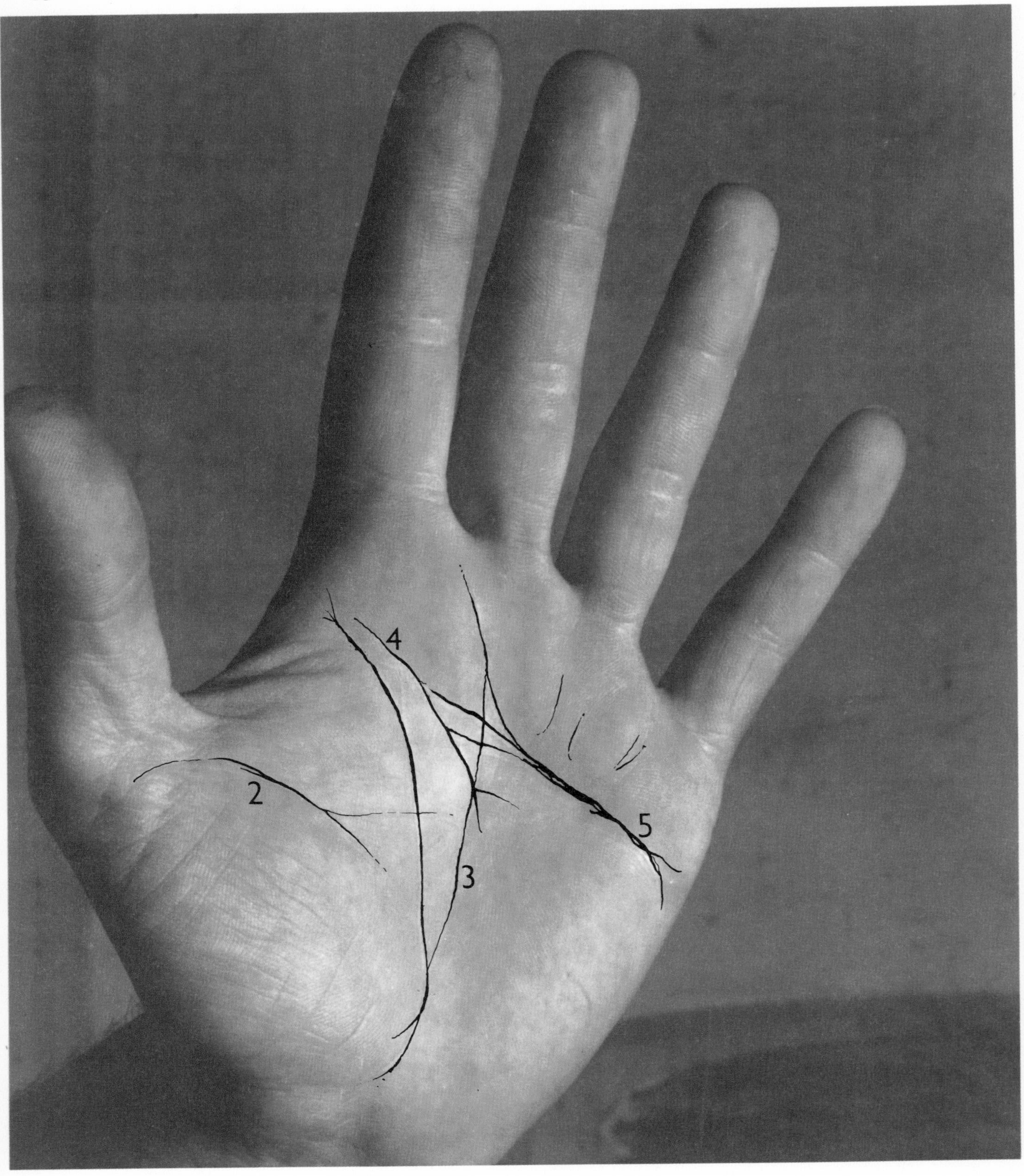

135. *The photograph opposite, and the schema below indicate*
136. *how the lines may be conceived as being the conductors of energies from one area of the hand to another. For example, the line marked 2 brings energies of a Martian nature, through the material zone of Venus into the sensitive area of the imaginative Moon—this is equivalent of pouring Fire onto water, and an explosive situation must be expected from such a line. Traditionally it is called an 'Influence' line, and is interpreted as some unexpected outer event, or meeting, which influences the subject's life at the time when it crosses the Life line. The other lines may be read in like manner.*

136

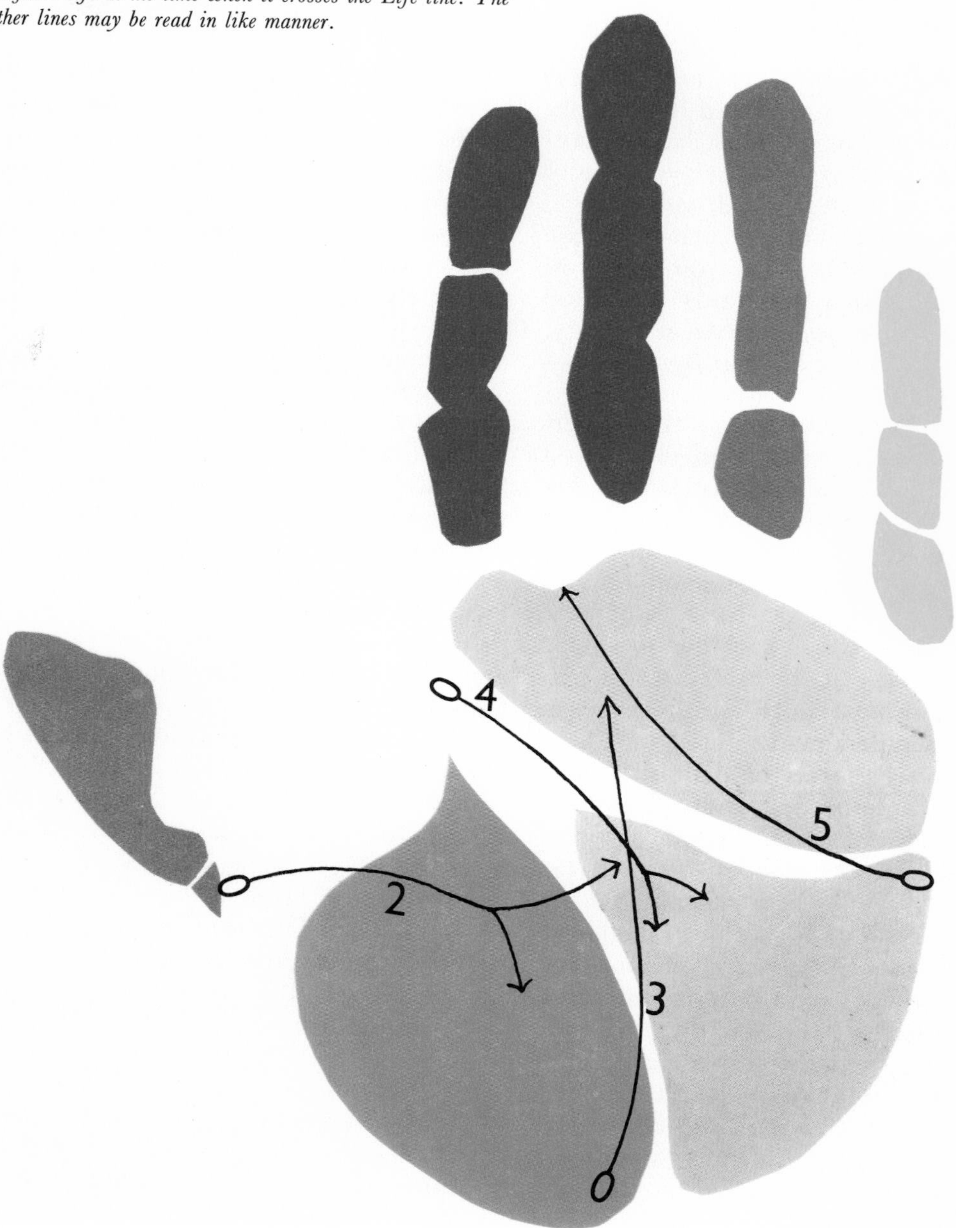

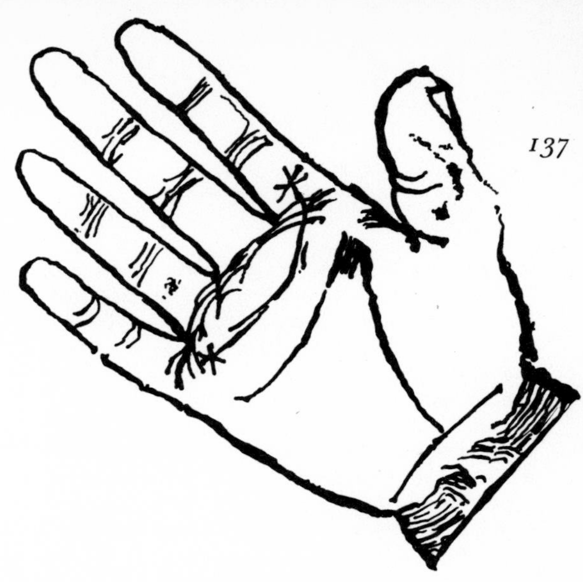

137

137. The Line of Venus with two crosses, which is supposed by the palmist Saunders to indicate 'Modesty'. See below.

shews the Party to be weak, and inclin'd to Modesty and Virtue; indeed it generally denotes Modesty in Women, and therefore those who desire such Wives, usually choose them by this Standard. (52)

Perhaps a misogynist will agree that if you are going to choose a wife, then you might as well not go by such standards as moral goodness, purity of soul, physical beauty, intellect or quality of being–but by two small crosses on the Girdle of Venus . . . And yet it is in such a tangled hedgerow that superstitions thrived, and the relatively honest observations concerning the relationships between hand forms and the temperament were completely covered and choked by lines run riot. It was not until the nineteenth century that theories relating to the hand form were to take precedence again, and thus to enable people to look once more at the quite perceptible relationships which the lines might hold with the temperament.

Almost all early forms of palmistry were involved with interpreting individual lines and symbols on the hand, though Richard Saunders, drawing an analogy between the lines and vegetative life, did suggest that the basic temperament of the subject might be expressed in terms of the quality of the hand:

. . . lines long and broad, shew a callid and hot complexion, lines long and small, intimate a hot and dry complexion, lines gross and short, intimate a super-abounding of evil, noxious humours in the Body, and cold constitution; Lines slender, small and disjoyned, plainly demonstrate a cold and dry temperament. (53)

In fact the modern classification, which relates the basic quality of line formation to the four elements of Earth, Air, Fire and Water, puts a quite different slant on the matter, and we may take the examples given in figures 56, 59 and 62 as definitive and accurate. What should interest us in the seventeenth century example, however, is the fact that the general quality of line is considered at all, for those words were penned at a time when few palmists appear to have considered the hand as a whole, but depended exclusively on the nature of individual signs and symbols in the hand. It was not the *quality* of the line which interested palmists at that time, so much as the graphic symbol which the line traced on the hand. In its worst phase such a level of interpretation was a travesty of palmistry, as the four samples at 140 indicate, and the following quotations, culled from Saunders, confirm this:

The Letter E in the Triangle of the Hand, Denotes a man contentious, of sordid qualities, Living Laciviously, with Women of vild (sic) condition, not regarding marriage, yet being married, becomes the murtherer of his own Wife. (54)

Fortunately an E in the Triangle of the hand (figure 140) is rare–indeed, so rare that I have never seen one. Wife murder must have been more common in the seventeenth century, if such palmistry is to be taken seriously:

The Character of (Venus) on the mount of the thumb, signifies such a person to murther his own wife, or other Women . . . (55)

138

138. Signs and marks that signify violent death, according to the English palmist Saunders.

139. Portrait of Richard Saunders the seventeenth century English palmist

139

And so on, and so forth, to the point of tedium, until one begins to ask what the *bad* palmists must have been like, for Richard Saunders was highly regarded both as a palmist and astrologer in those days, and himself warned the readers of his book about the quality of certain palmists who abounded at that time.

> . . . let me warn my *Readers* of those *Syncophats* and desulive *Ignorants* through whose *fides* the *Pretious Science* is dayly Wounded, such Spawn of Shame, that impudently make Profession of Art, not only in Several Countryes, but lurk in Obscure corners, in and about the Famous City, many *Illiterate* pieces of Non-sense and Impudence, of the *Female* kind, whose Ignorance transcends the Vulgar *Gypsies,* and Impudence sufficient to out face a *Whipping* Post. (56)

Our phrases may not be quite so forth-right today, but we must admit that much nonsense still abounds, simply because *real* palmistry is not easy to practise. Yet certain things have changed for the better. Although the interpreting of personality and destiny from isolated symbols in the hand has not entirely disappeared, even in modern times, the general agreement among palmists is that the hand form as a whole must be related to the overall structure of lines before any pronouncement may be made concerning the personality of the subject. It is indeed this willingness to regard the hand as a whole which separates modern palmistry from the traditional forms. However, it is evident that certain important lines do relate to specific functions within the human

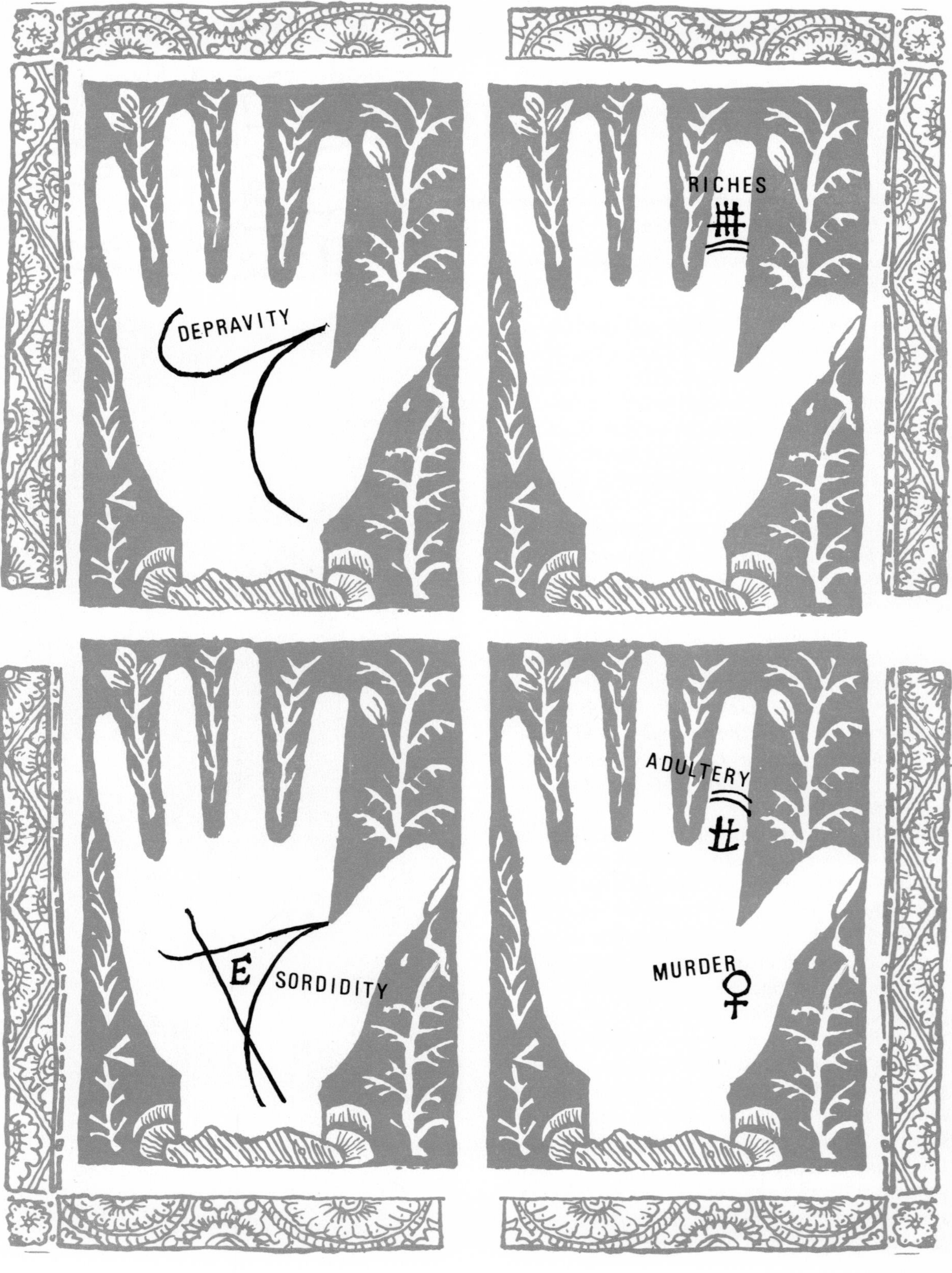
DEPRAVITY
RICHES
E
SORDIDITY
ADULTERY
MURDER

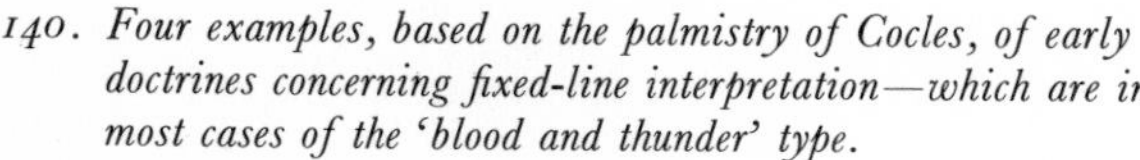

140. Four examples, based on the palmistry of Cocles, of early doctrines concerning fixed-line interpretation—which are in most cases of the 'blood and thunder' type.

141. Adda Nari *and the system of hand nomenclature put*
142. forward by Desbarrolles, who linked the hand with Kabbalistic systems. It is curious that Desbarrolles, for all his understanding of the occult, did not propound a useful chirognomical system.

141

temperament and psyche. Whilst one no longer looks for the likes of a letter E in the middle of the hand as denoting a wife murderer, one might examine the relationship between the thumb, which indicates energy, the line of Heart, which denotes the emotions, and a Simian line, and come to the conclusion that the type is rather hot-tempered, if not exactly violent. Modern palmistry will see tendencies in the hand, rather than events.

The palmist Desbarrolles belonged more to the cheiromantic tradition of palmistry than to the chirognomical, for his system is more involved with the study of lines and symbols, and in those cases where he does describe hand forms and finger forms, he still considers lines separately from the chirognomical forms enclosing them. This is a danger which is by no means entirely obviated today. One cannot help seeing such a subconscious feeling manifest in Desbarrolles when he reproduces in his classic work, the picture of *Adda Nari* (figure 141), which in spite of his following analysis of the symbolism of the goddess, is virtually irrelevant to his following study. And yet, the fact that the figure contains within its symbols the four elements of Earth, Air, Fire and Water in itself points to the great lack in the ideas of Desbarrolles, for he fails to present a consistent and inclusive system by which the forms of the hand may be recognized, and by which the individual line markings on hands may take on a pertinent and significant meaning. The *Adda Nari* is almost minatory, for it calls for a system of presenting the various temperaments as they manifest in the human hand.

142

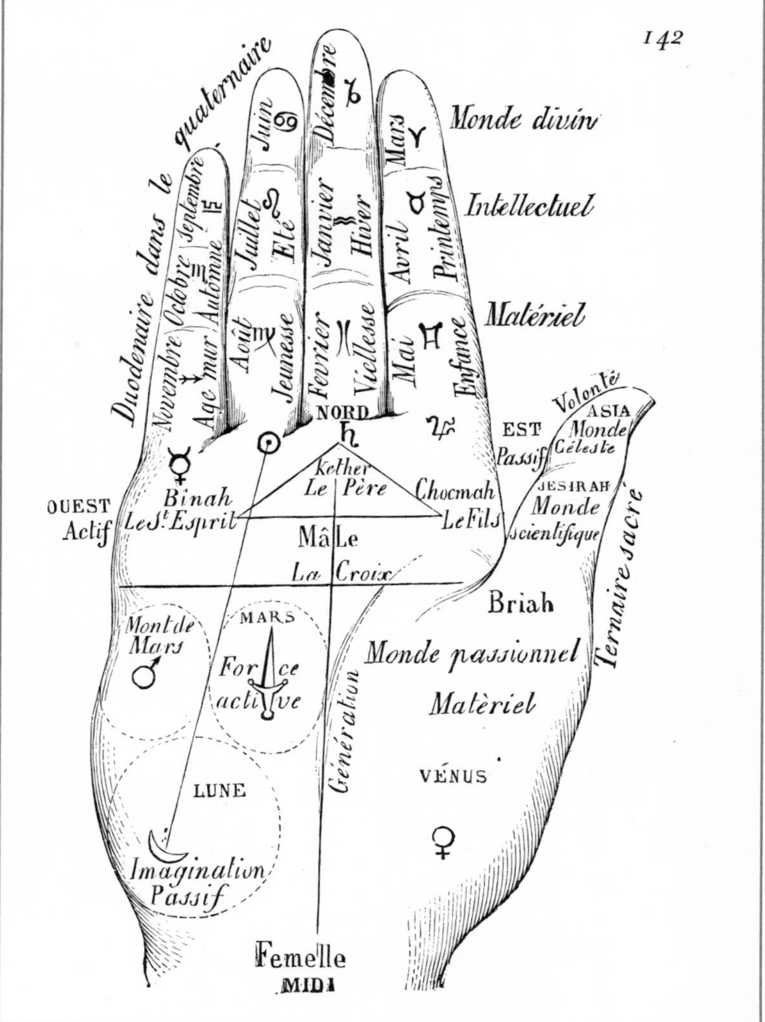

143. The normal sweep of a heart line.

144. A broken line, with an extensive Girdle above it.

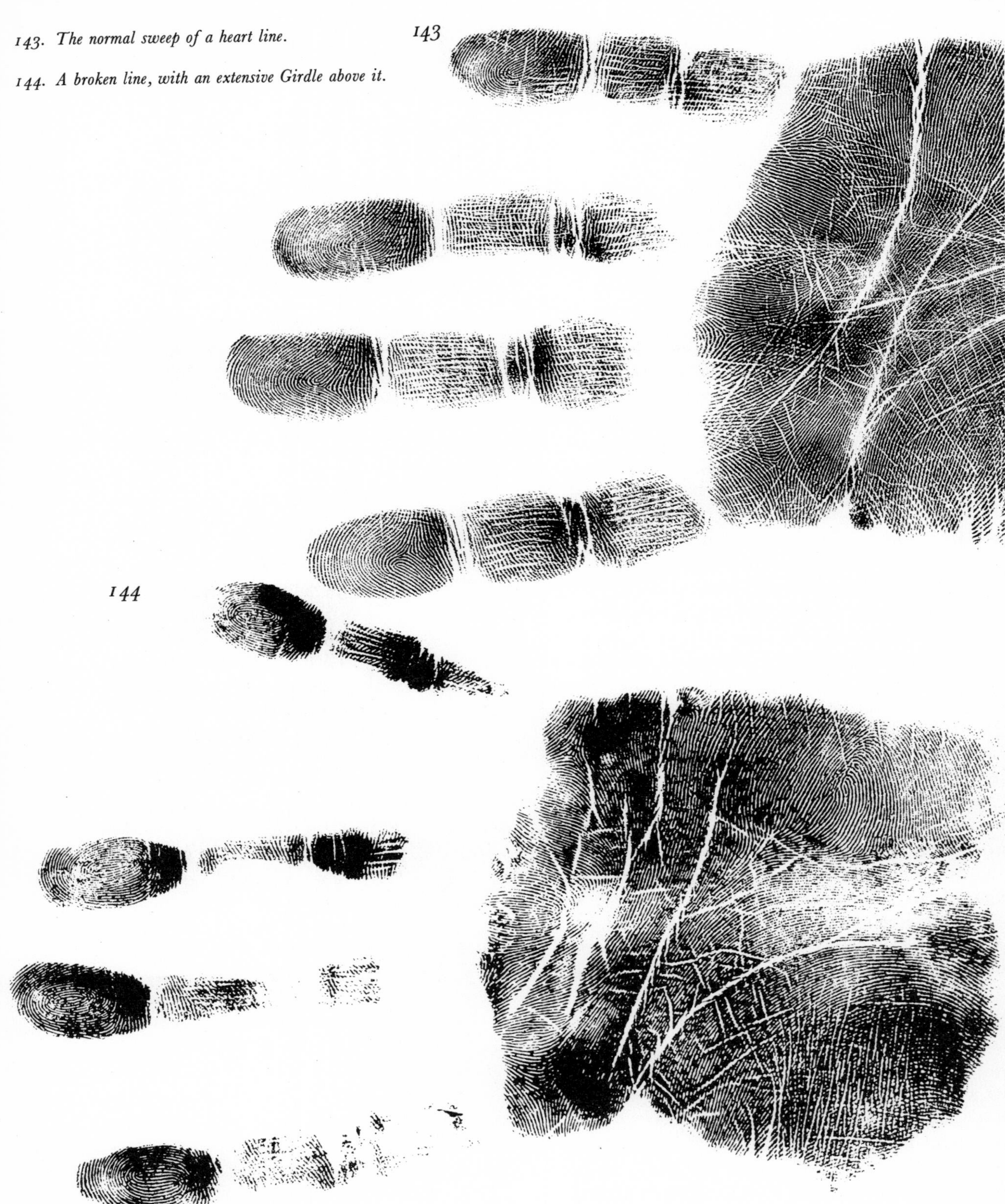

The Heart line

We have already noted the connexion which the tradition draws between this line and sexuality (page 7), but we must observe that it is more common to regard the line as an index of the emotions on the old chiromantical basis that 'strong lines indicate strong energies'. It is very common for a line of Heart to curve up strongly towards the root of the index finger (figure 143) and this is nowadays usually taken as a sign of a strong and healthy emotional life–indeed, even of a strong sexual life–in the subject, who will be open and constructive in emotional expression, and generally secure. This was not always held to be true, however, as the following observations of the seventeenth century palmist Richard Saunders make all too plain:

> The *Mensal* line *Naked*, without Branches, and touching the Root of the Index, Prognosticateth Poverty, Losses, Shipwrack of a Fortune and Calamaties. (57)

Perhaps this merely touches upon a puritanical streak in Saunders himself, expressing the idea that sexual and emotional enjoyment, covered by this line, should be cabined and confined, otherwise the rough justice of life would bring Shipwrack of Fortune. The fact remains that if we are to understand the natures of the individual lines as they may in reality be applied to the unriddling of the human temperament, we must turn to relatively modern literature, for the ancient system of fixed symbol interpretation appears to have prevented any growth towards a theory rulerships of lines over specific human qualities. The prevalent idea which emerged during the nineteenth century was that of the lines as conductors of energies, from one part of the hand to another, from one area to another. For Desbarrolles, the importance of the line of Heart lay in the fact that it ran from the area of Jupiter or Saturn, over to the mount of Mercury:

> The line runs towards the domain of Mercury, and Mercury is the messenger of the gods, the one who carries the astral line which communicates with materiality, whilst Jupiter represents the supreme ideal of spirit. Thus we see that the more this line reaches up into Jupiter the more you will love with the heart, the more your feelings will be noble and pure, though less material. The higher the line, the more idealistic the love; the lower it is, the more sensual is the love.

If one strips out the nineteenth century concepts, then one is near to reaching into the truth concerning this line. In astropalmistry the line conducts energies from the Piscean domain of Jupiter, right through the areas which are connected with emotionality, finally to separate the sensitive lunar influences of the Mount of Moon from the Mercury of Virgo (figure 74). The line runs thus the gamut of emotionality, and it is not surprising that one should read into its structure the inner nature of the 'emotional life' of the subject.

> Thus the Heart line is, in truth, a revealer not only of the muscular, vital strength, and action of the heart itself, but, as a result of these conditions, also of the strength and character of the affections . . .
>
> There are three well-verified readings attached to three starting points, and these

145

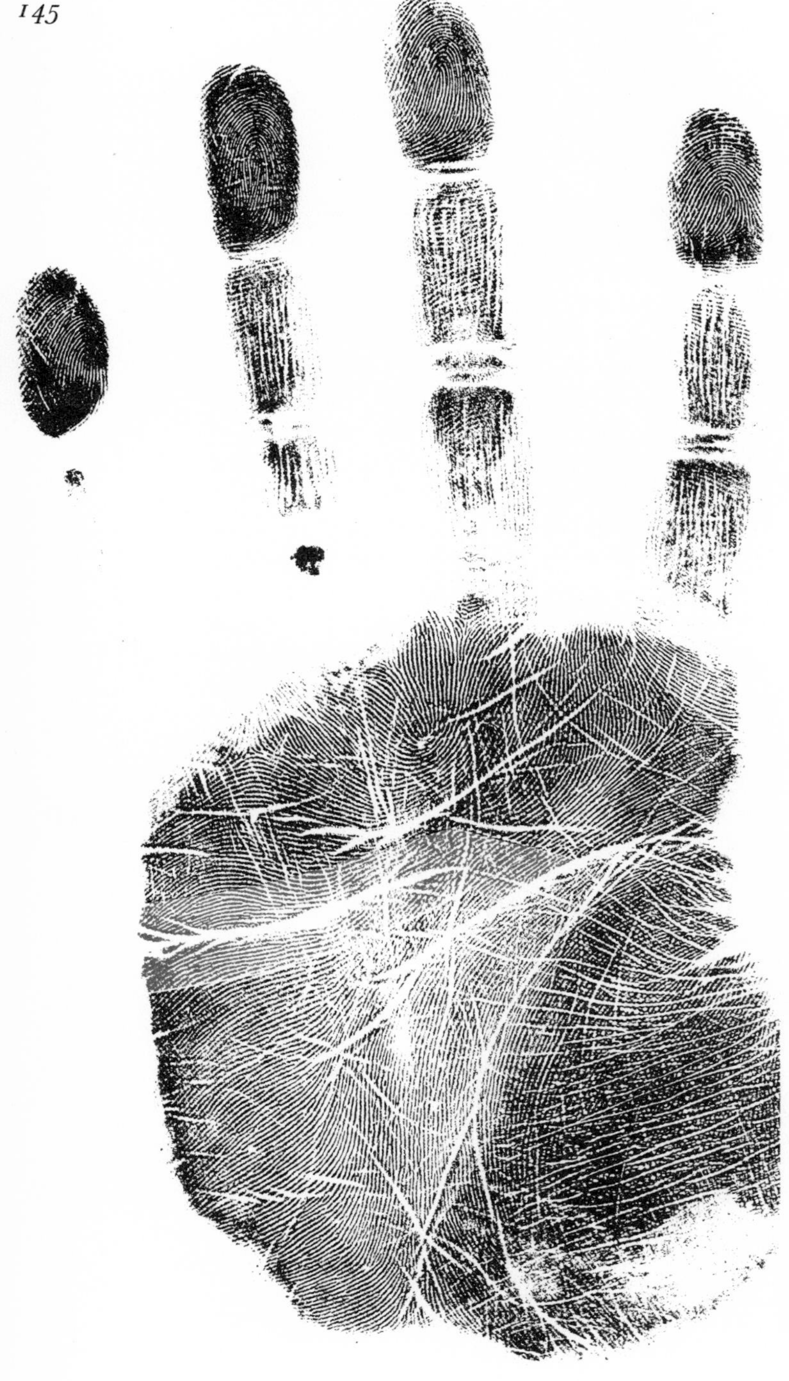

145. The Heart line sweeping towards the Head line. See text.

146. The Heart line sweeping up to Jupiter. See text.

147. A straight Heart line. See text.

should be used as a basis for your work, modifying and changing them in accordance as you see the starting points vary. 1. Rising from the Mount of Jupiter (figure 143), we read the development of the sentimental side to the affections. The subject is one whose love is ideal, to whom love is an adoration, and to whom love, even with poverty attached, is attractive. 2. Rising between Jupiter and Saturn (figure 144) the line shows the common-sense, practical, 'middle ground' with the affections, indicating one who is not carried away with sentiment, but who views love from a practical standpoint; is not 'soft' or 'spoony', but who is inclined to think that love in a cottage without plenty of bread and butter is a myth. This person is never carried away by sentiment, and whilst strong in affection is sensible and not foolish. 3. Rising From the Mount of Saturn (figure 169) the marking shows the sensualism in the affections of one whose love is tinged with the idea of pleasure from sexual relations. This is infallible if with it is seen a large Mount of Venus of pink or red color, and with strong Life and Mercury lines. (59)

There are two reasons why Benham insists on the 'sexuality' of a Heart line which terminates on Saturn: first, the line is a short one, and therefore unhealthy–which by nineteenth century standards could well have meant 'over-sexed'–but more important is the association with the planet Saturn, into which the line is seen as discharging its energies. This is the Saturn of Capricorn, who was rightly or wrongly linked with the goat, and is

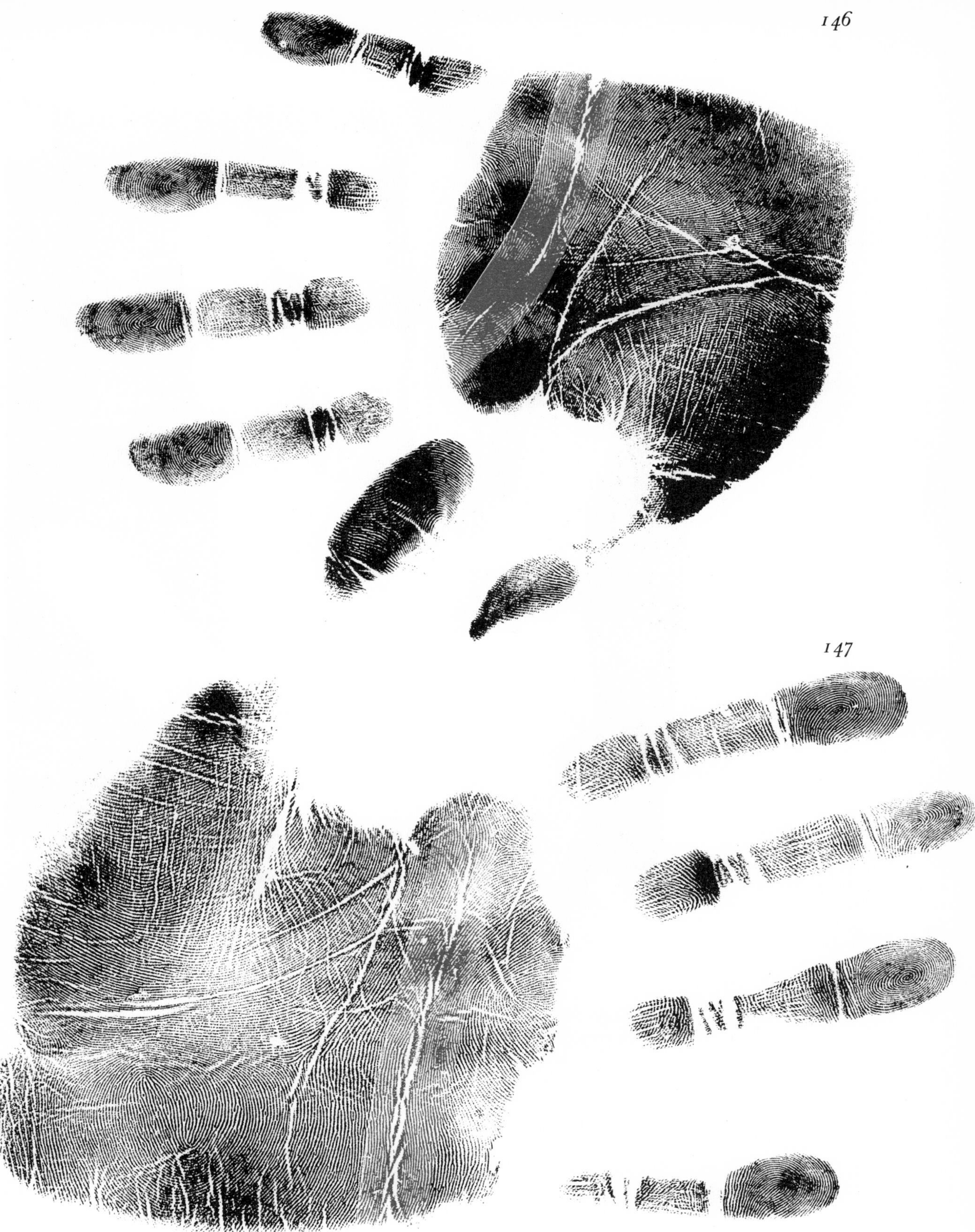
146

147

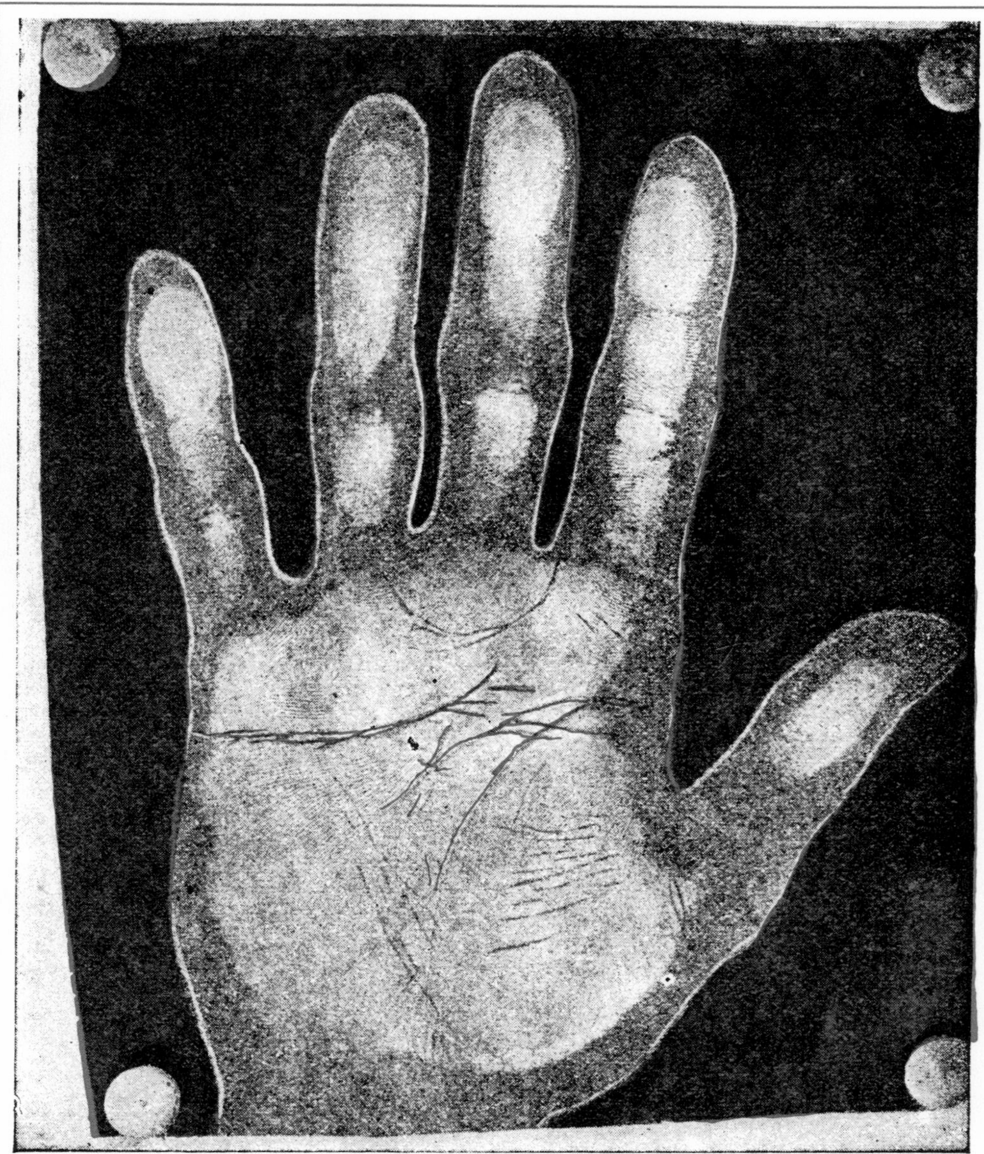

IRA MARLATT

The "Prison Demon," serving a life sentence for murder. He is very cunning, and, soon after his incarceration, procured weapons of various sorts with which he attacked and nearly succeeded in killing a number of guards. Nothing could be done to tame him, and finally a steel cage was built with no opening but a small door, in front of which a guard was constantly stationed. He seemed able in some mysterious way to procure wire, which he sharpened on the sides of his steel cell, with which terrible weapons he assaulted all who came near him. Kindness, and every conceivable means of punishment, has failed to subdue him. He has been fitly named the "Prison Demon." Marlatt has been the subject of great investigation by experts on insanity, who pronounce him sane. The day I secured this impression he came out of his cage, said he would do no violence, and kept his word. The guard with his gun stood near, however.

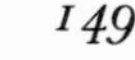

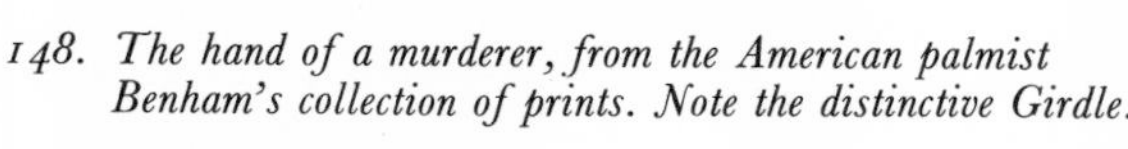

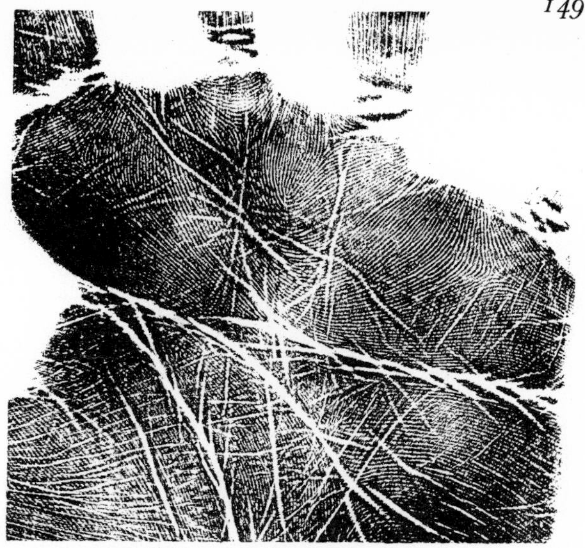

148. The hand of a murderer, from the American palmist Benham's collection of prints. Note the distinctive Girdle.

149. When the Heart line runs directly across the hand to touch the commencement of the Head line, it is called a 'simian' line, and represents a rather explosive meeting between Head and Heart.

150. The Head line commencing well inside the mount of Venus.

traditionally regarded as being over-sexed. However, the more common terminations for the line of Heart are found in three quite different positions: up towards the Mount of Jupiter, as Benham says, lower down towards the insertion of the line of Life (figure 147), and then even touching this insertion (figure 145).

> . . . should the line terminate in a swing downwards towards the commencement of the Life line or the Head line (figure 145) the resulting coldness of attitude will add a strong degree of idealism to the emotional considerations. In a male hand one can expect a strong female streak, not only in the attitude to sex, but in all emotional matters. Such a line on a male Fire hand, for example, will add a very strong feeling of insecurity, not at all proper to such a type . . . As a basic simplification we can say that the curve of the Heart line is the important characteristic – the curve will indicate human warmth, a wish to love, and a wish to be loved in return; whereas the straight path is significant of an independence and coldness which does not seek close relationships. (60)

The traditional explanation for this curious 'coldness' in a straight line of Heart is that the energies proper to the Heart are inclined towards the Head, to such an extent that sentiment is dominated by reason. Benham discusses the subject in such terms, but it is worth observing that among his interesting collection of prints is a superb example of such a 'straight' line of Heart – virtually a Simian line (see opposite) – in the hand of the 'prison Demon' Ira Marlatt (figure 148), who

150

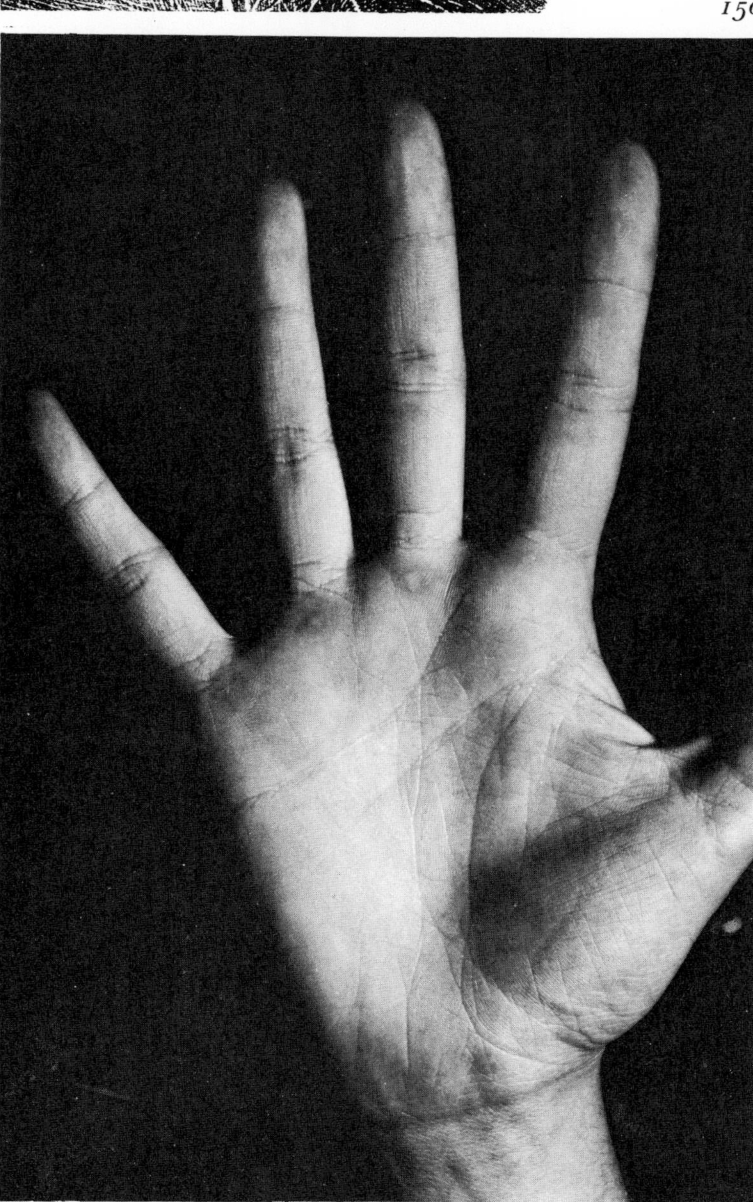

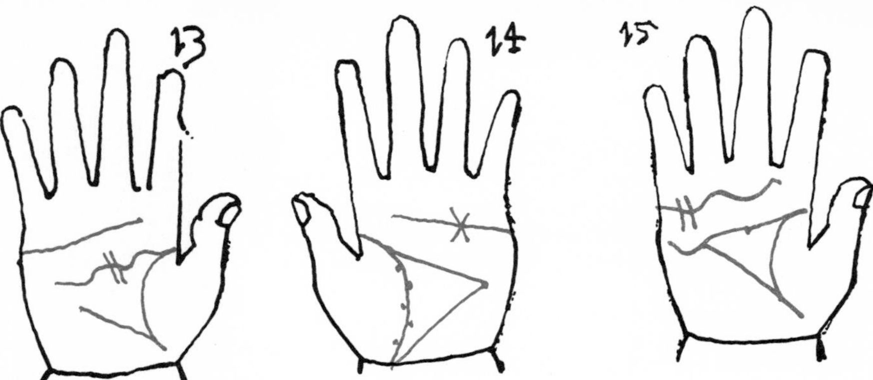

15 Menſalis à naturali, inæquali ſpatio diſtans, malam hominis complexionem oſtendit, & per conſequens infidelitatem notat.

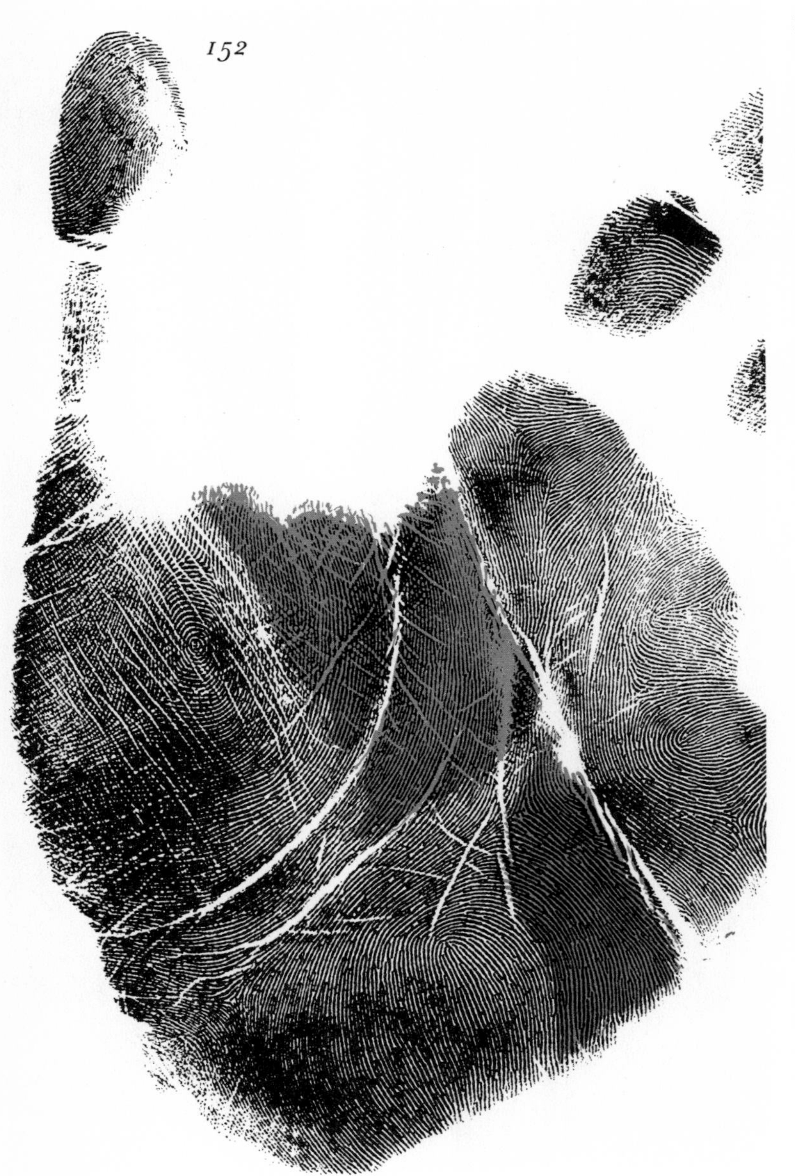
152

might in no way have been said to have 'sentiment dominated by reason'. The distinctive Girdle, the heavy chaining of the Heart line, and the strong simian nature of the line, would certainly be interpreted differently today. As we shall see, when we examine the Simian line, a straight line of Heart may often indicate 'excessive emotion' rather than 'sentiment dominated by reason'; however, there is always something unhealthy about the external expression of such excessive emotion. The modern polite term would be 'neurotic', one supposes, and whilst the Prison Demon may not have been pronounced insane, he might well have been pronounced *neurotic*, that marvellous cover-all label for emotional attitudes we do not understand.

The palmist Heron Allen had an entirely different interpretation for this straight line, though he does agree that a line which starts on the Mount of Saturn will render a subject 'more sensual than Platonic in his affections'. We may as well complete our survey of the traditions attached to this line by reference to this palmist's notes:

> Traced right across the hand, (from side to side) it indicates an excess of affection which produces jealousy and suffering in consequence thereof, especially if the Mount of Moon is high.
>
> If it is chained in its formation, the subject is an inveterate flirt, and, unless the rest of the hand be very strong, will be much subject to palpitations of the heart . . .
>
> The line should be close underneath, well up to the bases of the mounts; a line which lies close to that of the head throughout its

151. *This heart line, culled from Taisnier's collection, shows an evil disposition.*

152. *The Simian line which runs across the entire hand as in this example, has a reputation for violence. The reputation is in some ways theoretically justifiable in that it follows the course of the three areas of Mars—Upper and Lower Mars, and the Plain of Mars—across the hand. Mars in itself is the planet of violence.*

153. *A healthy line of Heart, according to Saunders.*

154. *A strong insertion of Heart into the gap between Jupiter and Saturn usually emphasises the mount of Jupiter, allowing the subject a more expansive approach to life.*

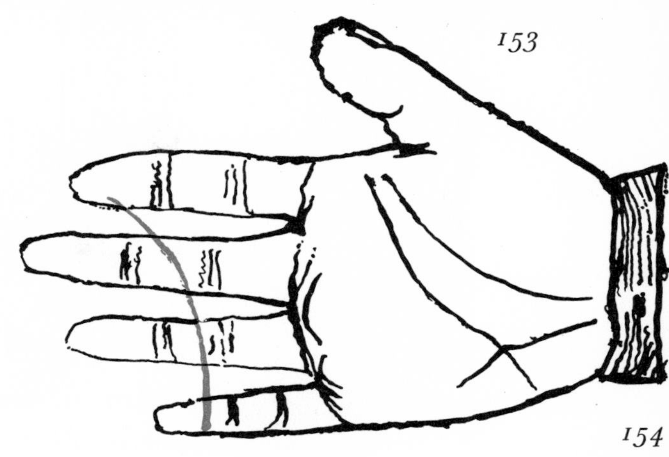

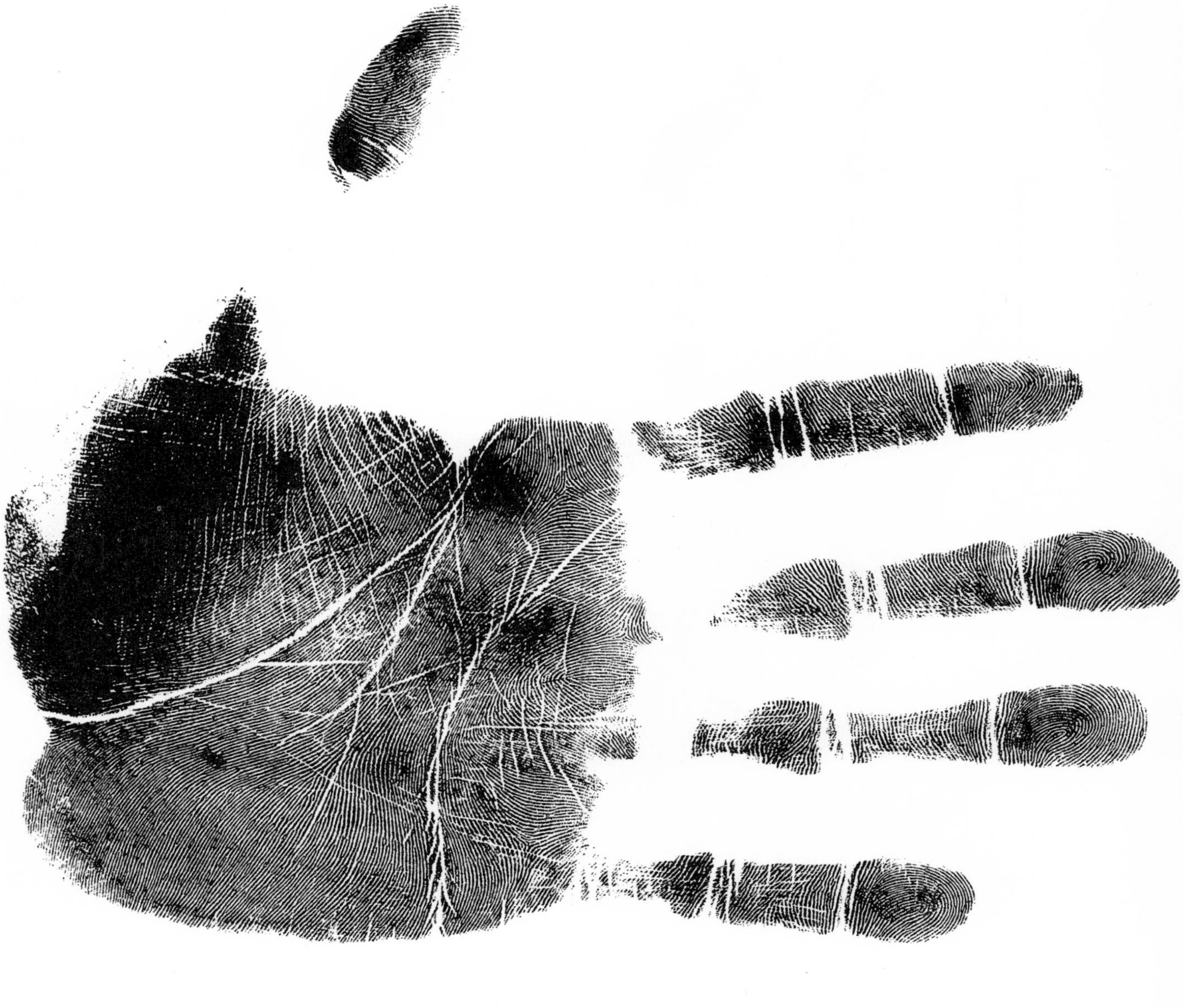

155

156

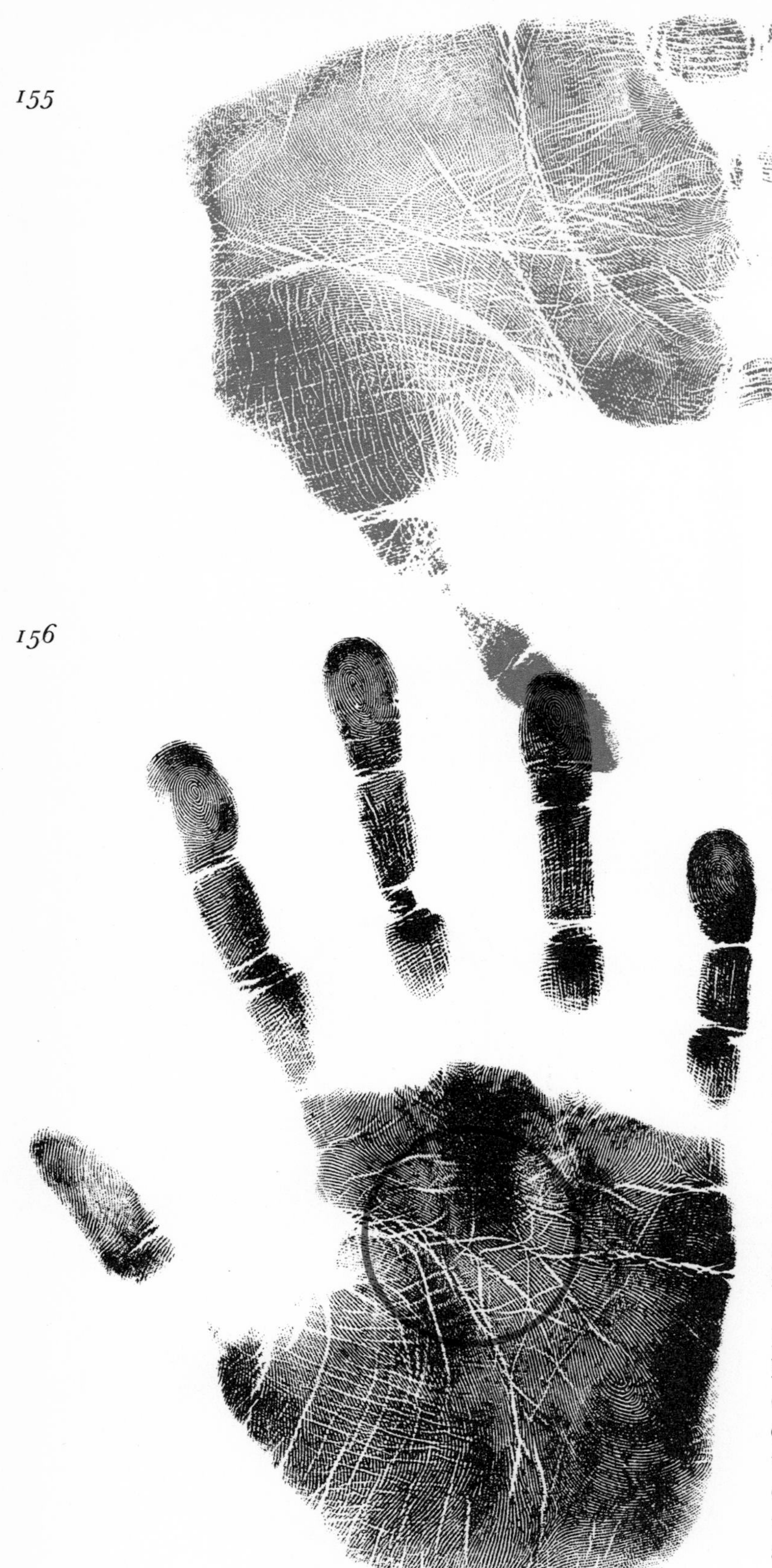

> length, betrays evil instincts, avarice, envy, hypocrisy and duplicity . . .
>
> If the line, instead of terminating on the Mounts of Jupiter or Saturn, seems to disappear between the first and second fingers, it betokens a long life of unremitting labour.

From this doleful picture above it would appear that one is unfortunate if one has a Heart Line of any kind – but then it seems that worse is to follow if one has *no* heart line:

> If in a hand there be found *no* line of heart, it is an unfailing sign of treachery, hypocrisy, and the worst instincts, and, unless the line of health be very good, the subject will be liable to heart disease, and runs a grave danger of a sudden early death. (62)

Even were we to take such information seriously, we might note that the Heart line is rarely absent, and whilst certain deviations in the Heart line do indicate a connexion with heart troubles, as well as emotional difficulties, there is no possibility of reading a sudden early death merely from the length of the line. Very often, the presence of a Simian line may lead the amateur to proclaim the Heart line absent, which is not the case.

Each of the major lines has attached to it at least one important tradition which should have been scotched long ago – that, for example, the length of the line of Life indicates the length of life itself, that a rapid termination of the line of Head will mark death from a mental disease, and so on. In this respect the line of Heart is no exception, and the particular piece of rabid nonsense here is that white marks on the line

155. A heavily chained line of Heart.

156. A chained and deviant line of Heart, which forms a simian line. The Girdle is extremely pronounced. This subject has suffered from childhood from heart troubles.

157. An incipient Simian line, formed when the Heart line is distinguishable, yet pours its energies into the Head line. It is not regarded with the same awe as the full Simian.

> . . . denote conquests in love: a point on the line means grief of the heart, and according to its position, you can tell by whom it was caused, thus–under the Mount of Apollo the cause was an artist, or a celebrity . . . under the Mount of Mercury the grief is caused by a man of science, a lawyer, or a doctor . . . (63)

Observe that the male it is who seduces: one can almost see the waxed moustache, hear the deep-throated laugh of the villain. Such beliefs survived until late into the nineteenth century, and such parts of the tradition should be stripped away as being of no further value, save perhaps in their antiquarian spirit.

As far as the tradition is concerned, it is hard to summarize the beliefs concerning the line of Heart: certainly it seems to be in some way linked with the emotions, with the 'heat of blood', and certainly deviations in the line from a 'norm'–a smooth curve from below Jupiter out to the percussion of the hand (figure 156)–indicate deviations of an emotional kind. Any practising palmist will confirm that a person with 'heart troubles' of the ordinary physical type (we may speak in such terms since we live in a society which clearly separates the physical from the material) will always have a deviant line of Heart. Without a detailed study of the nature of this line, it is not possible to be more explicit, save to say that the line has been linked directly with the fifth sign of the zodiac, Leo, and a study of this sign will certainly enrich the understanding of the line itself. In the astrological tradition Leo rules the heart (figure 61).

157

158

Docebo vos per manum DEI.
Iob. 27. v. 11.
Et in sinistra Eius divitiæ et Gloria.
Pro. 3. v. 16.
Longitudo dierum est in Dextrâ illius.
Fautor utroque tuum Laudabit Pollice Ludum.
Horat: L.I. Epist: 18. v. 66.
ΞΥΝ ΘΕΟΥ ΠΑΛΑΜΑ
Pindar. Olymp. 10.
METOPOSCOPICUM
LUDICRUM
CHIROMANTICUM
PRÆTORIUM
Usus habet Laudem:
Sed abusus crimina gign
Cheiromantica: Hic omnia certa.
Chiromantice: Cichainer_tom.
Quod est Inferius est sicut id quod est superius.
Experimentum proprium docuit Chiromantiam esse veram.
DERISORES huius artis Contemplentur saltem locum ♀ in manibus proprijs. etc.
HERMES TRISMEGISTUS.
RODOLPHUS GOCLENIUS
Nullum Numen abest, si sit prudentia præstò:
Cavete vobis â Pseudo-prophetis. Matth: 7. v. 15.

The line of the Head

158. Title page from a seventeenth century collection of palmistic texts, called 'Ludicrum Chiromanticum'.

159. A line of Head which terminates in a fork is traditionally supposed to indicate dishonesty in the subject.

In certain respects the Head line is the most personalized line in the hand: the Chinese call it the 'line of Man', and visualize it as being placed between the line of Heaven (our Heart line) and the line of Earth (our line of Life), caught in a tension between the spiritual and the material (figure 159). In the West there has always been a tendency to read the lines of Head and Heart in intimate connexion with each other, on the principle that one may pinpoint the basic personality if it is possible to determine the emotional intensity and the intellectual calibre of the subject. Such a practice has been supported by the fact that in certain cases the two lines do combine to form one (figure 149), which is the notorious Simian line. Within the framework of Chinese palmistry, therefore, we may see the Simian line as representing 'Man' in too close a contact with 'Heaven' or with the powerful, masculine *yang* influence, a point which we shall elaborate in the appropriate section dealing with the Simian line. Taken in isolation, however, the Head line is quite clearly linked with mentality, and from it the palmist gauges the outlook and understanding of the subject:

If the Head line penetrates the Mount of Moon, then it is tapping the undifferentiated energies which manifest as dreams and imagination, and a strange, imaginative view of reality must be expected. Such a termination may result in someone who is 'lost in dreams', but if the other signs in the hand indicate considerable executive power, then such a view of reality may be utilized, and given form, through one of the arts–

159

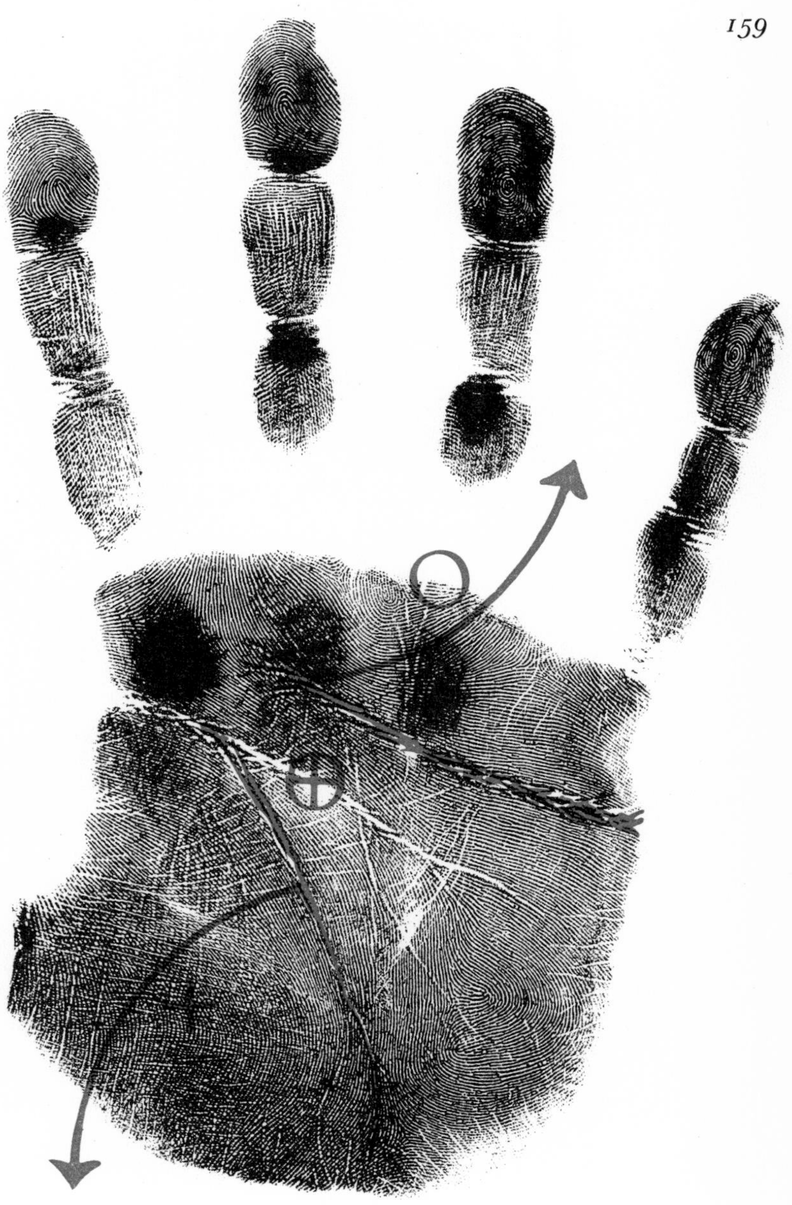

160

161

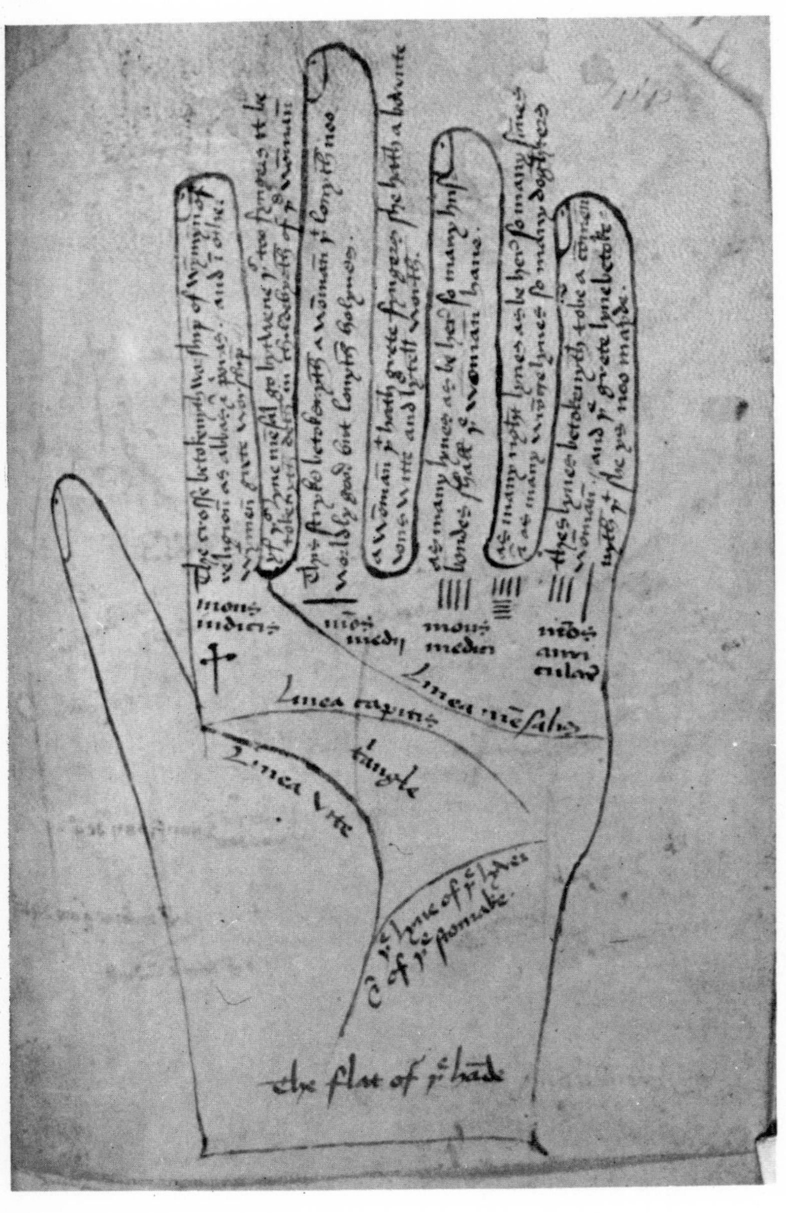

especially through literature. The low termination of Head in figure 157 is fairly typical of the creative writer or painter. The quality of the Head line, in terms of its intensity or chaining, will determine the flow of mental effort. It is for this reason that a chained line of Head is regarded by palmists as indication of poor concentration: each chain in the line symbolizes a damming up of the mental process, a weakening of the ability to transform matter and phenomena into abstract ideas. (64)

The tradition concerning the termination of lunar linking with the arts finds ample support in practice, and it even emerges in those few records of hands which have survived from the nineteenth century. For example, Desbarrolles, in discussing the hand of the French author Dumas, which he had presumably examined, says that this author had a long line of Head which descended into lunar; similarly, his description of the hand of Home, the famous medium immortalized by Browning, shows a line of Head descending through lunar down to the wrist. More recently, but still in the last century, the American Benham reproduced a superb example of an imaginative line of Head, strongly descending low into Moon (figure 46), and captions it as 'a celebrated author'. Similarly, the Irish palmist Cheiro gave us the hand of Gladstone with such a line (figure 162), whilst the present author reproduced the hand of a world-famous novelist with precisely the same descent into the lunar region, (figure 45). It is in fact one of the most common formations among artistic types, and is always indicative of

160. A strong, 'practical' Head line.

161. Palmistry of the fixed symbol type, from a mediaeval manuscript in the Bodleian Library Oxford.

162. The hand of Gladstone, from Cheiro's collection of prints.

imaginative faculties–one must, of course, determine from the rest of the hand whether or not the type would use such faculties.

As such considerations intimate, the line of Head must be conceived as channelling energies from the domain of Jupiter, that most expansive area of the hand, connected with ambitions and highly spiritualised energies, into various palmar zones. This is why the termination of the line is so important an index of understanding and mental outlook. Thus, a fairly long line makes contact with the mount of Moon, and so enlivens the spiritual outlook with the imagination associated with this area of the hand. One may see from this why a fork in the line (figure 164) is generally taken to denote intellectual dishonesty or a tendency to lie, as Benham's own comments make clear:

> This will indicate versatility, a union of practical and imaginative ideas which make the subject see things from a double point of view. I have seen this marking on the hands of successful theatrical people, and those who successfully appeal to the public in other ways. If the fork be slight, it must be read simply as versatility. If it be more marked, as in [fig. 164], it shows that the subject has a strong practical set of ideas and a strong set of imaginative ones. He can see things from both the practical and fanciful sides, and with this double point of view, he is less inclined to be narrow and one-sided. By noting which of the two forks is deeper and stronger, you can tell which side (practical or imaginative) will obtain the mastery.

162

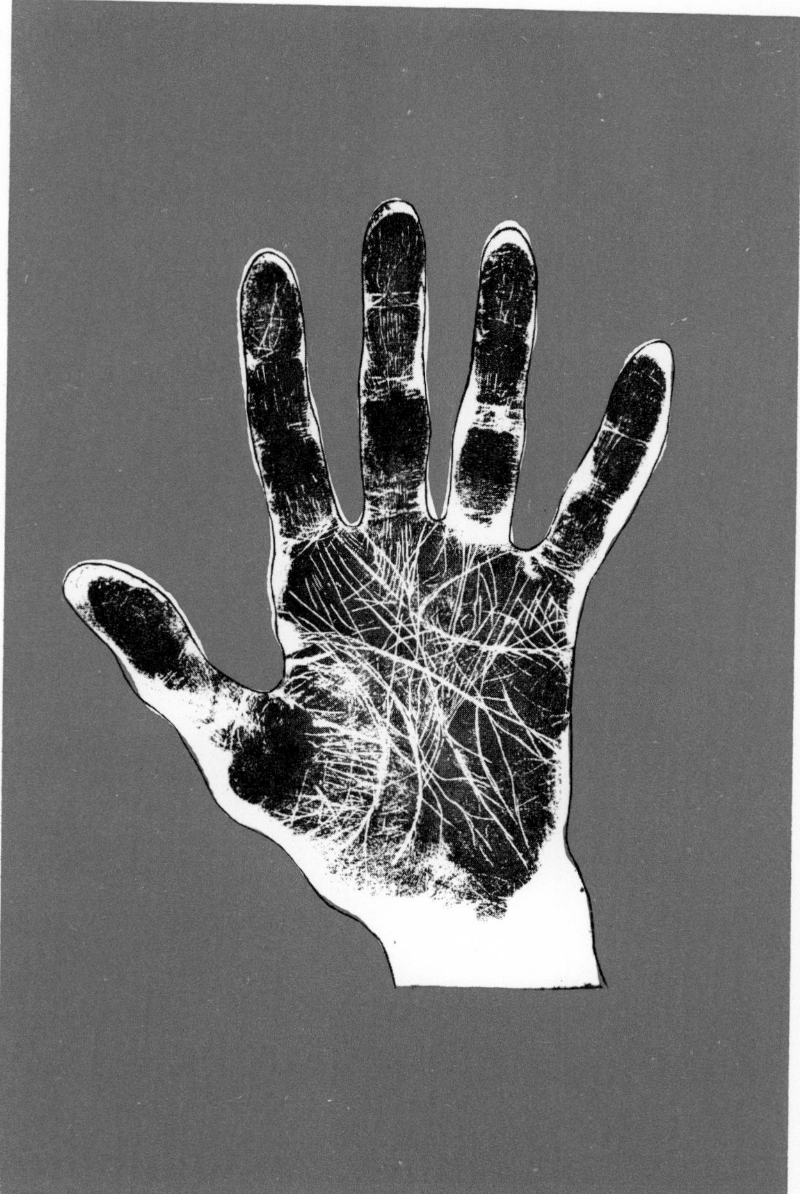

163

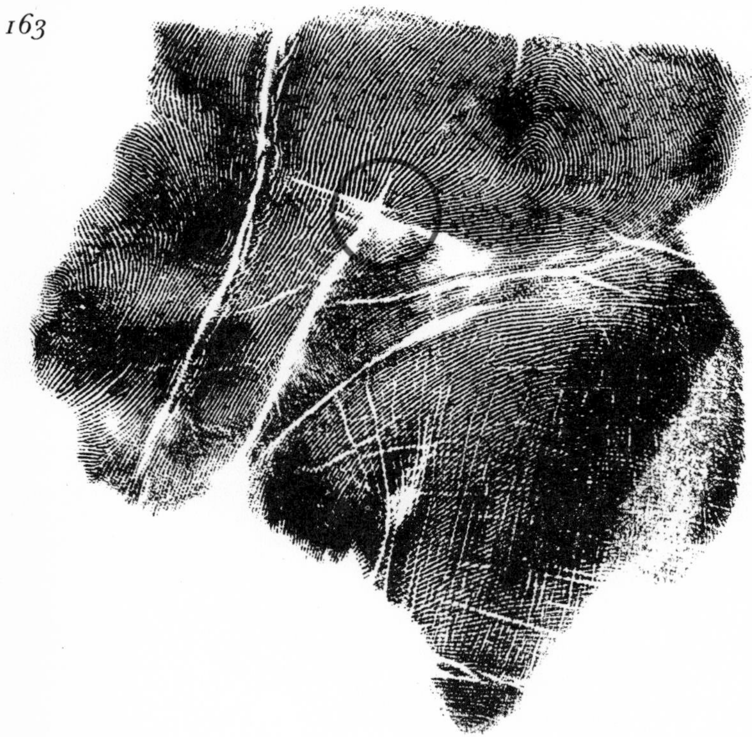

164

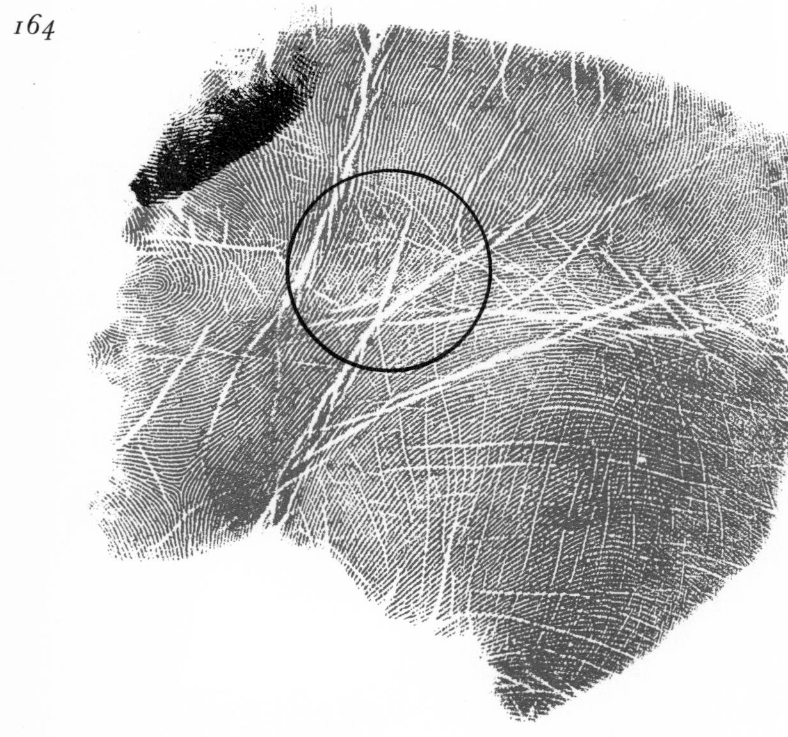

163. A short Head line, traditionally taken as a sign of a 'fixed', if not limited mentality. In some systems such a line is held to indicate violence, since it terminates on the Plain of Mars.

164. A forked Head line. In some systems a sign of dishonesty, in others a sign of creative potential.

165. The warlike Mars, ruler of the belligerent Aries, and the passionate, often violent, Scorpio.

166. Modifications of the lines, according to the system of the English palmist Heron-Allen.

This is a fine marking on a good hand. The double line, however, with its double point of view, often leads a subject into the habit of falsifying. He is not always an intentional liar; often he is not sure whether he is telling the literal story or the imaginative one. His imagination is vivid, and he sometimes makes himself think he is telling the truth when he is not. From the forking Head line is produced the liar, and when seen on an otherwise bad hand, it will make you sure of this interpretation. In habitual liars, I have found the forking Head line always present. (65)

If the line is a short one, then it terminates on that area which was called in traditional palmistry the Plain of Mars (figure 163). In such a case, energies are being transmitted into an area of unrest, since Mars is ever the restless, highly charged initiator, the activator of the cosmos, who will lead forward into battle regardless. We see spiritual expansion falling into a somewhat material area, and this will indicate that the personality may have a penetrating mentality, possibly a tenacious one, but the breadth which a strong imagination injects into the mental outlook will be lacking, and the type will be fixed or narrow. For these reasons it is difficult to see why a short line is traditionally supposed to 'betray weak ideas and a weak will', and why there should be a superstition that when a line of Head terminates under Saturn (which is to all intents and purposes on the Plain), then this 'foreshadows an early and sudden death'. In his palmistic descriptions of the seven deadly sins, Desbarrolles gives a short line of Head

165

under 'Sloth', but experience shows that the opposite of the traditions is more likely to be true. Certainly, a type with such short lines will be at least materialistic, whilst if other factors in the hand denote strong Martian or Fire impulses, then such a short line will certainly indicate a violent disposition. The hand of the murderer at figure 161, for example, taken from the collection of Benham, shows such a line. A hand of this kind reminds us that the symbol for Mars (figure 165), was originally a drawing of the cross of matter weighing down the circle of spirit (figure 130), and that the Mars of astrology and palmistry has always been depicted as a warlike, violent creature (figure 165). It is this Martian force which is being activated by the energies pouring into the Plain.

We have already noted the implications of a line which is long, for this usually ends above the Mount of Moon or upon the Mount of Moon, and in a relatively late quotation we may study the persistence of the belief that a long line of Head descending well into lunar indicates insanity:

> If the line . . . trace an oblique course to a termination *on* the Mount of Moon, it is a sign of idealism, imagination, and want of instinct of real life. If it comes very low upon the mount it leads to mysticism and folly, even culminating in madness if the line of health is cut by it in both hands. In an otherwise fairly strong hand this declension upon the Mount of Moon gives poetry and a love of the mystic or occult sciences, superstition, and an inclination to spiritualism. The line of head coming low upon the

166

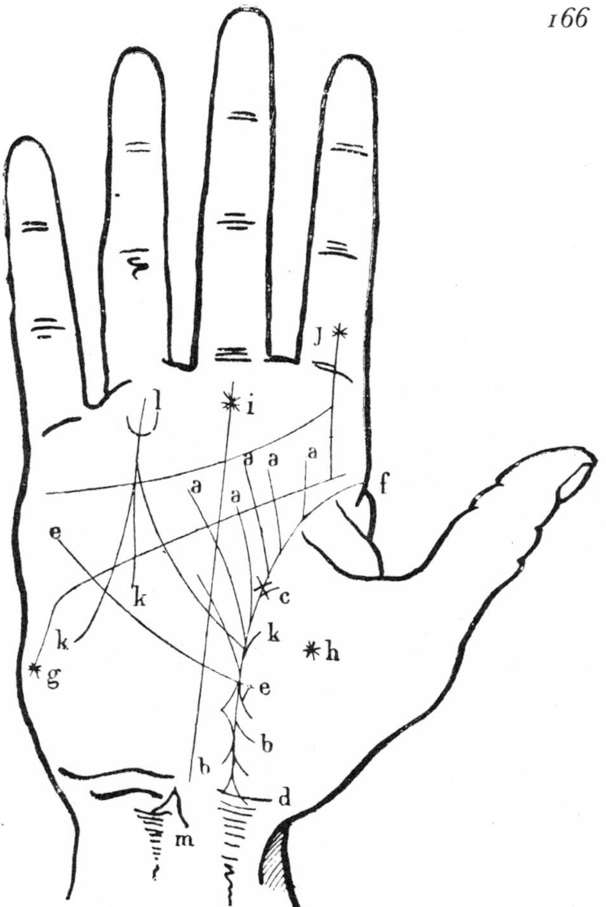

PLATE XV.—MODIFICATIONS OF THE PRINCIPAL LINES

Ed Heron-Allen

168

167

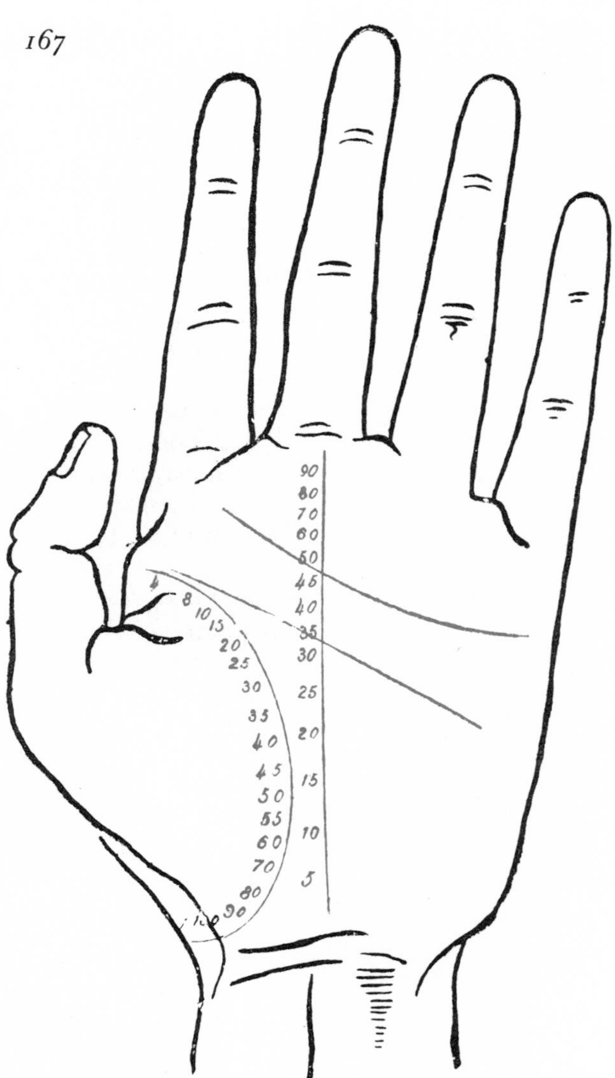

PLATE XI.—AGES UPON THE LINES OF LIFE AND FORTUNE

> Mount of the Moon to a star, as at *g* in Plate XV (figure 166), with the stars on the Mounts of Venus and Saturn, as at *h* and *i*, and a weak line of heart, are terribly certain signs of hereditary madness. This extreme obliquity of the line always indicates a *danger* of madness, and these concomitant signs prove it to be hereditary, and probably unavoidable.
>
> Again, if instead of going across the hand it turns up towards one of the Mounts, it will show that the thoughts are entirely taken up by the qualities belonging to the respective mounts; thus turning up to the Mount of Mercury, commerce will be the prevailing instinct, and will bring good fortune; or, turning towards the Mount of Apollo and Mercury, the signification is of success in art brought by scientific treatment. If the line go right up on the mount, it will denote a folly of the quality–thus, for instance, ending on Mercury it will denote occultims and deceit; on Apollo, the mania of art; and on Saturn, the mania of religion. (66)

One may not like the connexion drawn between occultism and deceit, and one may not understand what is meant by 'the mania of art', but we do see here a palmistic system which interprets lines as though they are the conductors of energies, the particular significance of which depends upon the zone into which these energies are released. The fact is that the line of Head is the one major line which has a wide latitude of insertion and termination, which is why it is such a useful indication of the unique personality, and why,

167. One of the numerous systems for locating dates, and the ages of events in the subject's life. This system is the one most commonly used by modern palmists.

168. A strong head line, commencing independently of the line of Life.

169. A forked Head line, with its commendement rooted in the line of Life at two points.

in the Chinese system, it represents 'the Man'.

Within the occult tradition the human head, in which thinking takes place, and from which the centre of being is experienced, represents the summation of previous incarnations, and it may therefore be taken as representing the most individualist phase in the development of man. This is why the highly personal and individualistic sign Aries is said to rule the head. In this respect, therefore, we find a connexion between Western palmistry and the apparently strange system of the orient. From the line we may be able to determine more precisely what is *unique* in the personality, for in many respects the understanding and intellect do manifest themselves in more diverse manners than emotional qualities.

The beginning of the line is just as important as its termination. Most frequently the Head line begins communally with the line of Life, and some palmists suggest that the point at which the two diverge (measured along the lines of the dating system in figure 167) will indicate the age at which 'the subject begins to think for himself, or to rely upon himself'. This theory is blown by the fact that in many hands the two lines are not joined at all:

> When the line of Head is distinctly separated from the line of Life (figure 168), it shows primarily self-reliance. The subject is original, is not bound down by the vies of others, acts for and depends upon himself, can plan well, is guided by his own judgement, is independent and courageous in his vies, and therefore this separation if not too wide, is a fine marking. The wider the separation the greater the degree of self-

169

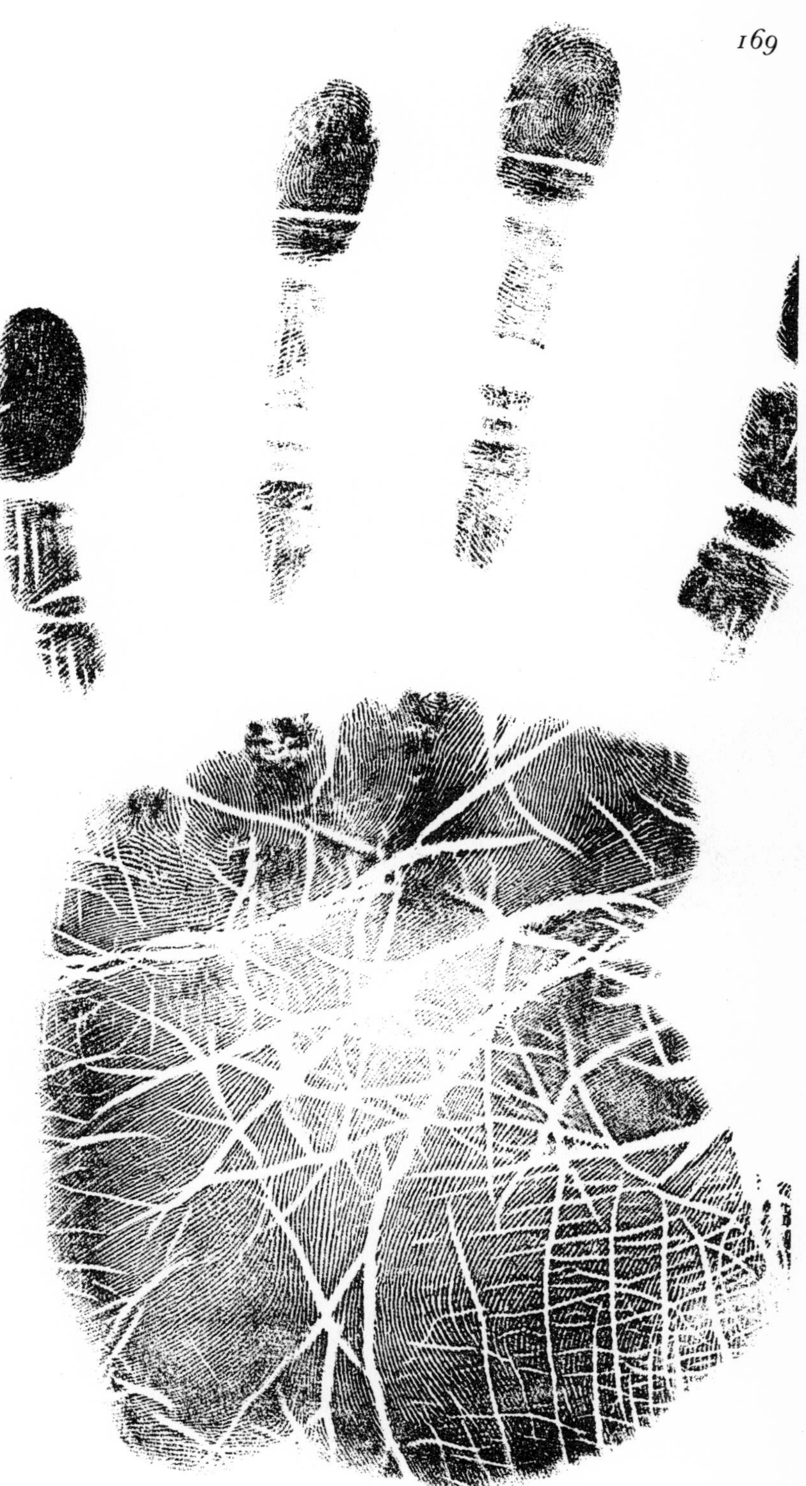

170

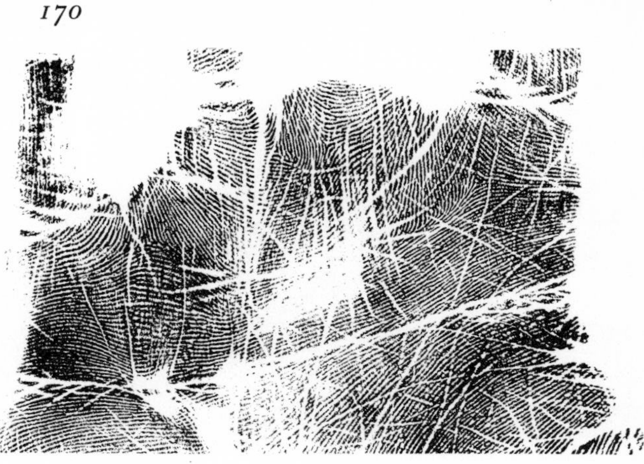

170. A simian line. See text below.

171. Five examples from the Italian Taisnier's section on the Head line. See the text in third column below.

172. A six-rayed cross on the Head line. See text in second column below.

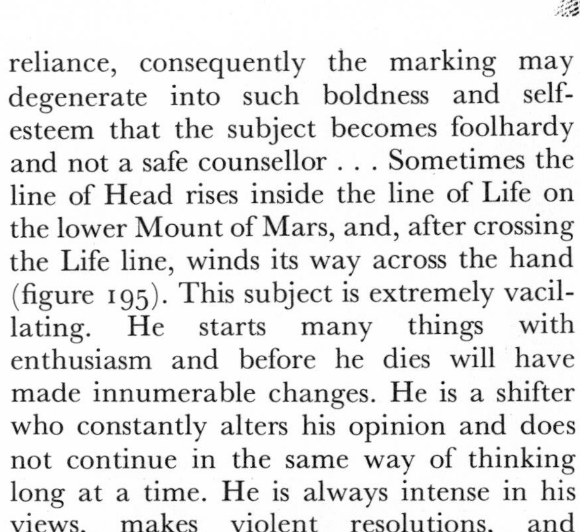

> reliance, consequently the marking may degenerate into such boldness and self-esteem that the subject becomes foolhardy and not a safe counsellor . . . Sometimes the line of Head rises inside the line of Life on the lower Mount of Mars, and, after crossing the Life line, winds its way across the hand (figure 195). This subject is extremely vacillating. He starts many things with enthusiasm and before he dies will have made innumerable changes. He is a shifter who constantly alters his opinion and does not continue in the same way of thinking long at a time. He is always intense in his views, makes violent resolutions, and changes his mind with facility, but always with the same vigour. (67)

Such interpretations spring from the fact that in Benham's system (figure 30) one finds a 'lower Mars', which runs above the Mount ot Venus, and forms with the Plain and Upper Mars (below Mercury) a martian barrier between the Mounts of Venus and Moon and the finger mounts. A line described above would therefore be tapping the lower Mars and this would activate too strongly in a wide variety of different directions. The opposite influence to the rapid energizing of Mars is the more steady emergizing of Jupiter, which will give an altogether more suitable influence where the head is concerned. We may see Benham's view of such an influence in figure 148, and we should note that the modern system of astropalmistry associates the entire line of Head with Jupiter by according it the rulership of Sagittarius, the sign which rules over philosophy, speculative thought and advanced education.

In the section of the Heart line it was mentioned that there are several ancient superstitions connected with the hand which are still widely believed by some people, for no less a reason than that they are frequently referred to by popular books on palmistry, and these we may as well dispense with once and for all. The line of head is no exception and with it we find various superstitions connected with fatality and insanity, a fair sample of which was still being perpetuated as late as the 1890s.

> The Line of Head broken in two immediately under the Mount of Saturn means, where the sign is on both hands, death on the scaffold, or at least, a fatal wound on the head. When this sign appears in one hand (no matter which), it indicates a probability of madness from an unfortunate passion, or a broken limb, or a blow, but not fatal, on the head.
>
> If the Line of the Head is long, thin, and not deeply marked, it shows infidelity and treachery. If, towards its close, it mounts suddenly to the Line of Heart, it signifies early death. When this line is cut by a number of small hair lines, it indicates a continuous nervous headache; a cross in the middle of the line is a sign of approaching death, or of a mortal wound. (68)

It is not uncommon for someone to have a six-rayed cross on the middle of the Head line: all that is required is for an influence line to run down from the Mount of Venus, and to intersect where the line of Saturn traverses the line of Head (figure 172). But then, the mere

171

18 19 21 22

18 Naturalis brevis & discontinua, mutabilitatē & levitatem animi cū vera

fact of having been born may be taken as a 'sign of approaching death', and we may quite properly relegate such ideas as those quoted above into the past, where they will do no more damage. Indagine gives some interesting traditions concerning this line (figure 171). A short line of Head, much broken, indicates a highly changeable personality, superficial and unreliable in speech, whilst a line which originates at a point separated from the line of Life may be taken as a sign of liberality and a love of show. When the line is crossed by many small lines, as indicated in the fourth diagram of figure 171, it shows an insecure personality, who does not do what he should do, and who is generally faithless in his intentions. Perhaps the most unfortunate sign from the collection is the final one, for whilst the Latin text does not agree in general with the information contained in the diagram, it is clear that a forked head line indicates one given over to all sorts of ingenious subtleties towards self aggrandisement.* There is an element of truth in such 'hell fire' interpretations, though we must remember that Taisnier was merely collecting various traditions from different historical sources.

We see from the brief examination of the tradition that there is no doubt whatsoever that the Head line is somehow connected with the intellectual processes, and that the course of the line reflects how the subject steers that delicate balance between a literal concern for truth and a pull towards the imagination. In this respect the line might be called the tightrope of the hand.

172

* The text reads 'Coniunctio vitalis cum naturali in opposito medii, miseriam animi, pravitatem et ingenii subtiltatem, et in acquirenda pecunia, hominem sollicitum facit, et nemini fidum.'

173

173. A reading from a book on palmistry by Cocles.

174. An eighteenth century gipsy chiromant.

175. The line of Life, surrounding and isolating the mount of Venus, the seat of sensual enjoyment.

174

The line of Life

The line of Life circles around Venus (figure 175) and is directly linked with the body and the corporeality of the subject: from its length, quality, strength and points of origin and insertion one may determine the vitality and health of the subject:

> This line should be long, completely encircling the ball of the thumb, strong, not too broad or too fine, without curvature, breakage, cross bar, or irregularities of any description. Thus marked in a hand, it denotes long life, good health, a good character and disposition.
>
> Pale and broad, it indicates ill-health, bad instincts, and a feeble and envious character. Thick and red, it betrays violence and brutality of mind; chained, (figure 156), it indicates delicacy of constitution; thin and meagre in the centre, it indicates ill-health during a portion of the life; a spot terminating this thinness indicates sudden death. If it is of various thickness through its course it denotes a capricious and fickle temper. (69)

Generally, when referring to health and temperament, the palmist Heron-Allen is fairly exact, but he does have a disconcerting habit of relapsing into a mediaeval state of mind, as for example when he speaks of a spot on the line as indicating 'sudden death', or when he infers that the length of the line is related to length of life. It has been necessary to reprimand Heron-Allen before:

> The length of the line has nothing to do with the length of life, as so many palmists claim, nor do breaks in the line necessarily indicate 'danger of death'. As we have

175

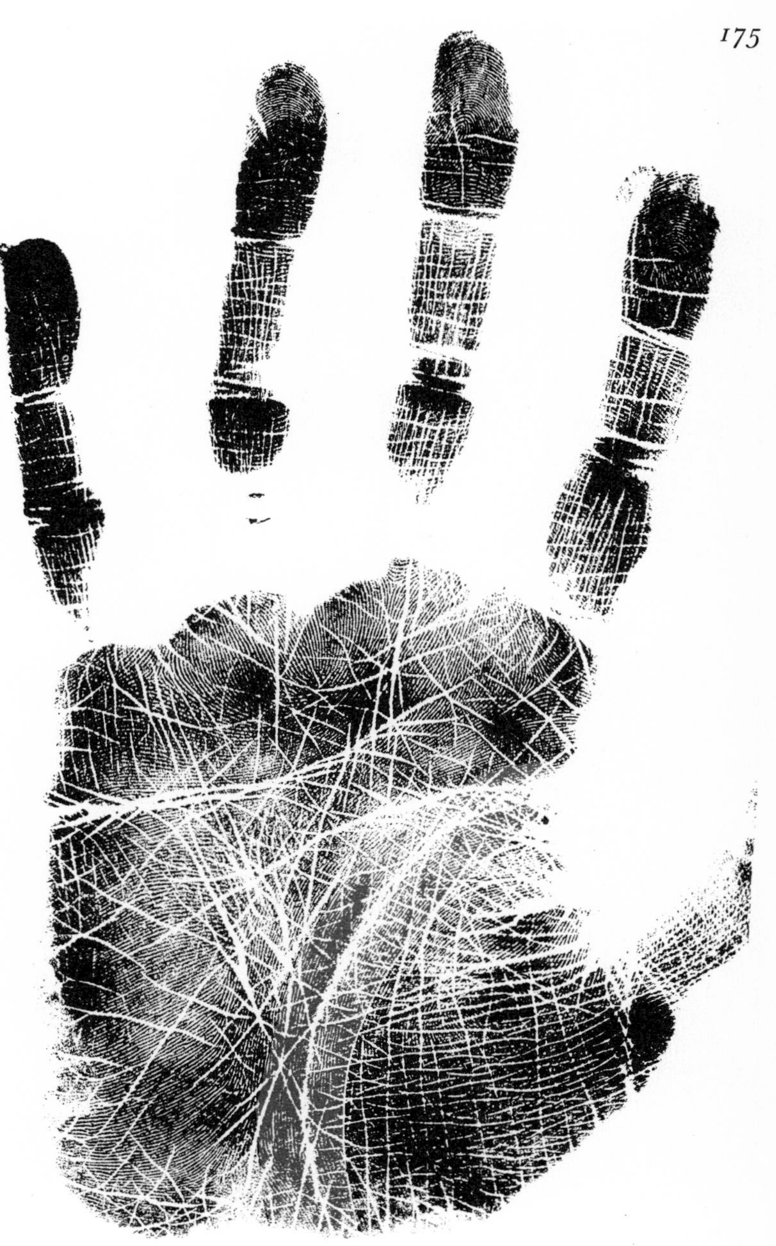

176

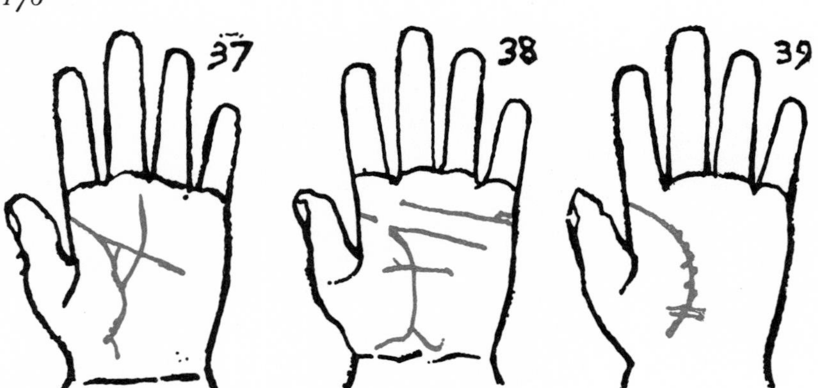

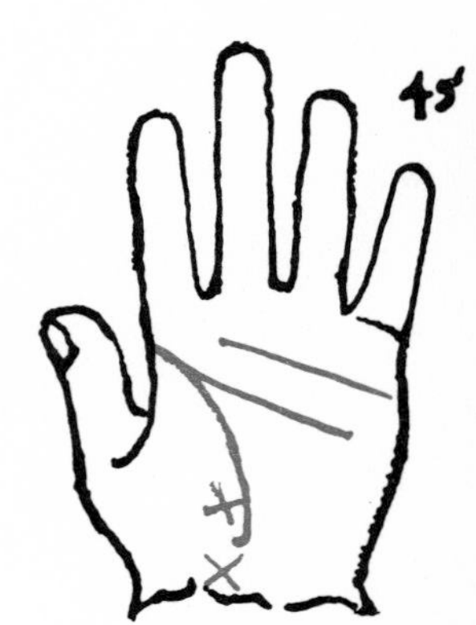

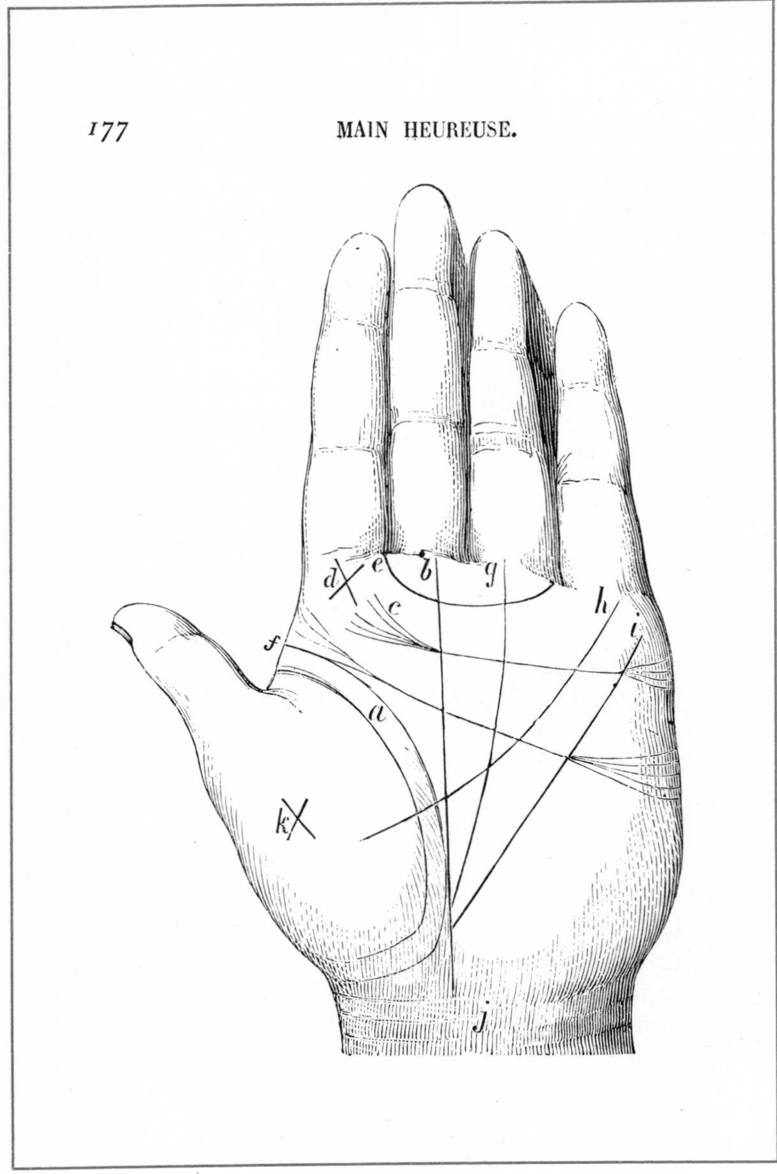

177

> already observed, a prediction may lead to a subconscious state of apprehension which can, in itself, create the event. When Heron-Allen predicted the death of a young man from the length of his Life line ('I told the subject that a fatal illness would attack him at thirty-seven, which would kill him at forty-one'), it is quite possible that, albeit in good faith, he was the man's executioner. Heron-Allen's qualifying remark ('to make deliberate statement like the above would be a brutal and dangerous thing to do, unless one spoke with *absolute* certainty') boomerangs, for one cannot speak with absolute certainty. Not only is the palmist himself fallible, but the lines themselves are not completely static, and may change to mark some corresponding inner change within the subject. (70)

No wonder that, with such a tradition, the Frenchman Desbarrolles should include in his description of the 'fortunate hand' a double life line (figure 177). A similar urge to personify the Life line is found in his teaching that if the Life line is separated from the line of Head at commencement (figure 180), this is a sign of an unfortunate and stupid character, since the native will lead a life without the guide of intelligence . . . We are fortunate with the line of Life that few other unreasonable superstitions have been attached to it, other than those already indicated; this is possibly because the line is one of the most constant in the hand:

> In its course through the hand the Life line varies little, the principal deflections being when the line runs close to the thumb

176. *Some of the sixteenth century traditions concerning the Life line, culled from Taisnier. See text below.*

177. *Desbarrolles version of a 'fortunate' hand, showing the most felicitious lines. Few modern palmists would agree that a Girdle might be called 'fortunate'.*

178. *Taisnier's traditions concerning the Life line. See text below.*

178

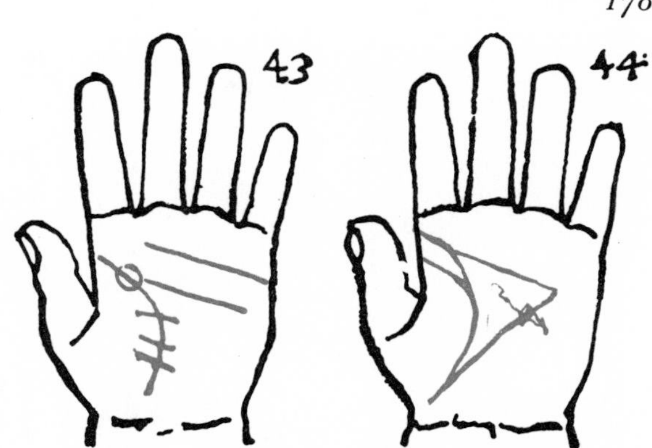

(figure 183), in which case it reduces the size of the Mount of Venus, thus checking the operation of that Mount, and the subject is cold, unsympathetic, lacks sexual desire and attraction for or to the opposite sex. This is a most important marking when you desire to estimate the probability of a fruitful marriage, for the less Venusian sexual desire present, the less likely is the subject to have children. It shows one who repels advances from the opposite sex instead of courting them, and for such reasons this line was used by the older palmists as an indication of barrenness. (71)

One observes, however, that this interpretation applies more to a restriction of Venus, than to any qualities connected with the line itself. We find most of the mediaeval traditions concerning this line collected in the vast compilation of Taisniers, for he presents us with sixty seven different woodcuts of the hand, each one descriptive of two or three variations relating to the Life line, all of them interesting.

(Figure 176) When a line runs from the Life line in a long furrow towards the middle finger, then this signifies a man who is proficient in the art of divination and the interpretation of dreams. However, if this same life line terminates in a fork towards its end, then it indicates a restless and unfaithful type . . . (Figure 176). If towards the end of the Life line there is a cross, then good fortune will continue towards the end of life. However, if this same cross is found under the Life line, near the rascette, then it indicates that good fortune and worth will be absent towards the end of life, and furthermore, if a small depression is found at the end of the line, then this threatens a sudden and violent death. (Figure 176) If near the beginning of the Life line one finds a line somewhat like a circle, then this suggests danger of death from poison or from drugs: the time of such occurrence may be determined from the position of this marking. (72)

It is in fact the very constancy of the line of life which drove the mediaeval palmists to reflect upon such signs as circles and crosses, and if we wish to derive any truth from the nature of the line we must concentrate more on its quality and upon its point of origin, and see how these may be interpreted by palmists:

The subject with a deep Line of Life has more ability to throw off worry and remain calm in moments of excitement. He is endowed with vigour of constitution, is filled with self-confidence, and inspires it in others. He is intense in everything he does, work and play alike . . . The strength and vigour will increase the Jupiterian propensities to 'eat, drink, and be merry,' and from this Life line and the Jupiterian type we get many drunkards . . . The same danger is present with a strong Martian type, especially with red colour and red hair. The deep Life line makes the Apollonian a strong, healthy fellow, one to make his way through the world with ease. The Venusian is intensely passionate, and so strong in health and vitality that the exercise of natural Venusian passions is

179

179. The triad of palmistry (see figure 80) related to the nature of the Life line, ruled by Gemini. See text below.

180. Cife line originating towards Jupiter.

181. Life line originating with the Head line.

182. Life line originating below the Head line, on the mount of Venus.

> much increased. In all cases it is the addition of good health and great vitality to the type, and with this idea in mind you can reason out the various combinations. A narrow and thin line indicates less vitality, less robustness, less resistance to illness, and greater liability of the subject to be overcome by various troubles of health. The thin line does not mean that the subject is necessarily delicate or sickly, but it shows that he cannot endure as much hardship, exposure, or resist disease as well as a subject with a deep Life line . . . The thin Life line is not distinctly a nervous line, yet the subject with such a line will be more nervous than one with a deep line. He will be apprehensive of coming evils, he seems instinctively to feel that the tension on health is great, and he fears the day when it will be overstrained . . . As strong vitality urges and feeds the desire of all types, so the thin Life line, indicating lack of robustness, minimizes and reduces the operation of every type, and makes each milder. These subjects are often lazy, and thin Life lines must be noted even with elastic consistency, for sometimes a lack of energy is accounted for by a lack of physical vigour. (73)

The three main areas from which the line of Life may originate are involved with the Jupiter/Venus polarity, so that some understanding of the natives of these planetary forces must be understood when one attempts to assess the importance of the Life line. The line may begin on the mount of Jupiter; it may arise with the line of Head, which is by far the most common beginning, or it may arise below the Head line, with a quite separate commencement. The first will imply a strong Jupiterian urge present in the vital expression of the subject:

> There will be a degree of ambitions calculations about the person's activities–he will always have some objective in mind when he does something. It is almost as if such a line facilitates a free passage of energy from that zone of the hand which is connected with the more passive and internal energies. To take the analogy a little further we can say that the energies which properly belong to one sphere are being passed into another. I find this line to be quite common in the extroverted Fire type, whose energy is so much directed towards dominating his surroundings. It is most usual to find that instead of the whole of the Life line crossing the Head line only one or perhaps two long lines run up towards Jupiter. I call this 'the line of ambition' . . .
>
> When the line of Life springs from the Head line the physical energies are controlled to some extent by the mind, and this leads to a certain degree of shrewdness. A clear and unchained fork between Life and Head is always indicative of a certain calculating shrewdness of character which tends to put emotional considerations in second place to 'hard headed' considerations. It is the typical marking of the businessman . . . Shrewdness is an excellent characteristic up to a certain point, but beyond that level it leads to a 'coldness' and emotionally inhibited state which, like all imbalance, can be disruptive to normal life

relationships. Benham calls an excessive displacement of the Head down the Life line 'a typical criminal marking' . . .

When the line of Life takes its point of origin below the Head line, and independently of it (figure 180) we must expect a less restricted use of life energy than in the former case. The fact that the Life line is divorced from the Head indicates that action is less inhibited, but that at the same time it is inclined to be impulsive, less controlled by reasoning. (74)

In astropalmistry this line has been accorded the rulership of Gemini, and its physical path, between the mounts of Venus and Moon, may be traced in the symbol for Mercury which is the planet of Gemini (figure 94). The course represents the spiritual path through life in which one is attracted to indulgence in the materiality of Venus on the one side and to the imaginative and spiritual impulse of Moon on the other side. Life must be lived within such a dichotomy in which the material is invested with the spiritual, since this is what incarnation is about, and why it might accurately be said that life becomes manifest in Gemini. Certainly such a connexion between Life and Gemini is a reasonable one, for it is in Gemini that life finds its external expression: pure spirit arises in Aries, and in order to descend into physical *expression* must pass through the material inertia of Taurus (figure 179). We see such a progression, a uniting of the spiritual with the material, each time we think, or undertake any action in the material world, for our ideas and intentions, though invisible,

180

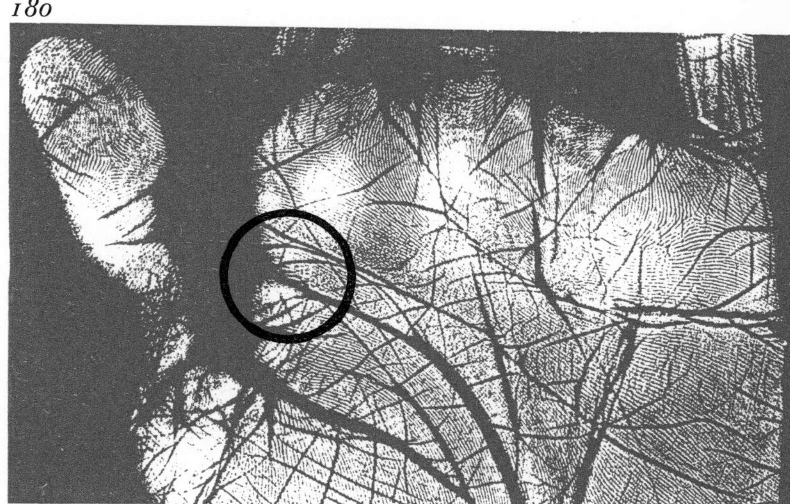

181

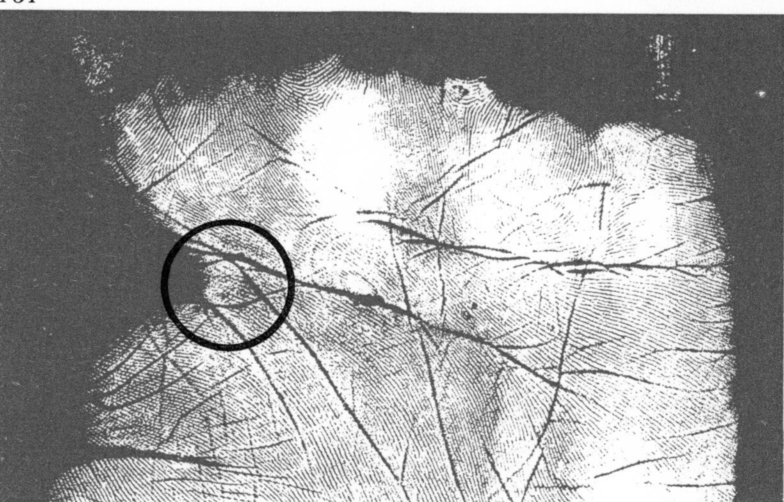

182

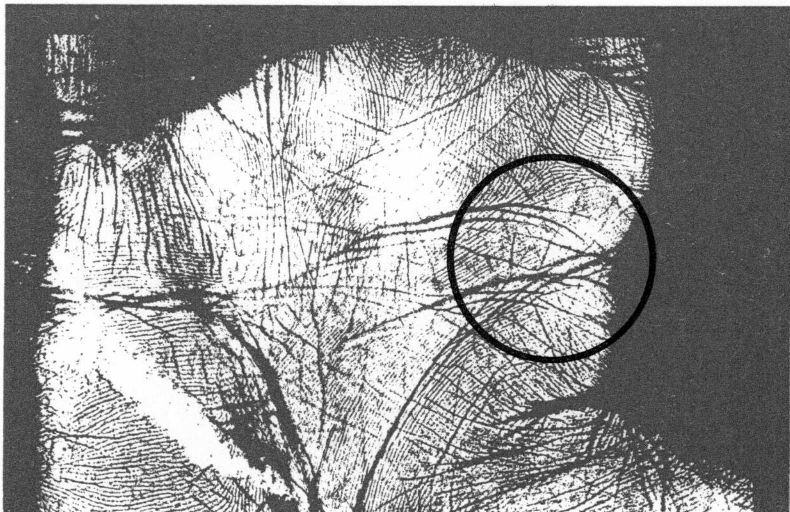

184

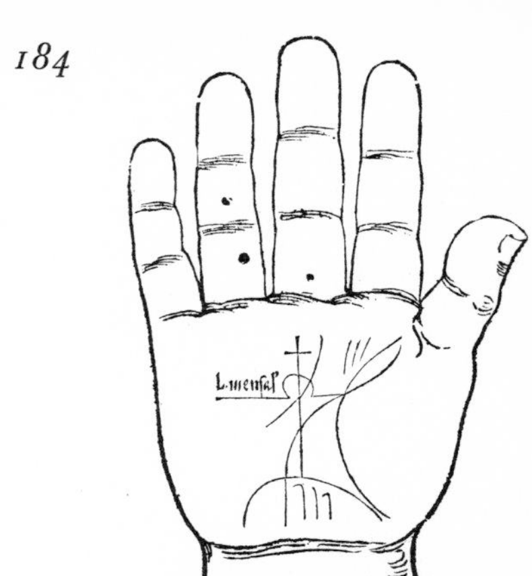

183

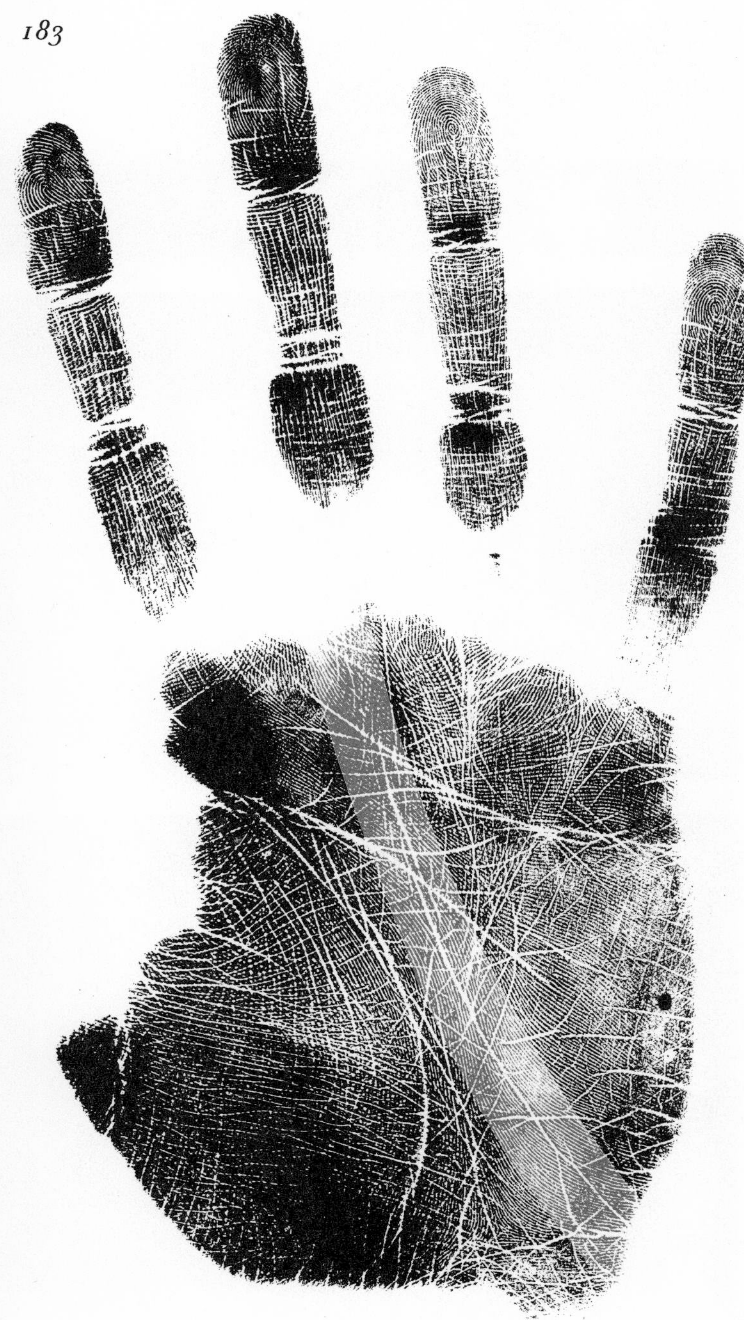

represent energy charges which are of the Arietan nature. Because we live in bodies, such ideas and intentions may be expressed only when they descend into the material world, symbolized in astrology through the materialistic bull of Taurus. All life may be seen in terms of a meeting of pure spirit with the inertia of materiality, and it is only on this deep level of interpretation that the true quality of Gemini, and of the line of Life, may be properly understood, for the inner conflict (superficially dubbed 'duality' in some astrological systems) of Gemini reflects the basic dichotomy of life, which is the meeting of the invisible spirit with the visible appearance of things. Perhaps it is for such reasons as these that one of the ancient Chinese systems calls this the line of Earth, for whilst the idea of earth may be far away from the Air element of Gemini, the Chinese still determine from this line the length of life, as well as the time and quality of accidents and ill-health, and they therefore have in mind the idea of corporeality which may be rightly associated with this line. When we reflect upon this relationship of the line to the Earth element, and note that in the greater proportion of hands the Head line, which represents the 'man', arises from the top of the Earth element, we may begin to see something of the sense contained in the ancient doctrine of the 'triangle' of the hand (figure 11), for it is the third line which binds together these two important lines of Earth and Man at the further extremities. It would seem that the ancients knew more than we usually give them credit for.

Subsidiary lines

183. The line of Saturn, sometimes called the Fate line.

184. A defective line of Saturn, after Indagine. See text on page 123.

185. A handprint from 'Cheiro's collection. Observe the curious twist of the line of Saturn toward the mount of Jupiter.

185

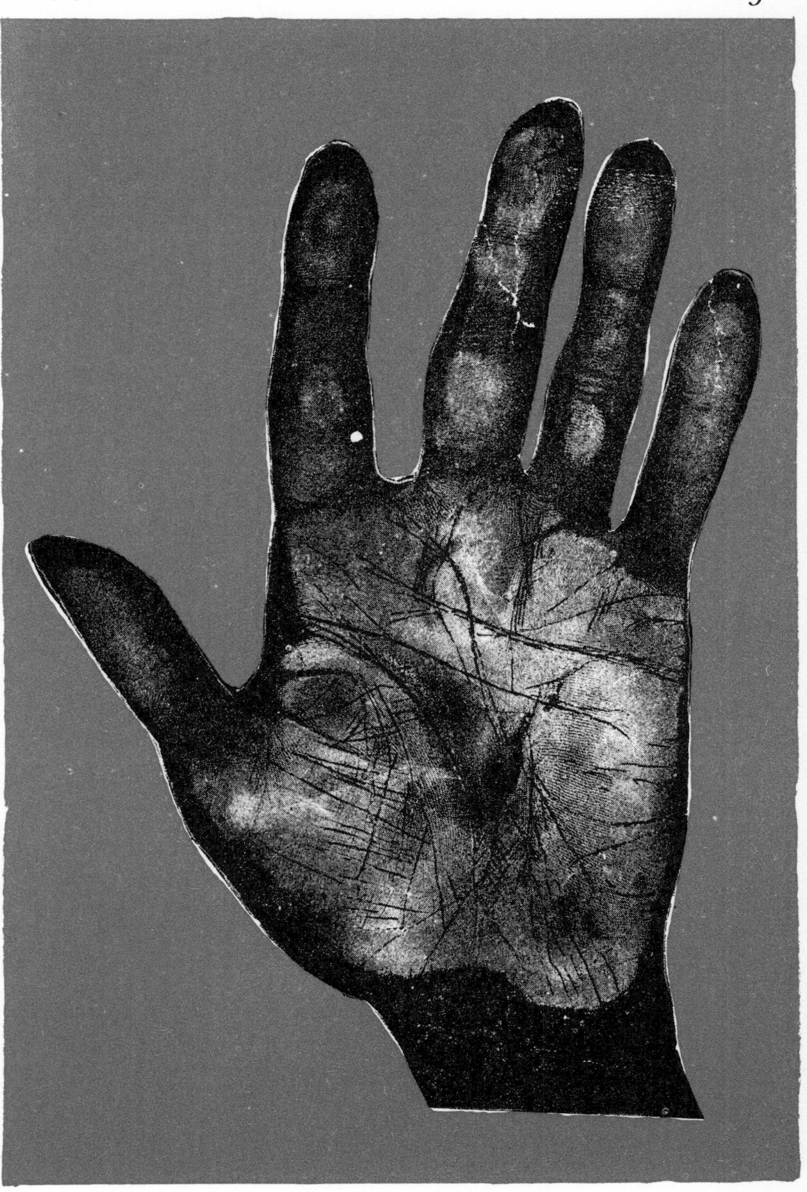

Beyond the three main lines of Head, Heart and Life, there often appear many other lines in the hand, but since these are not present in all hands, it is usual to consider them as being of lesser importance, though this is not always a realistic thing to do. The problem which faces any anthologer of the palmistic tradition is that in regard to these subsidiary lines one finds a wide variety of conflicting and contradictory traditions linked with each one of them, and it is hard to say precisely what truths may be gleaned from their examination. If we take the most important of the subsidiary lines by way of example – the so-called Fate Line (figure 183) – we may see how the relative degree of agreement which pervades the interpretation of the main lines is quite lost when we turn to the subsidiaries. The line (figure 183) does not appear on all hands, yet it has been accorded a great importance by most palmists, to the extent that it is sometimes included in descriptions of the main lines. Indagine, writing in the sixteenth century, associates it with character defects when it is afflicted, and with sound judgement when it is strong:

> If three small branches arise from the line of Fortune, and these join to the line of life, later descending down to the wrist (figure 184), then this indicates a good wit. If however it joins these lines in a distinctly crooked manner (figure 184), then it signifies an evil and wicked person, given to malicious slander and inclined to shed blood. (75)

In the same century, Taisnier was linking a long line of Saturn 'stretching from the

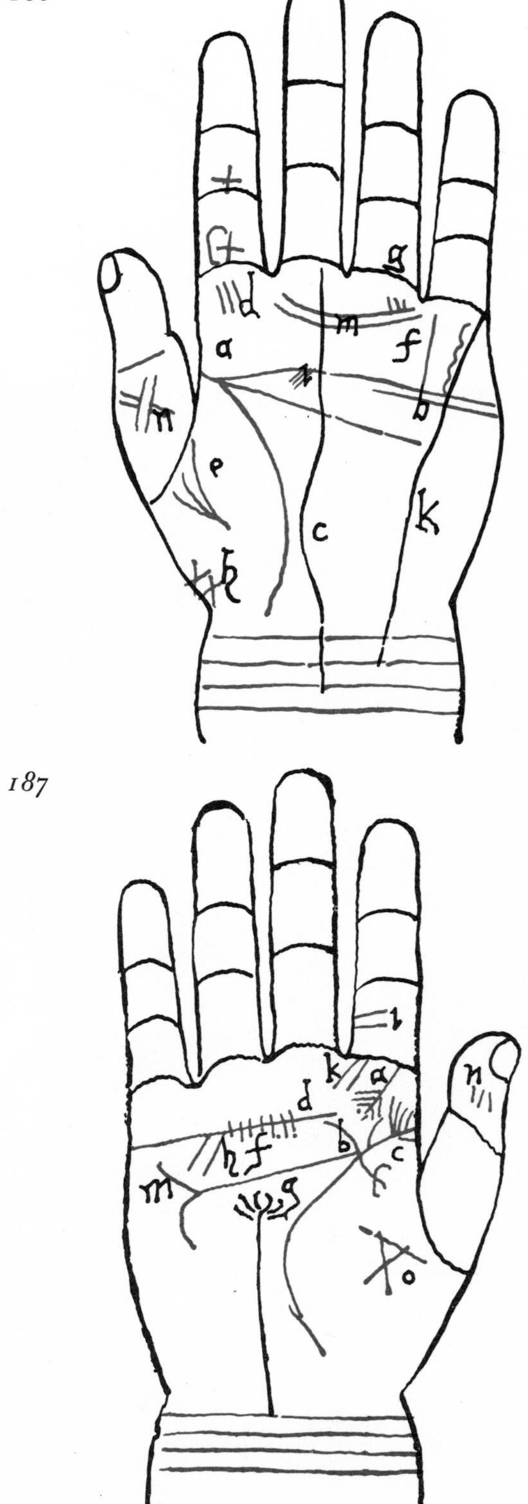

186. A long line of Saturn, a sign of 'melancholia', according to Taisnier. See text below.

187. A short line of Saturn, a sign of ill-health according to Taisnier. See text below.

188. The course of this line of Saturn is supposed by Taisnier to presage ill-health. Saturn was traditionally the planet dealing out illness, whilst Jupiter was the one supporting health.

189. Desbarrolles' reading of the line of Saturn suggests that the course of this line presages the course of the subject's life.

rascettes up to the middle finger' (figure 186) as a significator of melancholia, though in those days this would not be merely a sign of a miserable disposition, but also a sign of a serious cast of mind. A short line, ending in a series of small hair lines (figure 187), was taken as a sign of ill-health, though a line from the rascettes *crossing* the line of Fate and meeting with the life line is also supposed to presage the same condition according to his figure 188, and from this same diagram we learn that a Fate line running up towards the little finger is supposed to indicate a long life . . . The old tradition is confusing, to say the least, but even by the last century things were not less confused. Desbarrolles has no hesitation in affirming that the line is related to destiny and fatality, and although he is reluctant to say precisely what he means by this, he does appear at times to regard the course of the line as representing the course of life:

> If the line winds around in a screw-like pattern near the bottom (figure 189) and yet towards the top is straight and clear, this indicates great misfortune followed by good fortune. (76)

Yet in the very next sentence he indicates that the line may be regarded in itself as containing the evil forces of Saturn:

> It must be understood that as soon as the line of Saturn enters into the finger mount it injects the bad influence of Saturn, and is always more or less difficult depending upon the height to which it rises into the mount. This influence is just as bad if the line cuts the rascettes, that is to say if it goes

188

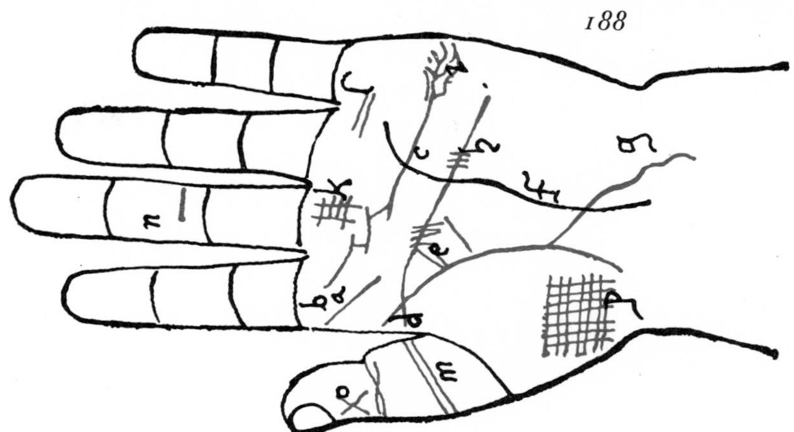

beyond the base of the hand and runs into the wrist: here again we find excess, and it is a sign of imprisonment and tribulations of all kinds. (77)

Almost the opposite interpretation is accorded such a line by Taisnier, and it is certainly quite removed from the interpretation offered by Heron-Allen at the end of the last century:

Starting from the line of life, the line of fortune indicates that the luck in life is the result of one's own personal merit. If it starts from the wrist, or rascette, the fortune will be very good, especially if it trace a fine strong furrow on the Mount of Saturn: in the same direction, but commending higher up from a point in the Plain of Mars, we get an indication of a painful, troubled life, especially if the line penetrates (as it often does) into the finger. If the lines start from the Mount of the Moon, it shows . . that the fortune is, to a great extent, derived from the caprice of opposite sex . . . Starting from the very base of the Mount of Moon, and ending on the Mount of Saturn, is an indication of prediction and clairvoyance.

Instead of going to the Mount of Saturn, the line may go up to some other mount, in which cases it will have special significations; thus, going to the Mount of Mercury, we get fortune in commerce, eloquence, and science; going up to the Mount of Apollo, we get fortune from art or wealth; going to the Mount of Jupiter, we find satisfied pride, and the attainment of the objects of our ambition. (78)

Such contradictions as these may not unnaturally lead us to question the whole value of the

189

LES MYSTÈRES DE LA MAIN. 241

cœur, bonheur qui doit être certain par la tendance vers Jupiter qui est toujours d'un heureux présage.

Si la saturnienne est droite et chargée de rameaux qui s'élèvent en haut comme des branches, c'est : passage successif de la pauvreté à la richesse.

Chaque rameau forme un échelle pour monter.

Si la saturnienne part de la vitale, c'est un bonheur acquis par le mérite propre.

Dans ce cas aussi, elle annonce un cœur généreux.

A la fin de la saturnienne, des lignes rassemblées ou qui la coupent, annoncent un bonheur suivi d'infortune.

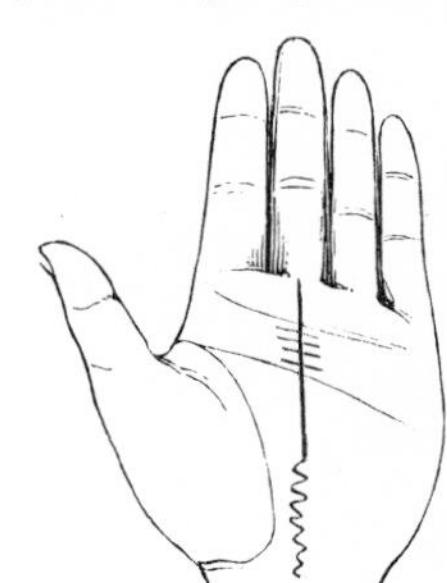

Si la ligne se contourne en forme de vis dans le bas, et que le haut en soit droit et pur, c'est un grand malheur suivi de fortune.

Il est bien entendu que dès que la saturnienne entre dans la racine du doigt, elle annonce la mauvaise influence de Saturne, et toujours de plus en plus fatale à mesure qu'elle s'élève; cette influence est de même mauvaise si elle coupe la rascette, c'est-à-dire si elle va plus loin que le bas de la main, et se trace sur la jointure en empiétant sur le poignet : alors il y a excès encore, et c'est un signe de prison et de tribulations de toute sorte.

Si la saturnienne part du bas de la main plus ou moins haut, qu'elle s'arrête à la ligne de cœur et s'y interrompe brusquement, c'est un bonheur brisé par une affaire de cœur ou une maladie de cœur.

14

190

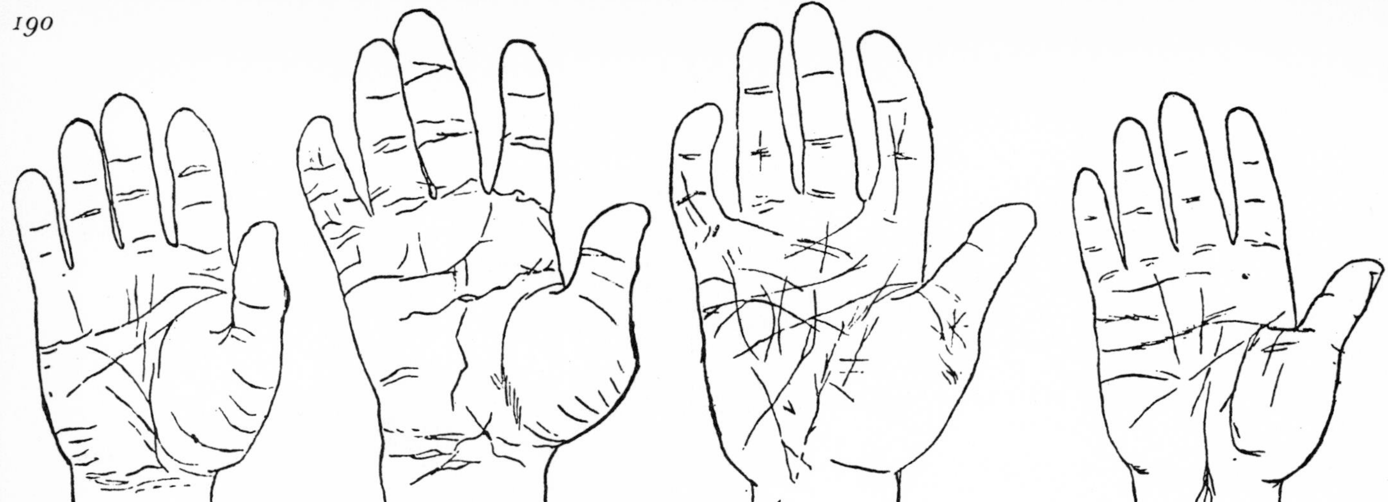

their seriousness by the depth of the cutting line, their cause from other lines and signs, and their outcome by the termination of the Saturn line. Breaks in the line (368) are most serious. At the time they occur some force has been sufficiently strong to check the career entirely, and if the line takes a new character, starts in a new direction, or does not start at all, these breaks indicate an entire change in the course of a subject's life-work. If the Saturn line be repeatedly broken it indicates a continual number of reverses, and the subject will have a laborious and troubled life. Each break indicates a different misfortune, and is more or less serious as the break is wide or is repaired. The age of each break can be read from the Saturn line. If the line be broken in many places but is repaired (369), the subject after numerous disappointments will fight his way eventually to success. It will be a continual fight, however, and such a subject will require great will power to carry him along. With breaks in the Saturn line both hands should always be examined, for from them you will read whether all of the

191

NO. 368 NO. 369 NO. 370

impediments in the line are a part of the natural plan or are the result of acquired habits, mistakes of calculation, ill health, or other causes. In a large majority of cases, the Saturn line is much better in the left than in the right hand, showing that a great many of our trials are brought on by ourselves. If a line of Saturn be uneven (370), alternately deep and thin in character, the subject will have intermittent

palmistic tradition. Fortunately, most of the contradictions may be understood when the changes in social conditions, and changes in attitudes to the planets themselves are fully appreciated. Saturn was always regarded as the ruler of the line of Fate, and whilst this rulership has remained constant, the attitude and beliefs concerning how Saturn affects human personality and life style has changed considerably, and it is largely such changes in attitude which account for so many apparent contradictions in the various palmistic systems. We tend to impose our own contemporary model of mankind on those people whom we study in the past, yet the evidence suggests that human beings have changed considerably, both in terms of social mores and as individuals, over the past few hundred years; consequently, we must anticipate that there be many changes in how 'the symbol of the model' – the human hand – may be interpreted. This is especially obvious in the case of the line of Fate, for the changes in the image of its ruler Saturn has been well documented by scholars, and at the same time the line is itself an index of the relationship which the individual holds the social mores of his time:

> Traditional palmistry has always maintained that Saturn had rule over this finger, but it rarely specified which aspect of Saturn was intended, and the line has been variously interpreted as relating to destiny, fate, inner balance and so on. Modern opinion is fairly united in the idea that it is related to the adaptability of the subject, as one might expect of a line which runs upwards to the 'sentinel' finger of the hand into the active

190. The hands of four murderer's drawn 'from life' to test the rules set down by Desbarrolles concerning the nature of a murderer's hand. (from 'The Palmist' of 1894)

191. Examples of a late nineteenth century reading of the line of Saturn, according to the American palmist Benham.

192. A weak line of Saturn. See text below.

> and passive areas, and the channel of the line may thus be regarded as being involved with acting as a mediator between the two: it may therefore be seen as an index of the subject's inner sense of freedom in relation to his life. In one sense the presence of this line in some strength may indicate a reasonable adaptability: in another sense it may show a developed sense of self-love, which permits of a harmonious relationship with the world. It is essential that a person should learn to love himself in the right way before he can hope to be in a position to love others and the world at large: it is in relation to this sort of self-love, which in a sense marks a certain freedom from the ego of Mars that the line must be studied.
>
> A weak line of Fate, or one which is badly broken (figure 192) implies a marked sense of insufficiency in these terms, as though the ego of Mars is strangling the subject and preventing a harmonious development with world demands . . . A strong line of Fate implies a creative and warm relationship to selfhood, which will permit the subject to relate in a warm and unselfish manner to the external world, and in particular to other human beings. (79)

As with the association drawn between the line of Fate and the mount of Saturn, we find that each of the finger mounts is associated with a particular line, though such lines do not appear in every hand. The interpretation of the line of Mercury (figure 197) has an interesting history, for even in the sixteenth century that indefatigable compiler Taisnier pointed out that a broken line of Mercury

192

193

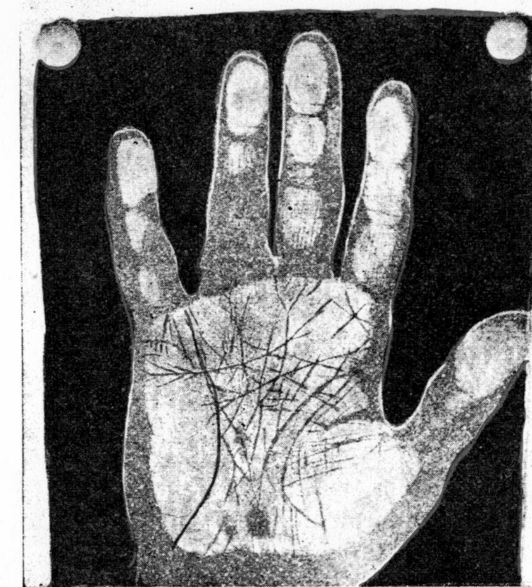

194

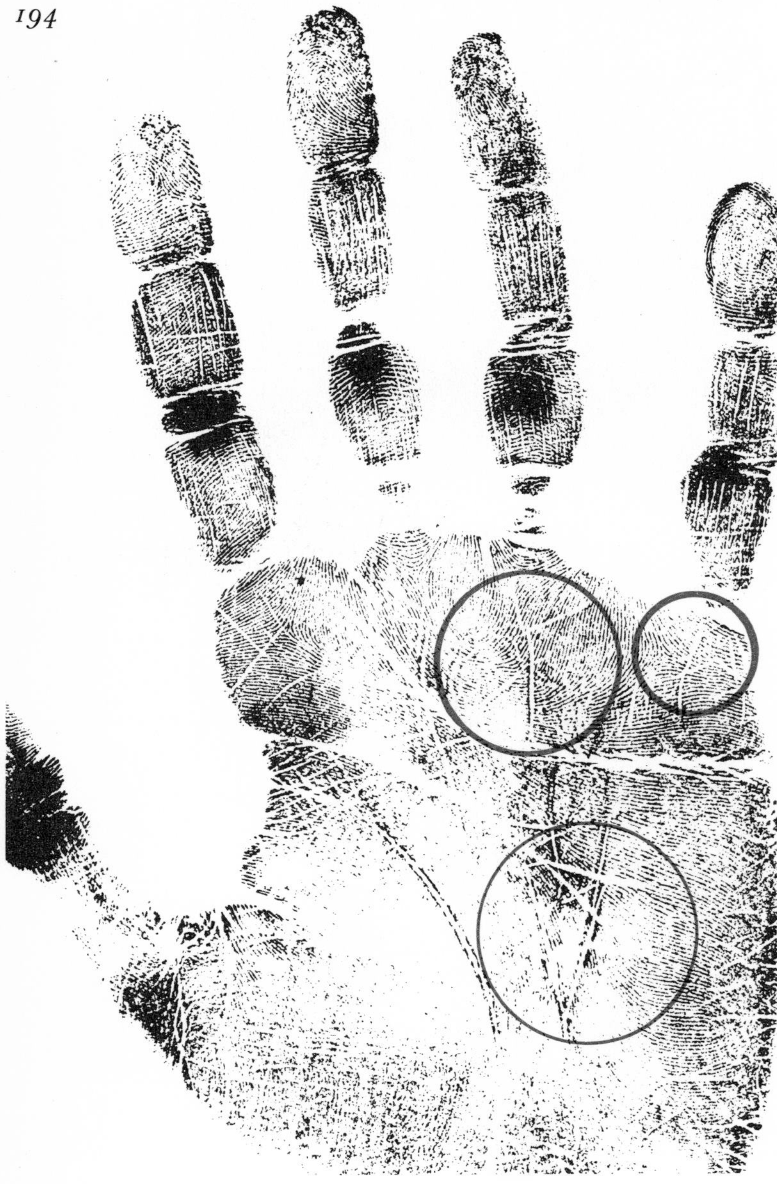

193. A strong line of Intuition, sometimes called the line of Mercury, sometimes the Hepatica. After Benham.

194. The print of a female artist. The three lines circled on the print are closely related to creativity—the line of Apollo, the small lines under Mercury, and a forked Head line all contribute to the qualities required by an artist.

195. A drawing of the hand of a Countess, from 'The Palmist of 1894. The chiromancer remarks that the deviations on the line of Fate are such that 'one only wonders that one so sensitive could survive such trials'.

196. A drawing of the hand of George Bernard Shaw, showing a strong line of Apollo and Mercury. The hand appears to have been of the Air type.

(figure 171) was linked with certain sexual difficulties, the gravity of which depended upon the degree of distortion in the line. In other respects, however, he preserved the tradition which regarded Mercury as the messenger of the Gods, and the line of Mercury as an indication of a strong intuition, which in occult terms implies a good close contact between the subconscious and the conscious mind. The later forms of palmistry tended to preserve this aspect of the tradition, even dubbing it the 'line of Intuition'. Eventually all the half-baked popular palmistry books harped on its link with intuition even when, in deference to the ancient tradition which linked it with the Liver, they called it the 'Line of Health':

> The Line of Health sometimes takes a curved form on *one* hand . . . In this case it is called the Line of Presentiment, and indicates vivid intuition, especially if Mercury is strong in his influence. When the Line of Health on *both* hands takes this form it indicates mediumistic powers, and powerful second sight . . . (80)

In relatively recent times, however, observation of the relationship between deformation of the little finger and sexual difficulties has led the modern palmist to link once more the Mercurial force of the finger and line with sexuality. Perhaps in any case the energies of sex are not unrelated to those energies which are used for the purpose of higher spiritual experiencing, and for mediumship.

The line of Apollo (figure 194) has inevitably always been linked with creative energies, and it is generally recognized that the presence

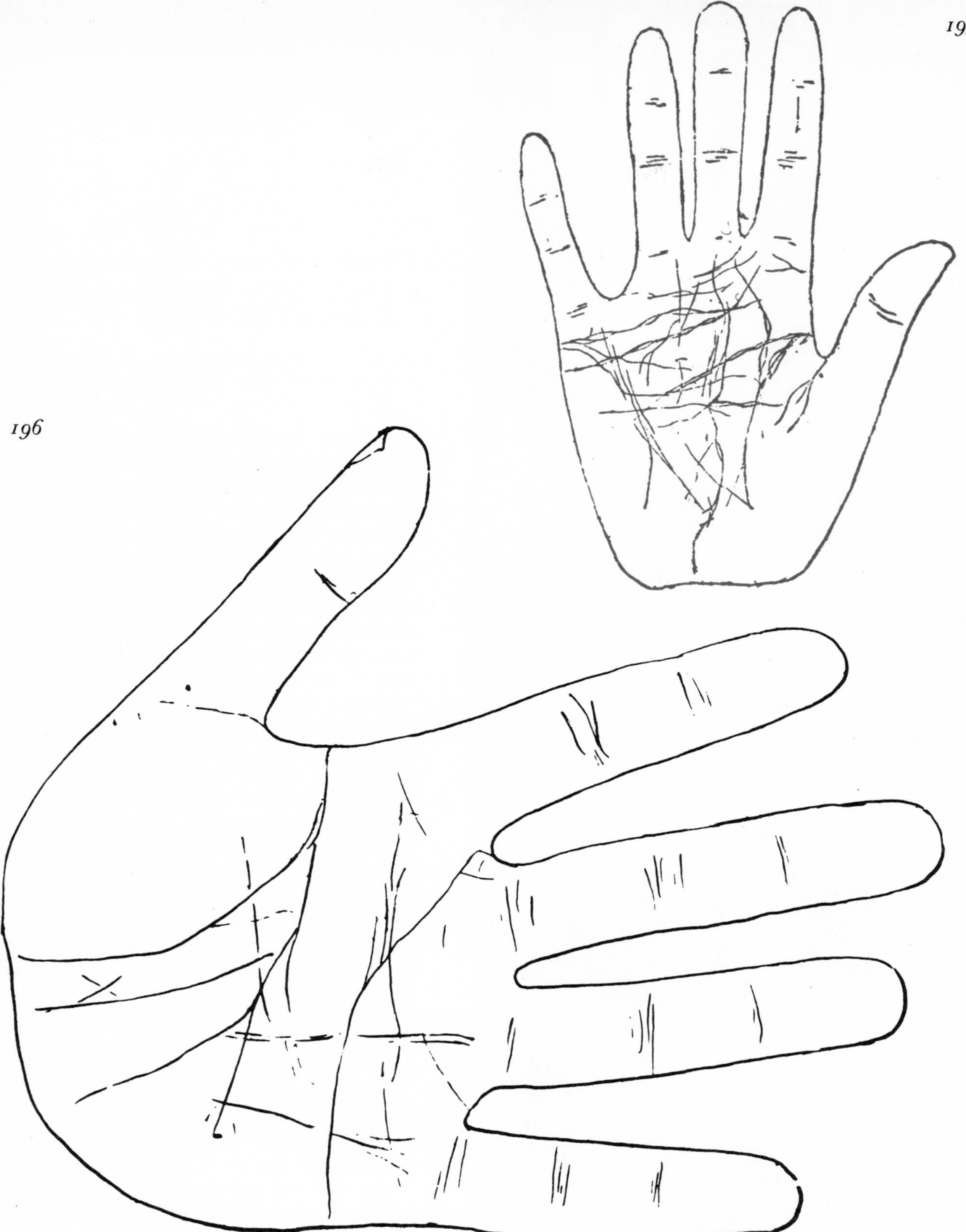

THE HAND OF MR. BERNARD SHAW.

(LEFT.)

197. A strong line of Mercury on the hand of a medium.

198. A drawing from the hand of a catatepltic, from the nineteenth century magazine 'The Palmist'.

199. A line of Ambition crossed by the so-called ring of Solomon, a line which encircles the mount of Jupiter. When isolated, these two form the so-called 'mystic cross'.

197

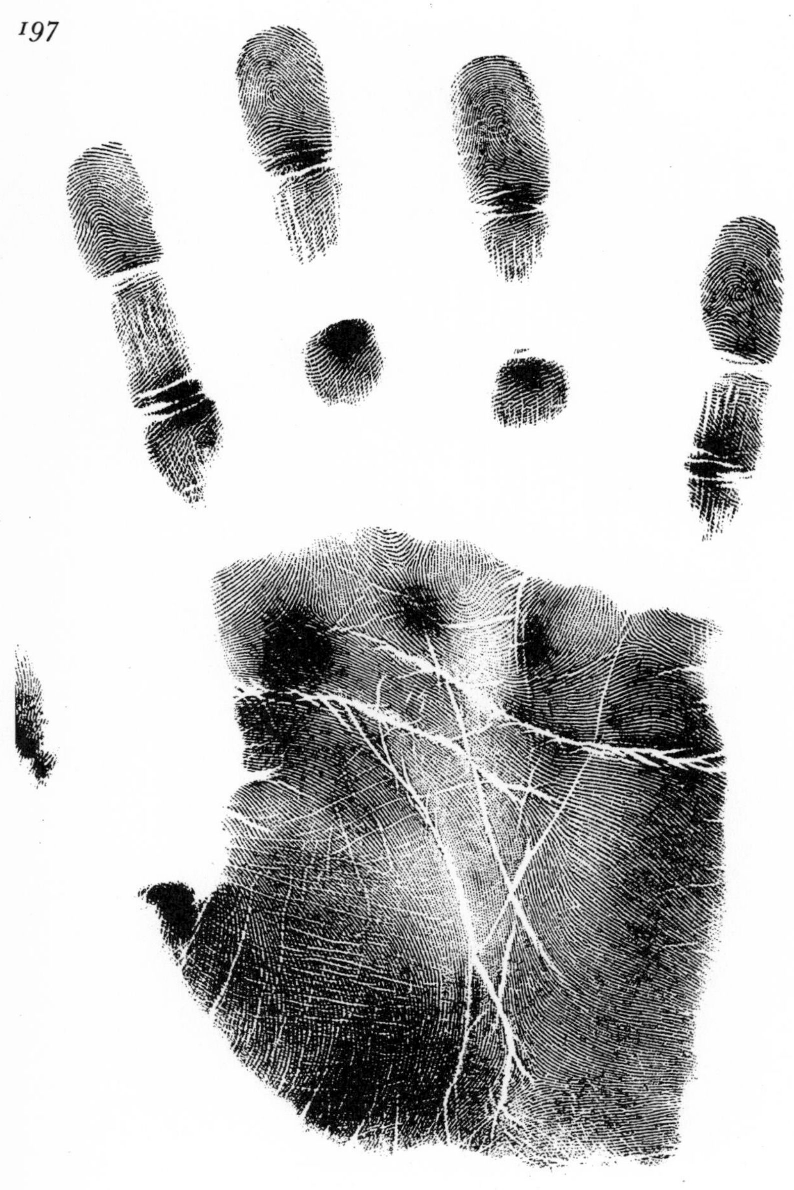

of this line is linked with creativity, to such an extent indeed that Benham felt constrained to add a note of caution concerning its interpretation:

> It has been variously called the line of the Sun, and the line of Brilliancy, and to it has been ascribed the gift of great artistic talents, wealth, and fame. It is one of the most thoroughly misunderstood of all the lines, and the mistaken reading of it has caused practitioners many mortifications. Whenever a good line of Apollo was seen, it has been customary to 'gush' about the wonderful talent the subject possessed for art, music, the stage, and various other artistic callings, of which perhaps no idea had previously entered his mind. Often a subject especially well fitted to be a good housewife has been made to feel indignant towards her parents by some well meaning palmist because alleged latent talents were not discovered and developed.
>
> It is the attempt to make the line of Brilliancy always indicate brilliancy in *art*, which is only one of the directions it may take, and the disregard for the fact that a subject may be brilliant in many *directions*, that has made the reading of the line of Apollo so inaccurate . . . It is only accurate when the subject has first been understood and the line has been applied *to him*, and it never has been and never will be accurate when the attempt is made to force every subject to fit the line. No better name has ever been given this line than the *Line of Capability* . . . It indicates a *capability* or *possibility* of accomplishing a great deal,

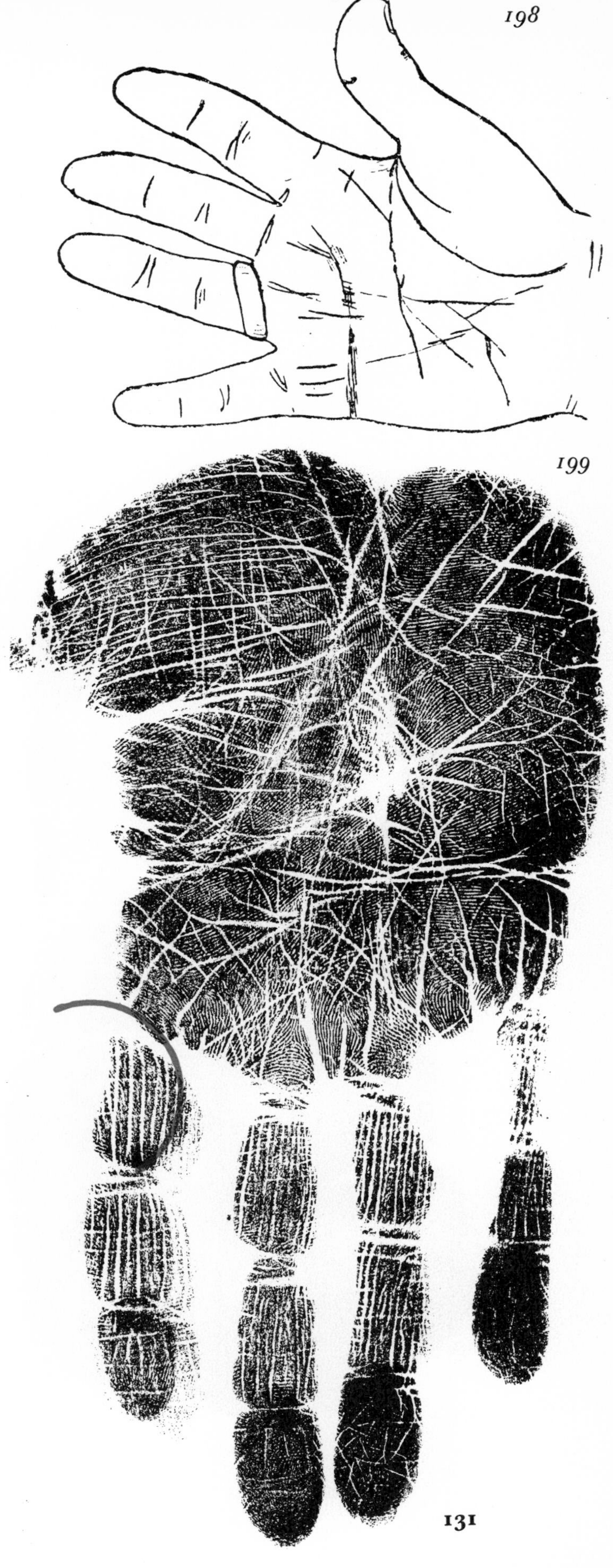

> the *field* in which the capability will best operate to be shown by Chirognomy, indicating the forces *behind*, which will direct the ability in some calling which produces results . . . The presence of a fine line of Apollo is an indication that the subject has been endowed with exceptional talents for getting on in the world, and if other parts of the hand be good, he most surely will do so. (81)

We see, then, that a strong Apollo, when examined in terms of the chirognomical system set out on page 40, will suggest in a Fire hand (figure 63) emotional talents and creativity involved with painting and the like; in an Air hand (figure 61) intellectual talents will be suggested, creativity involved with literature and so on; in an Earth hand (figure 67) the force will be towards talents concerned with physical expression or with rhythms, whilst in a Water hand (figure 57) the talents will be found in highly sensitive and refined directions, perhaps finding expression through relationships or dealing with people.

Strictly speaking, there is no line of Jupiter, though the line which arises from the line of Life and crosses deeply into the mount of Jupiter is nowadays called the 'line of ambition', which by its very name implies a link with exuberant life-enhancing Jupiterian characteristics: it might well be called the line of Jupiter. Although the term is a new one, given us by a psychologist furthermore, Heron Allen, writing at the end of the last century, points in this direction:

> A line starting from the commencement of the line of life, going to the Mount of

200

IOAN TAIS. HAN. LIB. IIII. 181

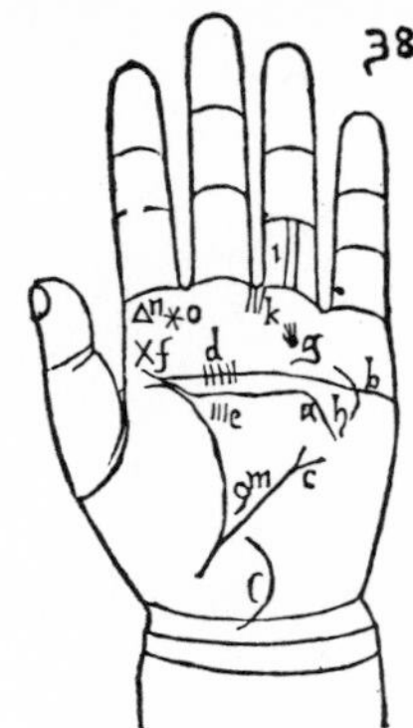

A Naturalis inclinata verſus menſalem, ſignificat hominem iniquum, & iuuenem moriturum.

B Naturalis ſcindẽs vitalem, & menſalis ipſi in principio vnita, homicidiarium notat, & aſtutum in malum.

C Linea hepatis bifurcata in fine, mortem violentam minatur, et hoc ab vno capite, quantum ab alio.

D Multæ lineæ ſecantes menſalem in oppoſito medij, damnum notant in ſubſtantijs.

E Lineæ tranſuerſales in angulo ſupremo, nõ ſcindentes tamen, notant hominem pœnitere ſuæ prodigalitatis, & eò magis quò angulus fuerit diſiunctus.

F Lineæ interſecatæ ſupra montem indicis, notant perſecutiones ab eccleſiaſticis.

200. *A plate from Taisnier showing an early example the doctrine that the simian line ('B' in the illustration) is a 'murderer's' line. The superstition lasted up to the beginning of our own century, and is not entirely lost in certain books on palmistry.*

201. *The 'mystic cross', which is traditionally supposed to confer an interest in the occult, or in deeper religious studies. It is associated with the ninth house of the horoscope figure.*

202. *A Girdle of Venus, composed of several delicate lines. This is its most common form.*

203. *A Girdle of Venus composed of several very strong lines, following the curvature of the Heart line, and acting as a kind of second Heart line.*

201

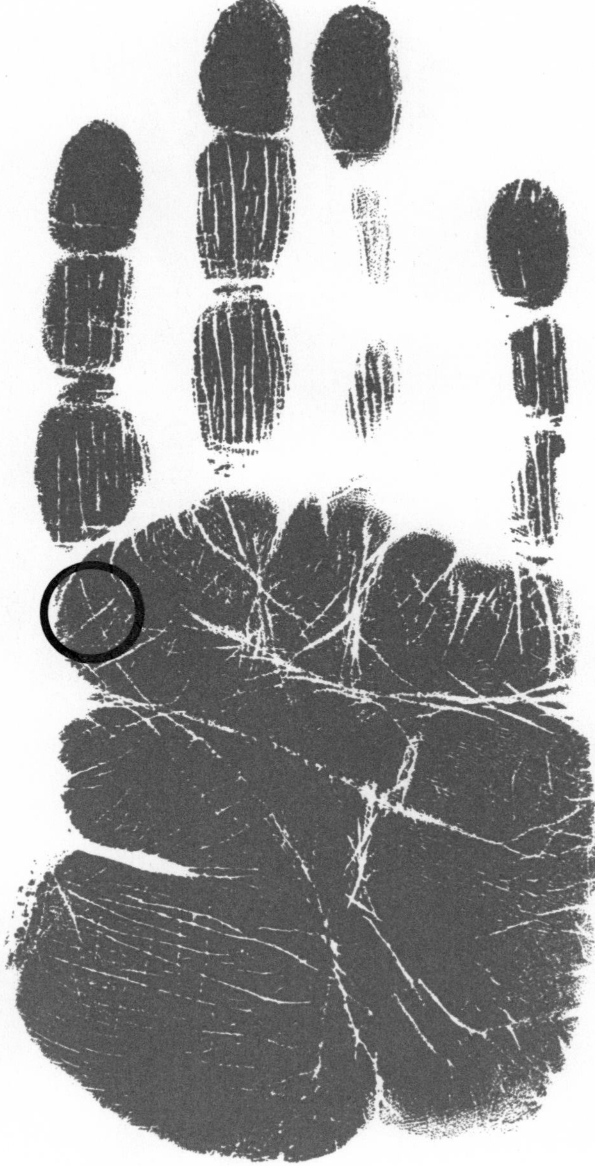

> Jupiter, and then turning on to the Mount of Saturn, as at figure 166, ca, denotes a disposition to fashionable fanaticism. If such a subject is religious *at all* it will be, that he is actuated mainly by a desire to become eminent in that particular line. (82)

Sometimes, on the mount itself, there appears a cross, which has been accorded great significance by many palmists: this is the so-called mystic cross which is supposed to give a deep insight into the spiritual world, but which Desbarrolles dismisses as a sign of 'superstition'–whatever that may mean, thus bowling over the beliefs of his contemporary Proudhon simply because he possessed a mystic cross, and yet claimed to be an agnostic. In between the mounts of Jupiter and Mercury one frequently finds a line which runs above the heart line, as a kind of 'sister-line' to it. This is called the Girdle of Venus, and it is a line which has been roundly discriminated against by almost all palmists: of all lines in the hand, this has perhaps the most unfortunate reputation. It has received this treatment mainly because it deals with the darker side of Venus, with her wanton nature (figure 205), and we see the tradition at its most casually unenlightened when we study Desbarrolles' words concerning the hand which would show the sin of luxury:

> Girdle of Venus: an irresistable urge to luxury without sense of limitation. If the Girdle of Venus is broken, then: sodomy infamous and coldblooded debauchery–Double or triple girdle of Venus: even more horrible debauchery . . . (83)

These are words very strong in their indigna-

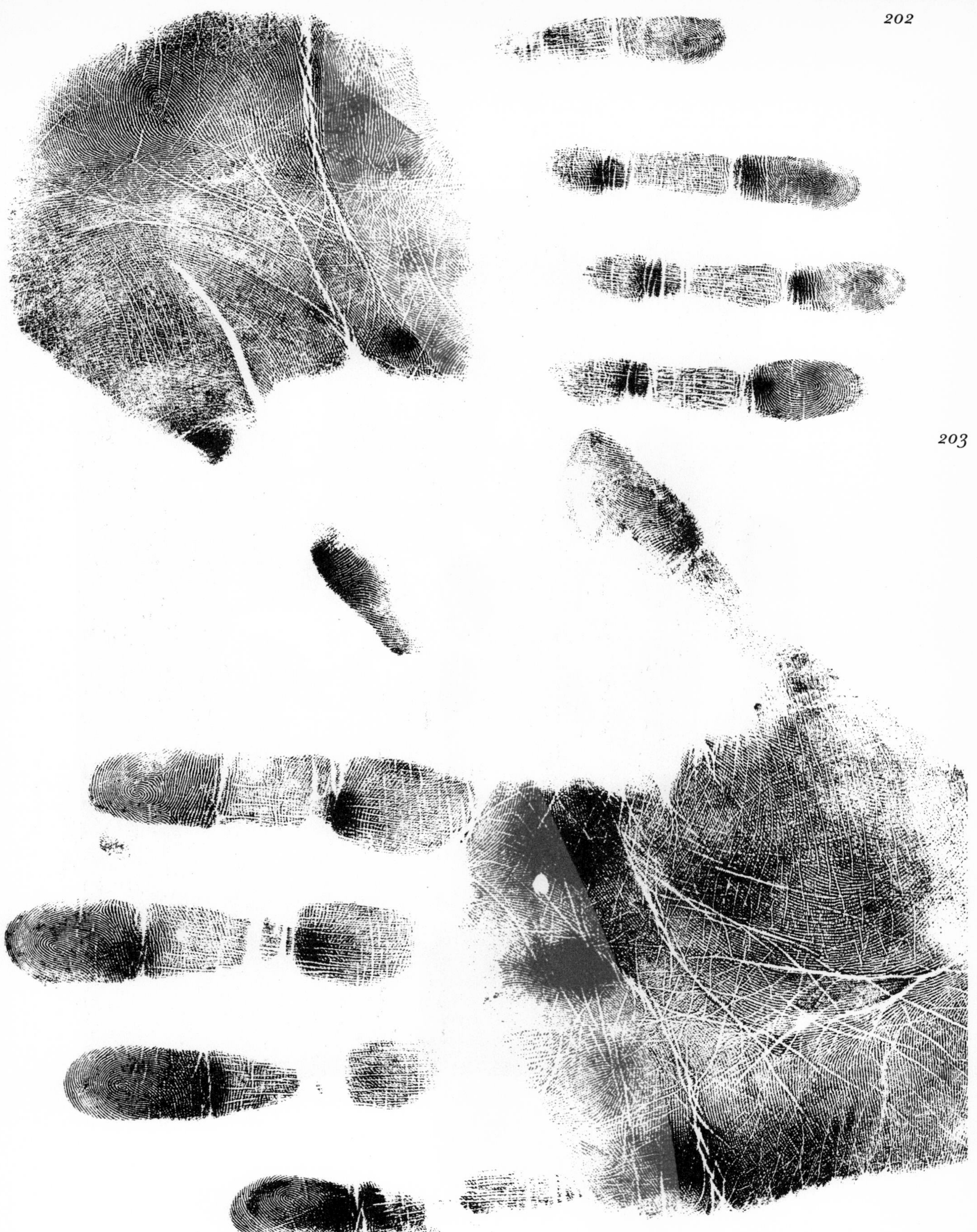

202

203

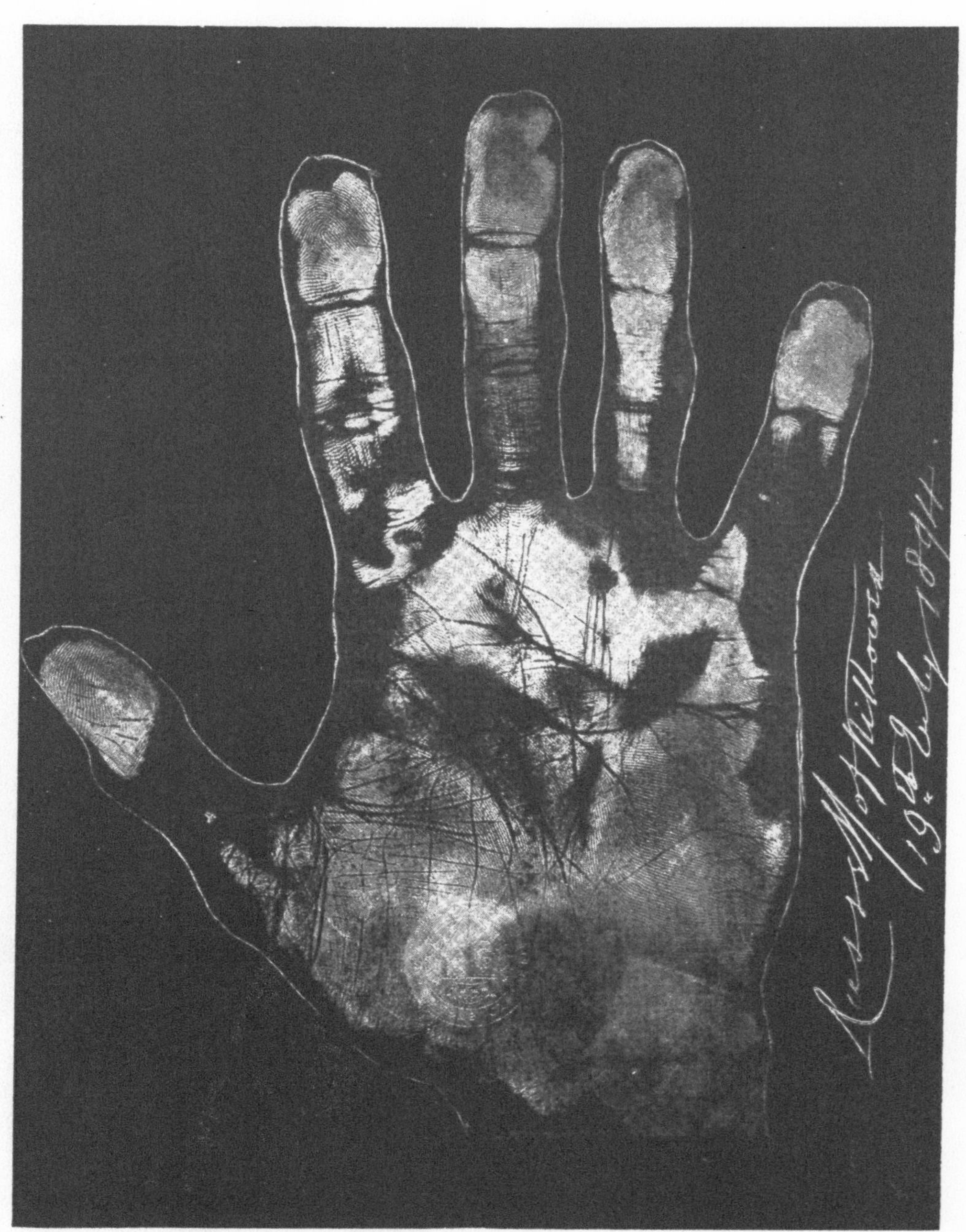

THE HAND OF THE LORD CHIEF JUSTICE OF ENGLAND.

LORD RUSSELL OF KILLOWEN.

Plate XXXVII.

205

204. *The hand of Lord Russell of Killowen, from 'Cheiro's' collection. Note the strong incipient Simian line, associated at that time with criminality.*

205. *Venus, ruler over the arts, music, love and lechery—this is why the 'excessive emotionalism' associated with the second line of Heart (figure 203) is named after Venus.*

206. *A strong Girdle of Venus. See text below.*

tion, yet similar attitudes could be culled from almost all palmistry books (one such, taken at random, reads: 'when fully developed, signifies unbridled passion and debauchery of all kinds' – 1889) until well into our own century. Even the restraint of modern times, without wish to escape the blood and thunder of the ancient systems, is not sufficient to blot out entirely the unfortunate associations of this line:

> It may be regarded as an adjunct to the line of Heart, and in some cases this is precisely what it is. In itself the line adds a degree of emotional sensitivity to the hand. Chiromantically the line acts as a connection between the external conscious and the inner conscious quality of the personality. It links the self-assertive elements with the emotions, and therefore tends to be a dangerous marking. People with marked girdles are in constant need of excitement and variety; I have seen the line strongly marked in the hands of drug addicts, and others in continual need of artificial emotional stimulation. A short girdle is itself a good sign of emotional alertness, but when it extends across the palm in a series of broken and chaotic lines (206) the sensitivity of the individual is so high and erratic as to be dangerous. (84)

It is hard to generalize about the subsidiary lines, particularly as the tradition contains so many conflicting teachings concerning their import. However, the modern systems of palmistry appear to have provided a satisfactory theoretical and practical account of their natures, in their teaching that these must be regarded as the 'conductors of energies' from

206

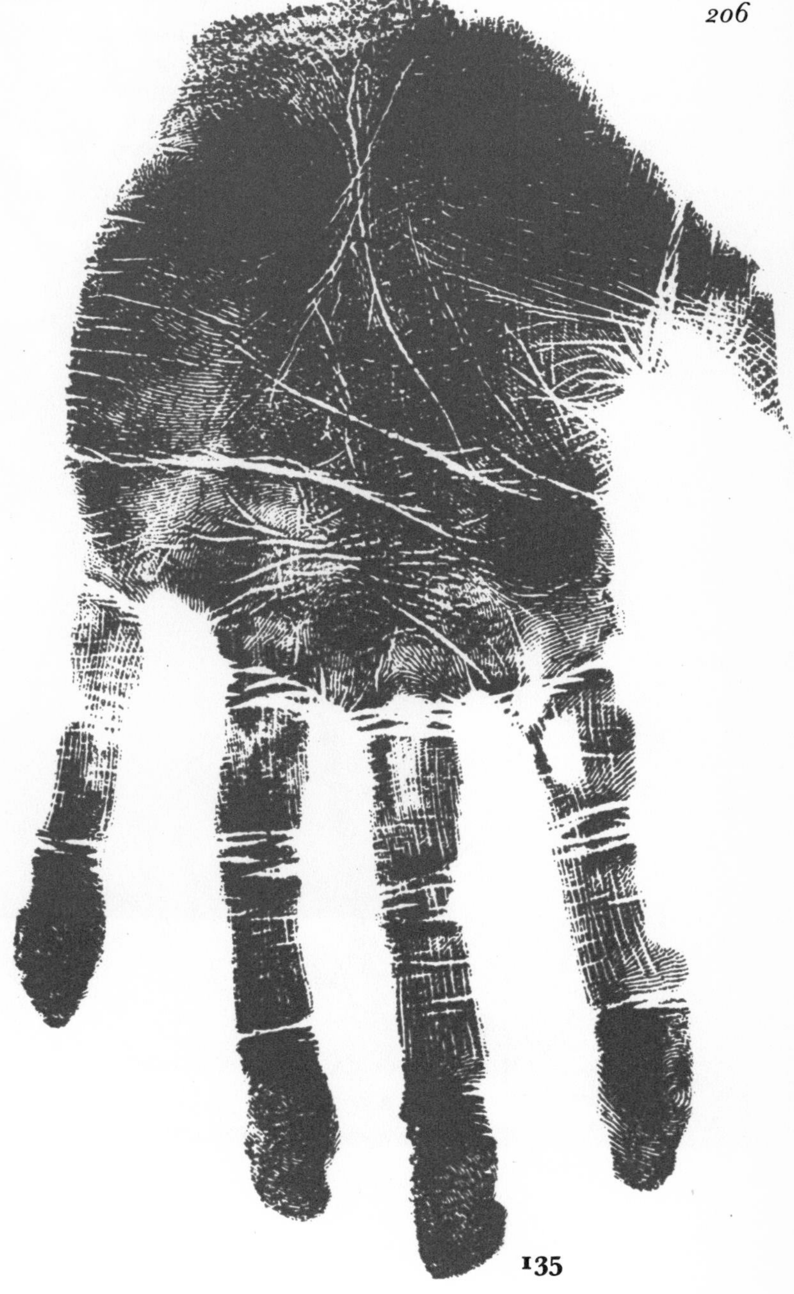

207. *Portrait of Indagine, the sixteenth century German chiromancer.*

208. *Some subsidiary lines are so erratic that they may be understood only in terms of the theory of planetary zones. The example shown here is clearly transfering Venusian energies across the line of Saturn.*

207

CHIROMANTIA.

2 Physiognomia, ex aspectu membrorum Hominis.
3 Periaxiomata, de faciebus SIGNORVM.
4 Canones astrologici, de iudicijs AEgritudinum.
5 ASTROLOGIA NATVRALIS.
6 Complexionum noticia, iuxta dominium Planetarum.

one zone of the hand to another. Provided one is sufficiently familiar with the planetary associations, then one may be able to work out which energies are being conducted, in what manner, and how the appearance of such energies in particular areas will interact within the personality as a whole. We have seen such considerations applied, to some extent, in our examination of the line of Apollo, which must be thought of as carrying energies from the Lunar mount, through the line of Heart, into the creative zone of the solar Apollo – that is, discharging energies proper to the subconscious into an area which seeks artistic and creative expression: the *kind* of expression permitted such a discharge of energy will, as we have seen, depend upon the structure of the hand as a whole.

This last observation points to what is perhaps the greatest difficulty which faces the palmist, for it would seem that he is required to do the impossible each time he analyses a hand. In order to see the full significance of a line, or a relationship of lines, he must bear in mind the picture of the 'whole' – of which these very lines or relationships are an integral part! The implied difficulties are enormous, but in practice it will be found that if one can catch a general 'image' of the subject from a preliminary examination of the hand – an 'image' which springs from a nice balance between intuitive judgements, informed knowledge and wide experience, then the working from this larger 'image' down to the individual parts, such as lines, fingers and patterns, towards the individuality of the subject will prove, if not exactly easy, at least to be possible!

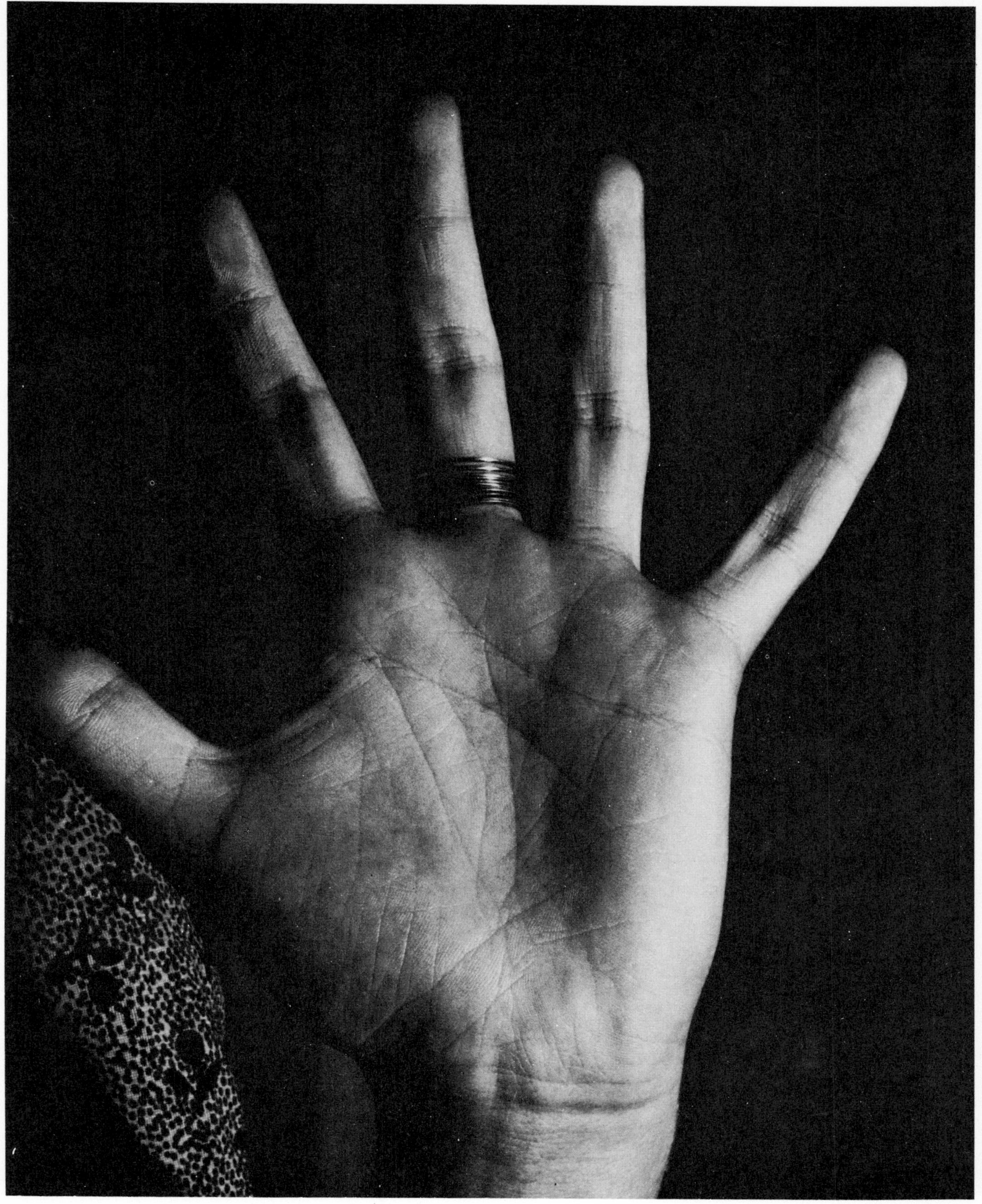

209

210

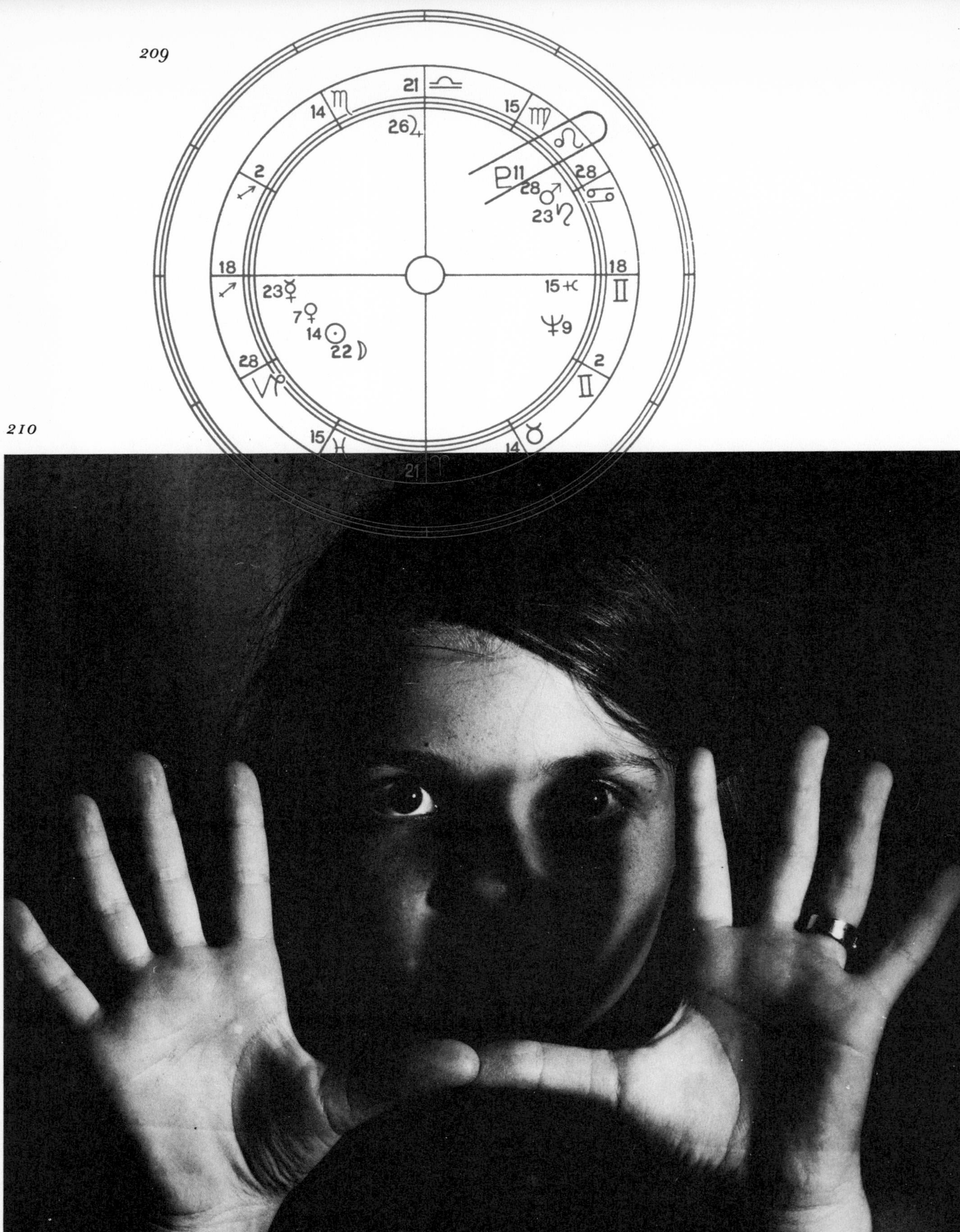

Conclusion

209–212. *The occult theory of palmistry was in its earliest forms intimately bound up with such studies as strology and physiognomy. A proper research programme in modern times would of necessity require a study of birth charts, physiognomy, as well as the detailed study of cheirognomy and line markings, to be of any real value.*

Perhaps the most that anyone may hope for a book of this nature is that it stimulates an interest in the subject of the hand itself. Much of the palmistic tradition is sterile–fit for entertainment and amusement, but no basis for arriving at truth . . . And yet, without such success and stumblings in the past, our own efforts, conscious or subconscious, by which we judge the inner state of a person from the outer appearance–by which we decide for instance that someone is happy because they are smiling–might not be quite so easy for us now. The more one studies the ancient traditions, especially those which are involved with the occult, the more one develops a sense of indebtedness to those who went before; the more one senses in such systems a remarkable unity of feeling and mentality which is quite lost in our own world-conception. Perhaps it is this sense of unity which we seek in such studies, for without it we are painfully aware of a schism in our being. It is easy to poke fun at Taisnier, at Indagine or at Desbarrolles, and yet once one begins to read what they have to say about the hand, it is hard not to become enchanted by their systems, by their world-conceptions, however far removed from our own they appear to be.

With such enchantment, the wish is easily felt to translate and make available all of Taisnier's innocent and deceptively simple aphorisms (which run into thousands), for these take on a new significance when related to the case histories of real-life hands which he preserves in his wood cuts. For, through the vast compilations of such men as Taisniers,

211

212

we see that even in the sixteenth century serious attempts were being made to link the theory of palmistry with the living symbol of the individual hand, in much the same way, and with much the same difficulties, as we do today. We might leap three centuries, in the hope that things will have progressed in that time, and feel again the same urge to translate the entire *Mysteries* of Desbarrolles, with all their intermixing of occultism and cabballa, and yet still feel the same sense of despair as with Taisnier, when we attempt to link the theoretical part of the book with the short accounts of incursions into practical palmistry through the hands of his famous contemporaries. For it is the strange lack of relationship between the theory of palmistry and the practice of palmistry which strikes one throughout the centuries, and yet it is in such an area that the real test of palmistry is found–not in the aptness, beauty, unity or depth of the theory, nor even in the unity of feeling and thinking–but in its *practical* value, in the way it may be used to help others in moments of crisis, or to help towards an understanding of self, which is perhaps the purpose of this crisis we call human life. The more palmistic systems one studies, the more one realizes that it is the *living* tradition which is important–the fact that certain sensitives and mediums are able to project their energies into the psychic life or subconscious natures of others by way of the hand, and then, hopefully, reveal all towards some useful end.

It is in the general failure to do just this–to help someone towards a useful end–that the real weakness of palmistry lies nowadays. Charlatans abound now, as always, but even the more serious minded tend to practise mainly in order to display their talents rather than to help, or to expound theories which, because they are isolated, like ourselves, from the living occult tradition which reflects the true nature of man and his cosmic role, are sterile speculations and ultimately of no value. The tragedy is that whilst there are very many different systems of palmistry–many truths by which we may arrive at an understanding of man through the hand–if they are used for the wrong purpose, then they are all quite wrong.

Palmistry works from the part to the whole–from the microcosm which is man, up towards the macrocosm of the celestial world, in order to place the individual in some significant relationship to the whole–the only valid way by which we may understand man. Astrology, the related science, works from a study of the macrocosm, and reaches downwards into the microcosm, which is intimately bound up within the larger pattern. Both the study of palmistry and the study of astrology are fraught with difficulties, especially nowadays in the face of so much superstition which passes for science, but particularly obvious difficulties face palmistry, for the system and systems which have survived are neither so ancient nor so compelling beautifully as a theory of existence as those of astrology. The realization of this may lead one to give up in despair, or it may lead one to see that it is for precisely such reasons that palmistry stands in need of urgent regeneration, if the real nature of man, and his place in the world, is to be grasped.

213. Desbarrolles reading the palm of a client.

214. (Over). A page from the earliest printed book on palmistry, the blockbook 'Die Kunst Ciromantia' of Hartlieb. (from the British Museum copy).

213

References

Bibliographical index of quotations in text

Pseudo Aristotle, 1738
ARISTOTLE'S MASTERPIECES
(quoted by Benham, see below) no. 51

D'Arpentigny, 1843
LA CHIROGNOMIE no. 14

R. Baughan, 1891
THE INFLUENCE OF THE STARS
no. 68, 80

W. G. Benham, 1900
THE LAWS OF SCIENTIFIC HAND READING
nos. 2, 4, 38–44, 59, 65, 67, 71, 73, 81

'Cheiro' (de Hamon), 1894
THE LANGUAGE OF THE HAND
nos. 9, 12, 17, 19, 23

CHOU I CHING
(Translated from a Sung blockbook) no. 50

A. Desbarrolles, 1859
LES MYSTERES DE LA MAIN
nos. 3, 58, 76–77, 83

J. Gaule, 1652
THE MAG-ASTROMANCER no. 6

F. Gettings, 1965
THE BOOK OF THE HAND
(quoted with kind permission of the publishers, Paul Hamlyn Ltd.)
nos. 26, 30, 35, 70, 74, 84

F. Gettings, 1966
PALMISTRY
(quoted with kind permission of the publishers, Bancrofts Ltd.) nos. 27, 28, 31, 32, 34, 36, 60

F. Gettings, 1973
THE HAND AND THE HOROSCOPE
(quoted with kind permission of the publishers, Trewin Copplestone Publishing Ltd.)
nos. 29, 33, 64, 79

Heron Allen, 1886
THE SCIENCE OF THE HAND
nos. 5, 7, 8, 10, 11, 13, 15, 16, 18, 20–22, 24, 25, 45–47

J. Indagine, 1582
INTRODUCTIONES APOTELESMATICAE
no. 75

G. Muchery, 1958
TRAITE COMPLET DE LA CHIROMANCIE DEDUCTIVE ET EXPERIMENTAL
(quoted with kind permission of the publishers, Editions du Chariot)
no. 37

R. Saunders, 1664
PALMISTRY, THE SECRETS THEREOF DISCLOSED
nos. 1, 52–57

Soulie de Morant
LES SCIENCES OCCULTES EN CHINE– LA MAIN
(quoted with kind permission of the publishers.)
nos. 48, 49

D. J. Taisniers, 1562
OPUS MATHEMATICUM
no. 72

(All translations from the above books have been made by the author)

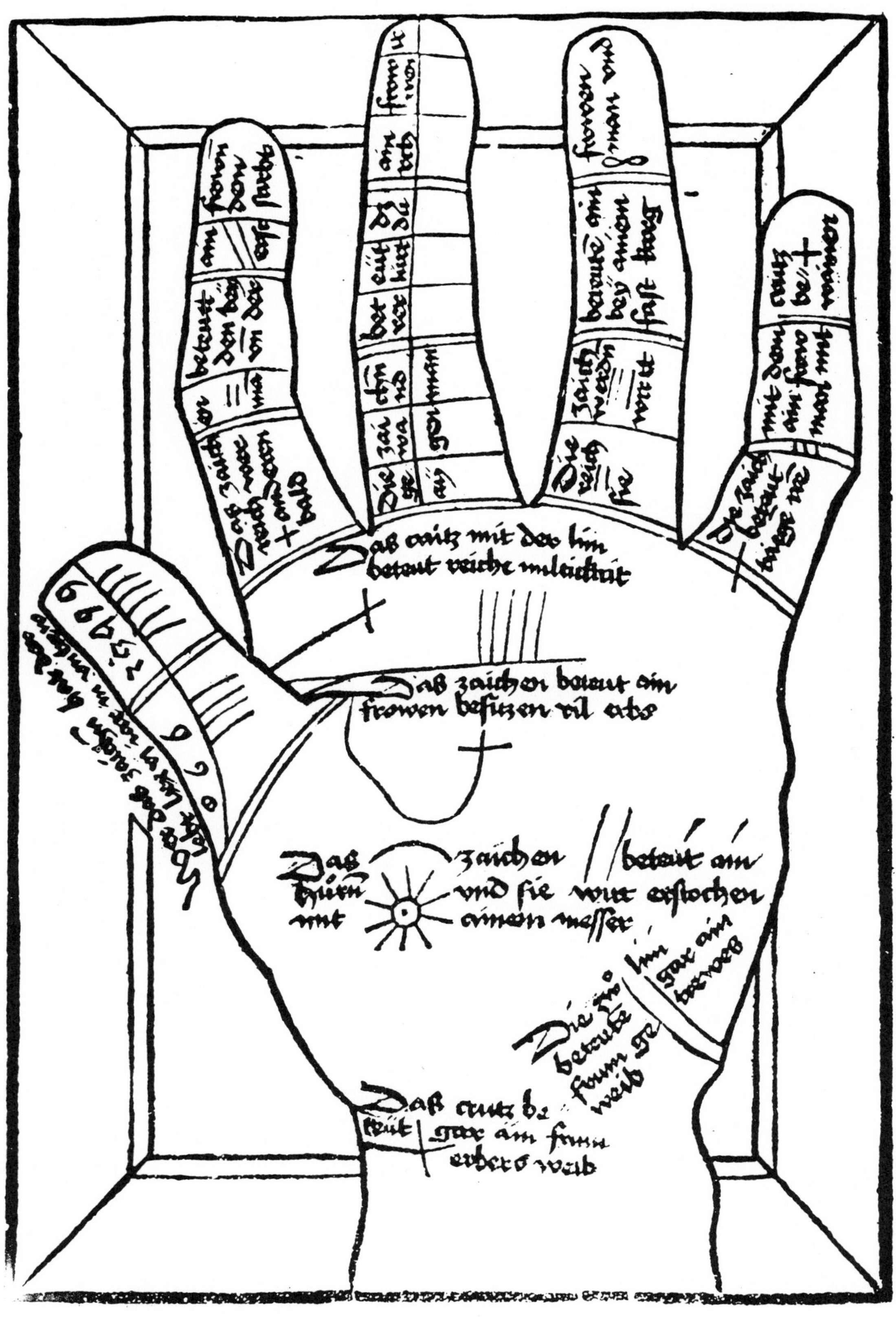
Daß zaichen betaut ain
frowen besitzen vil erbs
vnd sie wirt erstochen
ainem messer
erbers weib